CW00621222

PART 2

Paper 2.1

Information Systems

ACCA Study Text

ACCA
Approved Publisher

ftc

FTC Foulks Lynch
A **Kaplan Professional** Company

British Library Cataloguing-in-Publication Data

A catalogue record for this book is available from the British Library.

Published by:

FTC Foulks Lynch
Swift House
Market Place
Wokingham
Berkshire
RG40 1AP

ISBN 1 84390 587 6

© The Financial Training Company Ltd, May 2005

Printed and bound in Great Britain by William Clowes Ltd, Beccles, Suffolk

Acknowledgements

We are grateful to the Association of Chartered Certified Accountants and the Chartered Institute of Management Accountants for permission to reproduce past examination questions. The answers have been prepared by FTC Foulks Lynch.

Contents

Introduction

This is the FTC Foulks Lynch Study Text for Paper 2.1 *Information Systems*, and is part of the ACCA series produced for students taking the ACCA examinations.

This new edition has been produced with direct guidance from the examiner. It covers the syllabus and study guide in great detail, giving appropriate weighting to the various topics. Targeted very closely on the examination, this study text is written in a way that will help you assimilate the information easily. Numerous practice questions and exam-type questions at the end of each chapter reinforce your knowledge.

DEFINITION

- **Definitions.** The text defines key words and concepts, placing them in the margin, with a clear heading, as on the left. The purpose of including these definitions is to focus your attention on the point being covered.

KEY POINT

- **Key points**. In the margin you will see key points at regular intervals. The purpose of these is to summarise concisely the key material being covered.

ACTIVITY 1

- **Activities**. The text involves you in the learning process with a series of activities designed to catch your attention and make you concentrate and respond. The feedback to activities is at the end of each chapter.

SELF-TEST QUESTIONS

- **Self-test questions**. At the end of each chapter there is a series of self-test questions. The purpose of these is to help you revise some of the key elements of the chapter. All the answers to these questions can be found in the text.

EXAM-TYPE QUESTIONS

- **End of chapter questions**. At the end of each chapter we include examination-type questions. These will give you a very good idea of the sort of thing the examiner will ask and will test your understanding of what has been covered.

Syllabus and study guide

Objectives of the study guide

This Study Guide is designed to help you plan your studies and to provide a more detailed interpretation of the Syllabus for ACCA's professional examinations. It contains both the Syllabus and a Study Guide for each paper, which you can follow when preparing for the examination.

The Syllabus outlines the content of the paper and how that content is examined. The Study Guide takes the Syllabus content and expands it into study sessions of similar length. These sessions indicate what the examiner expects of candidates for each part of the Syllabus, and therefore gives you guidance in the skills you are expected to demonstrate in the examinations.

Syllabus content

1 MANAGING INFORMATION SYSTEMS (IS)

a   Business strategy and IS/IT alignment.

b   Delivering information systems – organisational arrangements.

c   Delivering information systems – accounting issues.

d   Organising information systems – structural issues.

e   Feasibility study.

f   Project initiation.

g   Project planning.

h   Project monitoring and control.

i   Software support for project management.

2 DESIGNING INFORMATION SYSTEMS

a   The information systems development process.

b   Investigating and recording user requirements.

c   Documenting and modelling user requirements – processes.

d   Documenting and modelling user requirements – static structures.

e   Documenting and modelling user requirements – events.

f   External design.

g   Developing a solution to fulfil requirements.

h   Software package selection.

i   Software support for the systems development process.

3 EVALUATING INFORMATION SYSTEMS

a   Technical information systems requirements.

b   Legal compliance in information systems.

c   Implementing security and legal requirements.

d   Quality assurance in the management and development process.

e   Systems and user acceptance testing.

f   Implementation issues and implementation methods.

g   Post-implementation issues.

h   Change control in systems development and maintenance.

i   Relationship of management, development process and quality.

Excluded topics

Detailed systems design – file / database design, program design is an excluded topic. Computer hardware will not be explicitly examined.

Key areas of the syllabus

The syllabus has three key areas, managing information systems, designing information systems and evaluating information systems.

Study guide

PART 1: MANAGING INFORMATION SYSTEMS

Overall

This section provides the candidate with an insight into how information systems (IS) and information systems projects are organised and managed. The intention is to concentrate on the following areas.

- Information Systems strategy, organisation and financing
- Project Management.

1   Business strategy and IS/IT alignment   Chapter 1

- Explain an approach that an organisation may follow to formulate its strategic business objectives.

- Discuss how information systems may be used to assist in achieving these objectives.

- Identify current trends in information technology (IT) and the opportunities they offer to organisations.

- Distinguish between a business strategy and an information systems strategy.

- Identify responsibility for the ownership of the IS strategy.

2   Delivering information systems – organisational arrangements   Chapter 2

- Describe the traditional structure of a centralised Information Systems department and the roles and responsibilities of each function.

- Explain the principles of a decentralised Information. Systems function.

- Discuss the advantages and disadvantages of centralising or decentralising the Information Systems function.

- Explain the principles of outsourcing the Information Systems function.

- Describe the advantages and disadvantages of outsourcing the Information Systems function.

3   Delivering information systems – accounting issues   Chapter 3

- Briefly describe the types of cost incurred in delivering information systems.

- Describe how the costs of the Information Systems function may be distributed between customer departments.

- Explain the principles, benefits and drawbacks of cross-charging costs.

- Discuss the issues raised by establishing the Information Systems function as a cost or profit centre.

- Describe the advantages and disadvantages of establishing the Information Systems function as a separate company.

- Explain the problems of accounting for shared infrastructure costs.

4   Organising information systems – structural issues   Chapter 3

- Describe the typical hardware, software, data and communications infrastructures found within Information Systems functions.

- Discuss the meaning and need for a disaster recovery plan.

- Discuss the meaning and need for a risk management process.

- Describe the meaning and implications of legacy systems.

- Discuss the relationship of Information Systems with end-users and the implications of the expectations and skills of end-users.

5   Feasibility study   Chapter 4

- Explain the purpose and objectives of a feasibility study.

- Evaluate the technical, operational, social and economic feasibility of the proposed project.

- Describe and categorise the benefits and costs of the proposed project.

- Apply appropriate investment appraisal techniques to determine the economic feasibility of a project.

- Define the typical content and structure of a feasibility study report.

6   Project initiation   Chapter 5

- Define the content and structure of terms of reference.

- Describe the typical contents of a Project Quality Plan and explain the need for such a plan.

- Identify the roles and responsibilities of staff who will manage and participate in the project.

- Define in detail the role and responsibilities of the project manager.

- Explain the concept of a flat management structure and its application to project-based systems development.

7   Project planning   Chapter 6

- Assist in splitting the project into its main phases.

- Participate in the breakdown of work into lower-level tasks.

- Assist in the estimation of the time taken to complete these lower-level tasks.

- Define dependencies between lower-level tasks.

- Construct and interpret a project network.

- Construct and interpret a Gantt Chart.

8   Project monitoring and control   Chapter 6

- Describe methods of monitoring and reporting progress.

- Define the reasons for slippage and how to deal with slippage when it occurs.

- Discuss the reasons for changes during the project and the need for a project change procedure.

- Reflect the effects of progress, slippage and change requests on the project plan.

- Discuss the particular problems of planning and controlling Information Systems projects.

9   Software support for project management   Chapter 6

- Define the meaning of a project management software package and give a brief list of representative products.

- Describe a range of features and functions that a project management software package may provide.

– Explain the advantages of using a project management software package in the project management process.

PART 2: DESIGNING INFORMATION SYSTEMS

Overall

This section provides the candidate with an insight into how systems are defined and developed. The intention is to concentrate on the following areas.

- The definition and agreement of business requirements
- The external design of the system
- The selection of a software package solution.

10 The information systems development process
Chapter 7

- Define the participants in the systems development process – managers, analysts, designers, programmers and testers.
- Describe the waterfall approach to systems development and identify its application in a representative systems development methodology.
- Describe the spiral approach to systems development and identify its application in a representative systems development methodology.
- Discuss the relative merits of the waterfall and spiral approaches, including an understanding of hybrid methodologies that include elements of both.

11 Investigating and recording user requirements
Chapter 8

- Define the tasks of planning, undertaking and documenting a user interview.
- Identify the potential role of background research, questionnaires and special purpose surveys in the definition of requirements.
- Describe the purpose, conduct and recording of a facilitated user workshop.
- Explain the potential use of prototyping in requirement's definition.
- Explain how requirements can be collected from current computerised information systems.
- Discuss the problems users have in defining, agreeing and prioritising requirements.

12 Documenting and modelling user requirements – processes
Chapter 9

- Describe the need for building a business process model of user requirements.
- Describe in detail the notation of either a data flow diagram or a flowchart.
- Construct a business process model of narrative user requirements using a data flow diagram or a flowchart.
- Explain the role of process models in the systems development process.

13 Documenting and modelling user requirements – static structures
Chapter 9

- Describe the need for building a business structure model of user requirements.
- Describe in detail the notation of either an entity-relationship model (Logical Data Model) or a class model.
- Construct a business structure model of narrative user requirements using an entity-relationship model (Logical Data Model) or a class model.
- Explain the role of structure models in the systems development process.

14 Documenting and modelling user requirements – events
Chapter 9

- Describe the need for building a business event model of user requirements.
- Describe in detail the notation of either a statechart diagram (state transition diagram) or an entity life history.
- Construct a business event model of narrative user requirements using a statechart diagram (state transition diagram) or an entity life history.
- Explain the role of event models in the systems development process.

15 External design
Chapter 10

- Define the characteristics of a 'user-friendly' system.
- Describe the task of external design and distinguish it from internal design.
- Design effective output documents and reports.
- Select appropriate technology to support the output design.
- Design effective inputs.
- Select appropriate technology to support input design.
- Describe how the user interface may be structured for ease of use.
- Explain how prototyping may be used in defining an external design.

16 Developing a solution to fulfil requirements
Chapter 11

- Define the bespoke software approach to fulfilling the user's information systems requirements.
- Briefly describe the tasks of design, programming and testing required in developing a bespoke systems solution.
- Define the application software package approach to fulfilling the user's information systems requirements.
- Briefly describe the tasks of package selection, evaluation and testing required in selecting an appropriate application software package.

- Describe the relative merits of the bespoke systems development and application software package approaches to fulfilling an information systems requirement.

17 Software package selection   **Chapter 11**

- Describe the structure and contents of an Invitation to Tender (ITT).
- Describe how to identify software packages and their suppliers that may potentially fulfil the information systems requirements.
- Develop suitable procedures for distributing an ITT and dealing with subsequent enquiries and bids.
- Describe a process for evaluating the application software package, the supplier of that package and the bid received from the supplier.
- Describe risks of the application software package approach to systems development and how these might be reduced or removed.

18 Software support for the systems development process   **Chapter 12**

- Define a Computer Aided Software Engineering (CASE) tool and give a brief list of representative products.
- Describe a range of features and functions that a CASE tool may provide.
- Explain the advantages of using a CASE tool in the systems development process.
- Define a Fourth Generation Language and give a brief list of representative products.
- Describe a range of features and functions that a Fourth Generation Language may provide.
- Explain how a Fourth Generation Language contributes to the prototyping process.

PART 3: EVALUATING INFORMATION SYSTEMS

Overall

This section provides the candidate with an insight into how systems are implemented and evaluated. The intention is to concentrate on the following areas.

- The definition and agreement of non-business requirements
- The quality assurance of the solution
- The implementation and maintenance of the solution.

19 Technical information systems requirements   **Chapter 13**

- Define and record performance and volume requirements of information systems.
- Discuss the need for archiving, backup and restore, and other 'house-keeping' functions.
- Explain the need for a software audit trail and define the content of such a trail.

- Examine the need to provide interfaces with other systems and discuss the implications of developing these interfaces.
- Establish requirements for data conversion and data creation.

20 Legal compliance in information systems   **Chapter 14**

- Describe the principles, terms and coverage typified by the UK Data Protection Act.
- Describe the principles, terms and coverage typified by the UK Computer Misuse Act.
- Explain the implications of software licences and copyright law in computer systems development.
- Discuss the legal implications of software supply with particular reference to ownership, liability and damages.

21 Implementing security and legal requirements   **Chapter 14**

- Describe methods to ensure the physical security of IT systems.
- Discuss the role, implementation and maintenance of a password system.
- Explain representative clerical and software controls that should assist in maintaining the integrity of a system.
- Describe the principles and application of encryption techniques.
- Discuss the implications of software viruses and malpractice.
- Discuss how the requirements of the UK Data Protection and UK Computer Misuse legislation may be implemented.

22 Quality assurance in the management and development process   **Chapter 15**

- Define the characteristics of a quality software product.
- Define the terms, quality management, quality assurance and quality control.
- Describe the V model and its application to quality assurance and testing.
- Explain the limitations of software testing.
- Participate in the quality assurance of deliverables in requirement specification using formal static testing methods.
- Explain the role of standards and, in particular, their application in quality assurance.
- Briefly describe the task of unit testing in bespoke systems development.

23 Systems and user acceptance testing   **Chapter 15**

- Define the scope of systems testing.
- Distinguish between dynamic and static testing.

- Use a cause-effect chart (decision table) to develop an appropriate test script for a representative systems test.
- Explain the scope and importance of performance testing and usability testing.
- Define the scope and procedures of user acceptance testing.
- Describe the potential use of automated tools to support systems and user acceptance testing.

24 Implementation issues and implementation methods
Chapter 16

- Plan for data conversion and creation.
- Discuss the need for training and suggest different methods of delivering such training.
- Describe the type of documentation needed to support implementation and comment on ways of effectively organising and presenting this documentation.
- Distinguish between parallel running and direct changeover and comment on the advantages and disadvantages of each.

25 Post-implementation issues   Chapter 17

- Describe the metrics required to measure the success of the system.
- Discuss the procedures that have to be implemented to effectively collect the agreed metrics.
- Identify what procedures and personnel should be put in place to support the users of the system.
- Explain the possible role of software monitors in measuring the success of the system.
- Describe the purpose and conduct of an end-project review and a post-implementation review.

- Describe the structure and content of a report from and end-project review and a post-implementation review.

26 Change control in systems development and maintenance   Chapter 18

- Describe the different types of maintenance that a system may require.
- Explain the need for a change control process for dealing with these changes.
- Describe a maintenance lifecycle.
- Explain the meaning and problems of regression testing.
- Discuss the role of user groups and their influence on system requirements.

27 Relationship of management, development process and quality   Chapter 18

- Describe the relationship between project management and the systems development process.
- Describe the relationship between the systems development process and quality assurance.
- Explain the time/cost/quality triangle and its implications for information systems projects.
- Discuss the need for automation to improve the efficiency and effectiveness of information systems management, delivery and quality assurance.
- Explain the role of the accountant in information systems management, delivery and quality assurance.

28 Revision

The examination

Format of the examination

	Number of marks
Section A: 3 compulsory questions (20 marks each)	60
Section B: choice of 2 from 3 questions (20 marks each)	40
	100
Total time allowed: 3 hours	

Section A is based on a short narrative scenario.

Section B contains three independent questions, one question from each main area of the syllabus.

Additional information

The study guide was previously vague about the diagramming requirements when documenting and modelling user requirements. The study guide has now been updated to clarify this matter — see Sessions 12, 13, and 14. Chapter 9 has been revised and a completely new Chapter 10 has been added to this text to reflect this.

There is more detailed clarification in the June 2004 exam notes, the full text of which is reproduced below.

Documenting and modelling user requirements

Paper 2.1 Study Guide Sessions 12, 13 and 14 require candidates to briefly describe different approaches to modelling and to describe and apply in detail one notation (each) for processes, static structures and events. Until now, no specific guidance has been given on which models to teach. However, it is now clear that tutors, publishers and candidates require clarification.

Session 12

Session 12 requires candidates to describe and apply a process model. The prescribed models for this session are **data flow diagrams** and **flowcharts**.

Either of these may be learnt in detail and applied in the examination.

Data flow diagrams have symbols for processes, data stores, external entities (sources and sinks) and data flows. They also have certain rules of construction. For example, one data store cannot be directly connected to another and data cannot flow directly from an external entity to a data store (or vice versa). A popular notation is that of SSADM, but alternatives such as the Yourdon/de Marco notation and the Gane & Sarson notation are perfectly acceptable. Candidates should understand how the data flow diagram is decomposed into lower-level data flow diagrams but they will not be expected to undertake such decomposition (or annotate it) in an examination.

Flowcharts are well-established process models. They usually have symbols for showing processes, decisions, data stores, documents and flows. The symbols used in Microsoft Word templates for flowcharts, together with arrow-headed lines for flows, should be sufficient for examination purposes.

The Unified Modeling Language (UML) includes the **activity diagram**, which is essentially a **flowcharting model**. This notation has symbols for initial and final states, action states, branches and concurrency. It is an acceptable alternative to the traditional flowchart. There is no requirement to show sub-activity states. Like most flowcharts, activity diagrams allow the symbols to be organised in 'swimlanes' to show who is handling the information. 'Swimlanes' may be organised horizontally or vertically.

Session 13

Session 13 requires candidates to describe and apply a business structure model. The prescribed models are **Entity-relationship models (Logical Data Models)** and **class models**.

Either one of these may be learnt in detail and applied in the examination.

Entity-relationship models have symbols for entities, the relationships between the entities and the cardinalities (degree) of those relationships (i.e. 1:1, 1:many, many:many). Learning entity sub-types and super-types bring these models more into line with the class models discussed below. A 'common sense' allocation of attributes to entities should also be understood. These attributes may be described within the entity or, perhaps more easily, in a simple list showing which attributes are in each entity. A formal approach to normalisation, the definition of foreign keys and the naming of relationships are not required. However, candidates should learn the decomposition of a many:many relationship to assist them in the allocation of attributes to appropriate entities.

The UML has an extensive notation for **class models**. Candidates should be able to identify classes, attributes within classes, simple associations and their cardinalities (i.e. multiplicities). Generalisation (inheritance) of attributes should also be learnt, as should association classes. However, it is unnecessary for candidates to handle composition and aggregation. Furthermore, operations, polymorphism, abstraction and association naming are also outside the scope of the syllabus.

Session 14

This session requires candidates to describe and apply a business event model. The prescribed models are **statechart diagrams (state transition diagrams)** and **entity life histories**.

Either one of these may be learnt in detail and applied in the examination.

The UML **statechart diagram** has symbols for initial state, final state, states, transitions, events and actions. The nesting of states should be learnt but there is no requirement for showing decomposition of states or the modelling of guards.

Entity life histories have a notation for showing the entity, the sequence of events affecting that entity, the iteration of events and the selection of events. There is no requirement for showing parallel events. Operations should be taught (as these make the entity life history clearer) but there is no need to show operations for forming or breaking relationships with other entities or for showing state indicators.

Examination tips

- Spend the first few minutes of the examination **reading the paper**.

- Where you have a **choice of questions**, decide which ones you will do.

- **Divide the time** you spend on questions in proportion to the marks on offer. One suggestion is to allocate 1½ minutes to each mark available, so a 10 mark question should be completed in 15 minutes.

- Unless you know exactly how to answer the question, spend some time **planning** your answer. Stick to the question and **tailor your answer** to what you are asked.

- **Fully explain** all your points but be **concise**. Set out all workings **clearly and neatly**, and state briefly what you are doing. Don't write out the question.

- If you do not understand what a question is asking, **state your assumptions**. Even if you do not answer precisely in the way the examiner hoped, you should be given some credit, if your assumptions are reasonable.

- If you **get completely stuck** with a question, leave space in your answer book and **return to it later.**

- Towards the end of the examination spend the last **five minutes** reading through your answers and **making any additions or corrections**.

- Before you finish, you must fill in the required information on the front of your answer booklet.

Answering the questions

- **Essay questions**: Make a quick plan in your answer book and under each main point list all the relevant facts you can think of. Then write out your answer developing each point fully. Your essay should have a clear structure; it should contain a brief introduction, a main section and a conclusion. Be concise. It is better to write a little about a lot of different points than a great deal about one or two points.

- **Case studies**: To write a good case study, first identify the area in which there is a problem, outline the main principles/theories you are going to use to answer the question, and then apply the principles/theories to the case. Include relevant points only and then reach a conclusion and, if asked for, recommendations. If you can, compare the facts to real-life examples – this may gain you additional marks in the exam.

- **Reports, memos and other documents**: Some questions ask you to present your answer in the form of a report or a memo or other document. Use the correct format – there could be easy marks to gain here.

Study skills and revision guidance

This section aims to give guidance on how to study for your ACCA exams and to give ideas on how to improve your existing study techniques.

Preparing to study

Set your objectives

Before starting to study decide what you want to achieve – the type of pass you wish to obtain. This will decide the level of commitment and time you need to dedicate to your studies.

Devise a study plan

- Determine which times of the week you will study.

- Split these times into sessions of at least one hour for study of new material. Any shorter periods could be used for revision or practice.

- Put the times you plan to study onto a study plan for the weeks from now until the exam and set yourself targets for each period of study – in your sessions make sure you cover the course, course assignments and revision.

- If you are studying for more than one paper at a time, try to vary your subjects, this can help you to keep interested and see subjects as part of wider knowledge.

- When working through your course, compare your progress with your plan and, if necessary, re-plan your work (perhaps including extra sessions) or, if you are ahead, do some extra revision/practice questions.

Effective studying

Active reading

You are not expected to learn the text by rote, rather, you must understand what you are reading and be able to use it to pass the exam and develop good practice. A good technique to use is SQ3Rs – Survey, Question, Read, Recall, Review:

1 **Survey** the chapter – look at the headings and read the introduction, summary and objectives, so as to get an overview of what the chapter deals with.

2 **Question** – whilst undertaking the survey, ask yourself the questions that you hope the chapter will answer for you.

3 **Read** through the chapter thoroughly, answering the questions and making sure you can meet the objectives. Attempt the exercises and activities in the text, and work through all the examples.

4 **Recall** – at the end of each section and at the end of the chapter, try to recall the main ideas of the section/chapter without referring to the text. This is best done after a short break of a couple of minutes after the reading stage.

5 **Review** – check that your recall notes are correct.

You may also find it helpful to reread the chapter and try to see the topic(s) it deals with as a whole.

Note-taking

Taking notes is a useful way of learning, but do not simply copy out the text. The notes must:

- be in your own words
- be concise
- cover the key points
- be well-organised
- be modified as you study further chapters in this text or in related ones.

Trying to summarise a chapter without referring to the text can be a useful way of determining which areas you know and which you don't.

Three ways of taking notes:

- **summarise the key points** of a chapter.

- **make linear notes** – a list of headings, divided up with subheadings listing the key points. If you use linear notes, you can use different colours to highlight key points and keep topic areas together. Use plenty of space to make your notes easy to use.

- **try a diagrammatic form** – the most common of which is a mind-map. To make a mind-map, put the main heading in the centre of the paper and put a circle around it. Then draw short lines radiating from this to the main sub-headings, which again have circles around them. Then continue the process from the sub-headings to sub-sub-headings, advantages, disadvantages, etc.

Highlighting and underlining

You may find it useful to underline or highlight key points in your study text – but do be selective. You may also wish to make notes in the margins.

Revision

The best approach to revision is to revise the course as you work through it. Also try to leave four to six weeks before the exam for final revision. Make sure you cover the whole syllabus and pay special attention to those areas where your knowledge is weak. Here are some recommendations:

- **Read through the text and your notes again** and condense your notes into key phrases. It may help to put key revision points onto index cards to look at when you have a few minutes to spare.

- **Review any assignments** you have completed and look at where you lost marks – put more work into those areas where you were weak.

- **Practise exam standard questions** under timed conditions. If you are short of time, list the points that you would cover in your answer and then read the model answer, but do try and complete at least a few questions under exam conditions.

- Also **practise producing answer plans** and comparing them to the model answer.

- If you are stuck on a topic find somebody (a tutor) to explain it to you.

- **Read good newspapers and professional journals**, especially ACCA's *Student Accountant* – this can give you an advantage in the exam.

- Ensure you **know the structure of the exam** – how many questions and of what type you will be expected to answer. During your revision attempt all the different styles of questions you may be asked.

Chapter 1

BUSINESS STRATEGY

This chapter investigates the need for information systems within organisations, and in particular how those systems are used to support business strategy. The difference between a Business Strategy and an Information Strategy is also explained, and links between these strategies are established.

Objectives

By the time you have finished this chapter you should be able to:

- understand the importance of business objectives
- discuss how information systems may be used to assist in achieving these objectives
- identify current trends in information technology (IT) and the opportunities they offer to organisations
- distinguish between a business strategy and an information systems strategy
- identify responsibility for the ownership of the IS strategy.

1 Strategic business objectives

All organisations should have objectives. Objectives define what an organisation is trying to achieve in the long term, as well as the short term. Without objectives, an organisation has no overall direction, and possibly no purpose for its existence. Objectives provide focus for an organisation allowing it to concentrate on the things it must do to be successful.

Organisations often have a hierarchy of objectives. For many companies, the primary objective is to increase shareholder wealth, possibly by seeking to grow long-term profits. For state-owned organisations, such as schools and health authorities, primary objectives are different and relate to providing value for money and high quality service.

Primary objectives normally generate a series of subsidiary objectives. These have to be achieved to ensure that primary objectives are met. Subsidiary objectives may relate to specific areas of business operation, including technological development, customer service and employee development. Organisations may also have a series of objectives to ensure development of required information systems.

1.1 Critical success factors (CSFs)

One method of quantifying objectives is to identify critical success factors or CSFs. This concept was originally developed by John Rockart in the 1970s.

CSFs focus the attention of senior management on what is really important to the long term success of an organisation.

Critical success factors are defined as:

The limited number of areas in which results, if satisfactory, will ensure successful competitive performance for the business. They are vital areas where 'things must go right' for the business to flourish.

Throughout an organisation there must be a clear and shared understanding of what the critical success factors are, together with an appreciation of how each unit or department can contribute to their achievement. The management process itself must be integrated in the sense of sharing a common purpose and approach.

Generally, corporate objectives are defined by broad issues around increasing profits, developing new products and diversification. Once identified, managers involved in strategy formulation will identify the critical success factors that must be achieved for the organisation to flourish.

1.2   Sources of CSFs

Sources of critical success factors can be wide ranging. Rockart identifies four sources:

1   **The industry that the business is in** – each industry has CSFs that are relevant to any company within it. 'Compliance with pollution requirements regarding car exhaust gases', for instance, would be relevant to the whole car industry.

2   **The company itself and its situation within the industry** e.g. its competitive strategy and its geographic location. CSFs could be to develop new products, create new markets or to support the field sales force. Actions taken by a few large dominant companies in an industry will provide one or more CSFs for small companies in that industry.

3   **The environment** e.g. the economy, political factors and consumer trends in the country or countries in which the organisation operates. Rockart points out that before 1973 very few chief executives in the USA would have cited 'energy supply availability' as a critical success factor. Following the oil embargo, many executives began to monitor this factor closely.

4   **Temporal organisational factors**, i.e. areas of company activity that are causing concern in the short term e.g. supply difficulties caused by transport restrictions during the Foot and Mouth epidemic in the UK.

Rockart identified two types of CSF:

- **monitoring**: keeping abreast of ongoing operations
- **building**: tracking progress of the change programs initiated by an executive.

Chief executives have both monitoring and building responsibilities. CSFs developed by an organisation will reflect this. CSFs of concern to senior management tend to involve building. For example, senior management may view decentralisation of the organisational structure as critical to future success. Middle management, tasked with achieving this, may have a series of CSFs designed to promote and monitor this change.

To obtain consensus, managers involved in strategy formulation should meet and confirm their understanding of the business strategy and the information needs it generates. Any conflict between management and departments must be minimised. Sufficient critical success factors should be established to cover all major business objectives, whilst ensuring that contradictory factors are not set.

Monitoring CSFs may involve use of several information sources. It will be up to the managers concerned to decide what information is required, the frequency of collection and the level of aggregation.

Examples of information that can be used to monitor some of the CSFs of a garden furniture manufacturer include:

CSF	Information needs
Achieve quoted delivery dates	• Production schedules
	• Inventory levels
Consistent performance to budget on major jobs	• Job cost budgeted/achieved
Market success	• Change in market share
Sound image in financial market	• Price/earnings ratio
Morale of employees to be high	• Turnover, absenteeism, sickness
	• Informal communication

1.3 Performance indicators

In addition to identifying CSFs, managers need to know how well or badly an organisation is performing, and whether its CSFs are being achieved.

For every CSF, there should be at least one identifiable and measurable performance measure (**key performance indicator/s**). Performance indicators are quantifiable targets and are used to monitor the degree of achievement of each CSF. Providing information on performance requires information to be supplied in a form that the executives and managers can use.

After critical factors success has been determined, two or three prime measures for each factor should be developed. Some measures use hard, factual data and these are the easiest to monitor. Other measures are softer, and involve opinions, perceptions and hunches. Capturing appropriate data for this type of measure is more problematic.

Not all the information needed will be available from existing information systems. If this is the case, new ways of acquiring information will need to be evaluated and developed.

One of the major problems with strategy implementation in many organisations is a failure to translate declarations of strategic purpose into a clearly defined set of critical success factors and key performance indicators. This is often compounded by failure to identify key tasks involved in achieving objectives and a lack of clear management responsibility for delivery.

These problems can be overcome by adopting a systematic approach.

Critical success factors for the specific strategy must be agreed and scrutinised to make sure that they are all genuinely necessary and that the list is sufficient to underpin success.

Key tasks, which are essential to the delivery of each critical success factor, must be identified. These may relate to activities in an organisation's value chain. Key tasks may include improvements in support activities or change in linkage within the value system. For example, an office equipment supply company, with a critical success factor of customer care, would underpin the CSF through three key tasks. These are responding to customer enquiries, supplying accurate information and provision of an efficient breakdown and maintenance service. These tasks are dependent on the company's information systems infrastructure, particularly its database of customer installations.

Management responsibility for key tasks should then be allocated. In the case of the office equipment supply company, a poorly maintained customer database will hamper customer care. Clear management responsibility for the maintenance of the database must be established, together with an effective communication system between the sales and maintenance teams.

1.4 CSFs and information needs

Effective implementation of strategy requires managers to make appropriate decisions to ensure that each CSF is achieved. This is illustrated below:

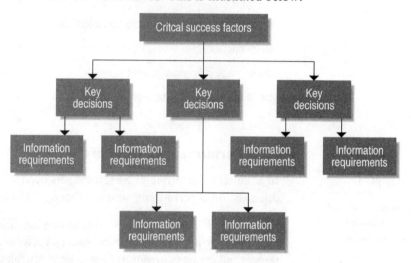

Making and monitoring these decisions in turn requires information. CSFs therefore help to define the information needs of an organisation, preventing the collection of unnecessary and costly data. A CSF relating to reduction of stock costs, for instance, would require collection of information on inventory levels and stock turnover times. In turn, appropriate company information systems can help to achieve this CSF by providing accurate demand forecasts, allowing managers to match purchasing with customer demand.

2 Information and systems

2.1 Strategy and information needs

CSFs and PIs generate information needs within in an organisation, both for their formulation and monitoring. This is in turn necessitates development of appropriate information systems to meet these needs.

2.2 Information technology and information systems

Information technology (IT) describes any equipment concerned with the capture, storage, transmission or presentation of information. Today IT is often referred to as ICT (Information Communications Technology), emphasising the importance of communications.

Information technology *per se* has little value to an organisation. Its application to meet specific information and communication needs generated by business activities can, however, bring enormous benefits.

2.3 Information systems

Information systems (ISs) are the systems responsible for the provision of information for management. They incorporate IT. However, they also include the people, business processes and procedures used to manage the capture and communication of information.

Information systems often involve complex and dynamic interaction between people, technology and process to ensure the delivery of appropriate and timely information to management.

2.4 Information as a resource

The characteristics of information required at different management levels varies considerably. The **Gorry and Scott-Morton model** presents a detailed picture of information attributes and how they vary with the level of management hierarchy.

Characteristics of information	Management hierarchy		
	Operational (day to day)	Tactical (medium term)	Strategic (longer term)
Source	Mainly internal		Mainly external
Scope	Narrow, well-defined		Very wide
Level of aggregation	Detailed		Aggregated
Time horizon	Historical		Future
Currency	Highly current		Quite old
Required accuracy	High		Quite low
Frequency of use	Very frequent		Infrequent

The changing characteristics of information at different management levels leads to different systems being developed.

Transaction Processing Systems (TPSs). These are used to capture and process transaction data in a routine manner. An example of a transaction processing system is a computerised accounting system. Another example of transaction processing is processing of customer sales via the Internet.

Management Information Systems (MISs). These provide routine management reports. An example is a system that provides budgetary control reports to management every month, by comparing actual results with a budget, and reporting on differences or variances between actual and budget.

Decision Support Systems (DSSs) Expert Systems (ESs) and Executive Information Systems (EIs). These systems provide information to middle and senior management and provide support for analysis of complex problems. Use of spreadsheets, for instance, to carry out scenario modelling or complex sensitivity analysis is an example of this type of system.

Although systems designed to support each management level have specific characteristics, effective information systems should have the following attributes:

- **decision oriented** – the system must produce material in an appropriate way to enable informed decision-making

- **data management** – the system should maintain the three Is of data storage – integrity, independence and integration

- **flexibility** – the system should be capable of adapting both to changing business information needs and to changes in technology

- **human computer interface** (HCI) – the interface should be intuitive and user friendly, and be capable of meeting the needs of novice and expert users alike.

2.5 Decision support systems (DSSs)

The purpose of many information systems is to provide information to support business decision-making. Decisions can be categorised into three types:

Structured decisions are routine decisions that are made according to a clear set of rules and procedures. Computer systems are often able to make structured decisions themselves, without the need for human intervention. Alternatively, computer systems might produce routine reports, and managers might use the information to make structured decisions.

Unstructured decisions are decisions where there are no clear rules, and the decision maker has to use judgement. The degree of uncertainty and risk could be very high. Information systems can help with an analysis of factors involved in the decision, and can help managers to reach a more rational and well-informed decision. Information systems that assist managers with unstructured decisions (and semi-structured decisions) are called **decision support systems**.

Semi-structured decisions have both rules and areas that require the application of judgement.

Expert systems are often mentioned in the context of decision-making. Unlike decision support systems, expert systems are capable of making decisions. They are commonly developed for use with problems that requires application of logical reasoning rather than computation. An example of an expert system is a medical computer system that can be used to analyse the symptoms of a patient's condition, to make a medical diagnosis.

2.6 Databases in decision support systems

A database is defined as a collection of structured data. Its structure is determined by the data themselves rather than the needs of a particular software application or group of users. In this way a database provides a flexible resource that can be adapted for multiple uses and can evolve as an organisation's information needs change.

An effective database will:

- avoid redundancy (duplication) of data

- support use by a wide variety of software applications and user groups

- be capable of adapting to changing data capture and storage requirements

- have clearly defined universal rules for addition, modification and deletion of data, together with a common protocol for data retrieval.

The following diagram shows the position of databases in the information systems hierarchy:

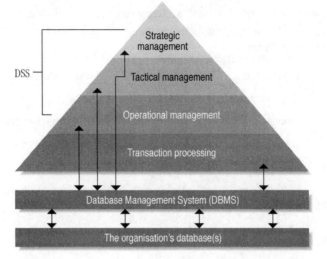

Database systems have a number of advantages:

- data only have to be input and stored once
- consistent data are used across an organisation
- flexibility to adapt to both technological change and changing business information needs
- the same data can be used to support all management levels.

2.7 Information management – a changing environment

Effective information management involves a blend of business skills, technological awareness, people and management skills. These skills are rarely found in an individual, requiring a multi-disciplinary team-based approach to issues of information management.

The complexity of information management has been increased by a number of organisational and technical changes:

- increasing user control over information system specification and use
- pressure to improve the cost-effectiveness of new systems
- pressure for increased access to and sharing of information from both users and customers
- increased pace of business and technological change.

3 Strategic planning for information systems

Effective use of information systems, in common with any other major business resource, requires strategic planning. Given the pervasive nature of information systems, it is arguable that strategic planning for systems should have a high management priority.

Failure to plan effectively can lead to:

- lead to development of inappropriate or ineffective systems
- compatibility problems across an organisation, preventing development of a corporate information infrastructure
- inefficient use of resources and unnecessarily high costs

- loss of competitive advantage through poor management and exploitation of corporate information resources.

Once a corporate business strategy has been developed, it becomes possible to ask, and begin to answer, a number of strategic questions relating to information systems. These include:

- what are the information needs of the organisation?
- what systems are required to meet these needs?
- what is the business role of these systems (mission critical or supportive)?
- what is the overall policy for development of these systems?
- what are the resources required?
- how is development and operation of systems to be managed, particularly who is to take strategic responsibility for these processes?

3.1 Ownership of IS strategy

For strategic planning of information systems to be effective, there needs to a firm and on-going commitment at board level within an organisation. Directors should be actively involved in developing and promoting strategy within an organisation. Without this commitment insufficient resources will be allocated to the process, and there will inadequate tie back into business strategy.

3.2 Linking IS and business strategy

An organisation's IS strategy should be firmly linked into its business strategy.

Clear identification of business objectives, CSFs and PIs does much to clarify the information needs of an organisation. An effective IS strategy will then ensure that these needs are met in an effective way, through the development of appropriate information systems.

In practical terms, implementation of an IS strategy will require an organisation to develop an IT strategy, with supporting hardware and software strategies. This hierarchy of strategies is illustrated below.

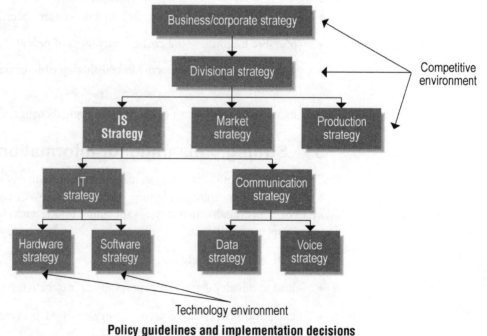

Policy guidelines and implementation decisions

(Adapted from *Strategic Management and Information Systems* Robson, 1997, Pitman)

3.3 The changing role of information systems strategy

Historically, an IS strategy was developed once the process of business strategy planning was completed. IS strategy was seen as supporting rather than driving key strategic business decisions. This tended to lead to ad-hoc or piecemeal systems development, with little overview of how systems should or could fit together.

From the 1980s onwards, the view of information as a key business resource gained momentum and there was a shift in the role of IS strategy. Rather than IS simply supporting business strategy it began to play a role in formulating strategy. Parallel to this was increased recognition of the role of users in specifying systems.

This change in role from passive business support to an active driver of business change is illustrated in the diagram below:

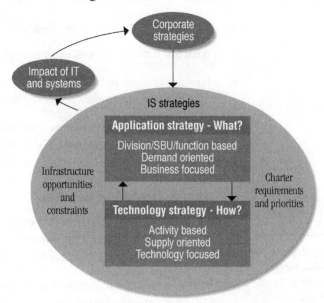

(Adapted from 'Integrating Information Systems into Business Strategies', Ward, *Long range planning* Vol 20, No 3 pp 19–20, 1987)

3.4 Objectives of IS strategic planning

Strategic information systems planning has a number of objectives, including:

- capturing business information needs through effective communication with users
- ensuring effective and appropriate systems development
- ensuring senior management engagement and commitment to the process.

IS strategic planning should be closely integrated with the corporate planning process, perhaps to the extent that the two activities are indistinguishable. Given the dynamic nature of both business and technology, strategic planning tends to be on-going, adapting to new business needs and changes in the competitive environment. Factors that can drive a review of IS strategy include:

1   Major organisational leading to significant change in business operations and information needs e.g. the acquisition of overseas operations.

2   External competitive opportunities and threats e.g. the emergence of low cost operators requiring aggressive use of technology to reduce costs and improve customer service.

3   Change in organisational maturity. As organisations begin to exploit information systems this tends to lead to identification of additional IS applications e.g. a gradual move away from standalone systems to development of an integrated corporate systems architecture.

4 Formulating an IT strategy

An IT strategy is concerned with development of a plan to deliver the technology and software needed to develop information systems identified in the IS Strategy.

Key issues addressed during development of an IT strategy include:

- what technology is needed to develop required systems?

- what software is needed to develop required systems?

- which solutions offer the best cost-benefit scenario?

- how is hardware and software to be obtained (in house vs. out-sourced; off-the shelf vs. bespoke)?

- how are new systems to be integrated with existing systems?

- what are the implications of proposed changes for staff?

- how are systems to be monitored and managed (performance indicators and management structure?

The level of effort and expenditure required to implement an IS strategic plan is likely to be high. It is therefore critical that an organisation considers thoroughly the issues listed above.

4.1 Implementation of plans

If carried out thoroughly, a combination of strategic business planning, IS strategy development and IT strategy formulation, should lead to clear identification and implementation of ideas to achieve business objectives.

Realisation of strategy will require formulation of a series of tactical and operational plans to ensure effective implementation. Much of the rest of this textbook explores the process of systems development and project management, together with the tools available to assist the process.

Backwater is a company with an established base of IT applications. The finance department has a fully computerised accounting system. The marketing department has a customer-modelling package and the production department does not see the need for technology.

The Finance Director is in charge of IT and he is proposing a 12% increase in IT expenditure to upgrade systems in the relevant departments, based on last year.

Briefly comment on the weaknesses in the IT provision at Backwater, and any improvements you might make.

Feedback to this activity is at the end of the chapter.

5 Developments in information technology

Technological developments pose a constant challenge to organisations, both opening up new opportunities and creating new threats. Whilst detailed knowledge of every new development in IT is not required, students are expected to have an awareness of current trends. A few are given below.

Here are just some developments in recent years.

Trading on the Internet

The possibility of trading online has both challenged existing business models and led to the development of new models. Buyer aggregation through the setting up of online markets (e.g. US motor manufacturers grouping together to buy parts) and customer to customer trading (e.g. eBay) have all offered new opportunities for business. Exploitation of e-tickets by low cost airlines has further increased the competitive pressure faced by established carriers.

Information on demand

Improved telecommunications infrastructure, the growth of networked systems and internet technology has led to development of an information on demand culture. Customers increasingly expect to control the flow of information between themselves and those they do business with rather than vice versa. This has led companies to develop systems allowing customers to access corporate systems to manage their own access to information e.g. Dell providing online access to maintenance databases for large clients.

Intranet

Intranets are in-house systems based on web technology. They are designed to provide a communication network to support shared access to information and collaborative working. Intranets do not recognise departmental boundaries, treating information and information systems as shared resources. In addition to improving access to corporate information resources and improving communication, many intranets provide interactive features such as staff bulletin and notice boards.

Broadband

The spread of high speed, high capacity broadband networks has been one of the most significant technological developments of the last three years. Broadband is now affordable for all businesses and for most consumers. Remote access to corporate systems is now a practical and affordable proposition for small businesses. Domestic use of broadband also offers companies an opportunity to harness the power of multimedia technology to promote their products.

Mobile computing

Mobile computing is becoming more and more common with laptop PCs having more power and communication capabilities. This has been supported by the spread of wireless networking and the integration of mobile phone and internet technologies. Staff on the road can now easily remain in contact with corporate information systems e.g. service engineers accessing the latest maintenance advice remotely from client premises.

ACTIVITY 2	Take 30 minutes to try and find out about new IT products and services that became available in the last month.

Feedback to this activity is at the end of the chapter.

Conclusion

Whilst the information needs of an organisation are driven by its business strategy and objectives, it is important to recognise the role that information systems and technology can play in formulating strategy.

In order to realise maximum benefit from information resources, companies need to plan their information systems at a strategic level and then develop an appropriate information technology strategy to ensure effective systems development and implementation.

SELF-TEST
QUESTIONS

Strategic business objectives

1   What is a critical success factor? (1.1)

2   What are the four sources of CSFs according to Rockart? (1.2)

3   Explain how CSF analysis helps managers determine their information
     requirements. (1.4)

Information and systems

4   Show how the characteristics of information change depending on the
     management level that information is being used by. (2.4)

Strategic planning for information systems

5   What must an organisation's IS strategy be consistent with? (3.2)

6   Draw a diagram showing the relationship between IS, IT and the corporate
     strategies. (3.2)

Formulating an IT strategy

7   Define 'Information Technology'. (4)

EXAM-TYPE
QUESTION

IS strategy

Many major organisations use formal strategies to identify development priorities
for information systems (IS).

Required:

Discuss the reason for this.   **(10 marks)**

For the answer to this question, see the 'Answers' section at the end of the book.

FEEDBACK TO
ACTIVITY 1

Successful provision of information technology is not simply about ensuring
adequate finance. The process should begin with a clear outline of Backwater's
strategic objectives and the information needs this generates. This would then
allow an effective IS strategy to be developed to develop systems to meet these
needs, and from this an IT strategy to ensure implementation. This would ensure
that all of the departments are involved and recognise the important of IS/IT in
supporting and developing business operations. It would also help to ensure that
systems across the organisation are developed and integrated. Without such an
approach being adopted, there is a real risk that extra funding proposed by the
finance director will not be spent effectively.

FEEDBACK TO
ACTIVITY 2

There are various sources of information to assist you in your search. The Internet is
probably the most easily-accessible source.

On the Internet check out search engines such as www.google.com or
www.yahoo.com and enter key words or phrases into a search. With a bit of trial
and error, you should come across some interesting sites to visit.

Lookout for PC related magazines such as PCPRO and Computer Weekly. Both
provide reviews of current technology as well as examples of how it is being used in
practice.

Chapter 2
DELIVERING INFORMATION SYSTEMS – 1

This is the first of two chapters investigating how organisations provide information to their employees or third parties. This chapter examines different structures that can be used by the information systems function and the benefits or otherwise of outsourcing systems provision.

Objectives

By the time you have finished this chapter you should be able to:

- understand the role of steering committees in guiding development and provision of information systems

- describe the traditional structure of a centralised information systems department

- explain the principles of a decentralised information systems function

- discuss the advantages and disadvantages of centralising or decentralising the information systems function

- explain the principles of outsourcing the information systems function

- describe the advantages and disadvantages of outsourcing the information systems function.

1 The role of the steering committee

Because of the size of investment involved and the importance of key systems to organisations, many firms are establishing committees to help manage information-processing activities.

Steering committees draw their membership from across an organisation to ensure a wide range of opinions and viewpoints. The purpose of a steering committee is to decide how to allocate scarce IT resources and to plan for future system developments. Other activities of the steering committee include:

- ensuring that all the IT activities are in line with the strategic plans of the organisation

- providing leadership at senior level for the exploitation and management of IT

- ensuring that resource allocation decisions are effective

- co-ordinating information system requirements created by organisational restructuring

- creating terms of reference for project teams

- monitoring progress of the various projects.

Some firms establish a corporate-level steering committee, whose objective is to review plans and determine the size of the firm's investment in information processing. The corporate committee reviews divisional plans, organises and approves education about systems, and seeks coordination of systems across the organisation

The problems that arise with steering committees are:

- the experience and skills of members do not match the purpose of the committee

- committee composition reflects internal businesses politics rather than underlying systems needs

- the committee fails to communicate effectively with the rest of the organisation

- insufficient commitment is made to the committee leading to under allocation of time and resources.

2 The information systems department

Information systems departments tend to have a broad range of company-wide responsibilities.

The main functions of a typical department are shown in the diagram below:

Information Systems Department

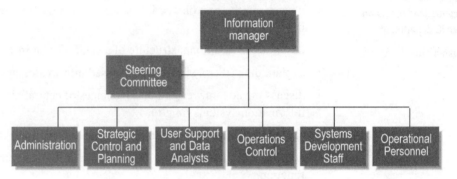

2.1 Information systems manager/director

The IS department will be under the control of the information systems manager or director, who will normally occupy a position on the board or similar executive decision-making body in the organisation.

In his book *Introducing information systems management,* Malcolm Peltu, describes the skills that the IT director should possess. These are:

- good management ability

- good understanding of how the organisation operates and the organisational activities

- good technical expertise in developing and running information systems.

These skills are difficult to find in combination. Many individuals having good technical skills often lack business experience or good people skills. In contrast, experienced managers and good communicators often lack technical skills. Many organisations employ information systems managers with strong business skills, relying on other members of staff to provide technical input.

The role of the information director is likely to include the following:

1 Ensuring development and implementation of an IS strategy that is compatible with the business strategy.

2 Actively promoting the use of IS within an organisation.

3 Responsibility for the information infrastructure, which incorporates the technical and software standards, establishment of databases and the provision of a systems support function.

4   Setting up and servicing links between IS staff and the rest of the organisation. This involves provision of technical assistance, discussion with users about their needs, discussion with finance and management accounting about the payoff of IS investments.

5   Participating in a steering committee to oversee the general direction of IS policy and taking decisions on individual IT projects.

6   Ensuring compliance with current data protection legislation.

2.2   Administration

Administration includes the secretarial, accounting and library services associated with the systems department. Key elements of departmental administration include budgeting and monitoring costs, together with maintaining records of hardware and software assets.

Particularly important here is maintenance of a software licence database to ensure compliance with licensing agreements and to assist upgrade and maintenance procedures. Detailed maintenance and problem logs should also be maintained.

2.3   User support

The IS department will provide user support in a variety ways. This can range from advice on software use and training through to development of corporate hardware and software standards to guide systems development occurring in user departments.

More specifically, user support includes:

- establishing hardware standards
- approving hardware suppliers
- establishing software, testing and documentation standards
- managing software upgrades
- ensuring data integrity
- enforcing security procedures including data backup and virus checking
- training in the use of languages and software development tools
- help when searching for reference publications on software, hardware, development methods
- assisting users to exploit corporate data resources
- technical assistance in dealing with particular problems when writing applications in programming languages
- ensuring that new systems developments do not create compatibility problems with existing (legacy) systems within the organisation
- guidance when purchasing hardware, software, application packages or external support services to maintain compatibility.

Much of the support offered by an IS department may be delivered through a centralised help desk. Typically this involves telephone support, supplemented by on-site visits. Increasing use is made of networked diagnostic software to reduce the need for visits. Training may be provided at the user's location or through use of dedicated training suites. Online training facilities are often made available to users.

2.4 Operations control

A key role of the Information Systems department is to ensure the continued operation of a company's information systems. Particular tasks that operations control will perform include:

- monitoring system usage and performance to ensure adequate system response times and capacity
- scheduling maintenance to minimise user disruption
- maintaining the IT infrastructure to ensure reliability and performance
- responding to faults quickly and effectively
- updating anti-virus software and firewall maintenance.

2.5 Systems development

In additional to operational responsibilities, IS departments play a key role in implementing corporate IS and IT strategies. Large IS departments often have permanent systems analyst and designer posts to help in the specification of new systems. A team of programmers may also be employed to write and maintain software applications for the organisation. Many of the key members for systems development projects (chapter 7) will be drawn from the department to provide critical systems and technical input into the development process.

3 Centralised vs decentralised provision of an IS department

Historically, IS departments were centralised, semi-autonomous departments within an organisation. More recently IS departments have become less centralised, with IS staff working and locating close to users. This section explores some of the reasons for this change, together with the relative merits of centralised and decentralised provision of IS services.

3.1 Decentralisation

The main reason for decentralising at least part of an IS department is to provide a more local service.

Other reasons for decentralising the IS functions are:.

Effective decision-making and user control

The process of decentralisation breaks up an IS department into more manageable units. This enables decision-making to proceed quickly and effectively. Decentralisation should also improve user control over system specification and development

Greater awareness of user needs

By working more closely with users, decentralised IS staff can develop a greater appreciation of user needs and the operational pressures faced by different workgroups. This should result in a more responsive IS team and development of appropriate systems, closely tailored to user needs.

Motivation

Decentralised IS staff are more likely to take ownership of specific user problems and systems issues.

Uncertainty and better 'local knowledge'

With ever-changing market conditions, decisions cannot be pre-planned or centrally planned. It is important to have local managers who are close touch with each particular part of the business environment to be in a position to respond quickly as problems arise. Decentralising the IS department means that changes can be made more quickly to respond to the individual needs of each user department. A centralised solution might not suit every part of the organisation.

Cost

Decentralising an IS department should empower user groups to determine the level of expenditure on IS systems. It is also arguable that decentralisation, by providing a scalable and flexible service, can reduce overall IS costs for a company.

Training

Training can be focused onto the requirements of the individual department, rather than generic training courses being produced for the whole organisation.

Software availability

For many applications, relatively cheap and well-tried software packages are available. It is therefore easier for departments in an organisation to select off-the-shelf software, without the need for centralised support or systems development work.

3.2 Centralisation

Though decentralisation of IS departments has been a recent trend in many organisations, there are a number of good reasons for retaining a centralised department. These are outlined below.

Economies of scale

Provision of centralised computing facilities may be cheaper than establishing a series of decentralised systems as unnecessary duplication of staff and IT equipment can be avoided.

Staff shortages/turnover

Centralisation mitigates the effect of both, so that individuals are less indispensable; they can also be provided with greater scope in their working experience. Fewer employees may be needed so higher quality staff and specialists may be affordable.

Ease of control

It is easier for senior management to coordinate and control the activities of a single department. This ensures consistent interpretation and implementation of a company's IS strategy. It also facilitates development and implementation of technical standards throughout an organisation.

Efficient hardware and software acquisition

A centralised department has the expertise to make effective decisions regarding purchase of hardware and software. It can also develop strong links with suppliers, together with negotiating significant discounts for hardware purchases.

4   Outsourcing

Outsourcing refers to organisations hiring/contracting–in services and expertise rather than providing them using their own staff and equipment..

Outsourcing can take a number of formats. At its simplest this may just involve outsourcing computer maintenance. At the other end of the scale, an organisation may outsource all of its IS provision, taking the decision not to own any information systems equipment or software or to employ an IS staff.

Facilities management, as a form of outsourcing, is growing in popularity as a solution to IS provision, and is discussed below.

4.1   Facilities management

Rather than maintain a computing department of its own, an organisation can choose to contract out its computer operations to a private company, which will be paid a fee for its services.

Facilities management is defined as the management and operation of part or all of an organisation's IT services by an external source, at an agreed service level, to an agreed cost formula and over an agreed time period. A facilities management contract may also include IT consultancy, management of IT services, provision of new services and ownership of hardware and software.

Facilities management companies are contracted to take over part or all of an organisation's computing facilities including:

- project management assistance
- complete control of systems development
- running an entire computing function.

Advantages

Possible reasons for using facilities management (FM) include:
- an organisation may not have the staff, management time or expertise to organise their substantial data processing requirements
- controlling costs as FM contracts have clearly defined costs
- economies of scale as FM companies can negotiate competitive prices for hardware and software
- the FM company may employ staff with specific expertise, which can be shared between several customers.

Disadvantages

Potential disadvantages and problems include:
- the provision of information is an inherent part of management and may be too important to contract out.
- technologies that play a strategic role in an organisation's success should be kept in-house.
- the process of outsourcing can be difficult to reverse. This can give the facilities management company great bargaining power.
- the organisation and the facilities management company have different objectives. The organisation will be anxious to maximise the performance and business benefits of systems. Conversely, the FM company will seek to minimise costs.
- facilities management might be used as a way to off-load problems rather than as a way of gaining significant business benefits.

4.2 Examples of IT outsourcing

Students might be asked to comment on the usefulness of outsourcing in particular circumstances, as part of an examination question. Some examples of outsourcing are:

- Payroll. Some companies, particularly small and medium-sized companies, outsource the processing of the monthly payroll to an outside specialist agency.

- Running of an entire computer system. In the UK, there are examples of large government computer systems, such as systems for processing social benefits claims and systems for storing and using criminal intelligence records, that have been outsourced to private sector companies.

- Software maintenance. Organisations that cannot (or do not want to) afford their own full-time IT staff for maintenance support will use the services of an outside firm. If any problem arises with an organisation's systems, such as a malfunction of the organisation's web site or its system for processing payments for Internet sales, the matter is referred to the outside software support firm.

Conclusion

Information systems departments can be either centralised or decentralised within organisations. Though there are advantages to both approaches, the recent trend has been to decentralise departments. Companies may also chose to outsource some or all of their IS provision in an attempt to cut cost and improve provision.

Information systems department

1   What is the purpose of a steering committee? (1)

2   What activities does the role of the Information Director include? (2.1)

Centralisation or decentralisation? The relative merits

3   Give five reasons for decentralising the IS department. (3.1)

Outsourcing

4   What services does a facilities management company provide? (4.1)

5   Outline the advantages and disadvantages of outsourcing the IS department. (4.1)

Centralising IT

Mugen Industrial plc is an industrial company serving international markets from factories in France, Germany, Portugal and Spain, North America and the UK. The company is a recognised leader in the manufacture of equipment for the automobile and aircraft industries. It also makes a wide range of engine mountings, hoses, plastic mouldings and rubber components. Turnover shown in the last published accounts was £450 million, of which £150 million was contributed by the UK companies.

All the overseas subsidiaries are wholly owned and operate principally in their own country. There is little transfer of goods across national boundaries. The group is managed from a small London headquarters and a great deal of autonomy has been given to the operating units. As a result each subsidiary has evolved its own information systems strategy.

In recent months the London headquarters has begun to press for a more centralised management structure. They argue it will enable more efficient use of resources and so cut costs. The Finance Director has asked you to investigate the options and report to him.

Required:

Prepare your report for the Finance Director setting out:

- the advantages of centralising the IT structure
- the disadvantages of centralising the IT structure
- any non-IT factors that might affect your final recommendation.

(15 marks)

For the answer to this question, see the 'Answers' section at the end of the book.

Chapter 3

DELIVERING INFORMATION SYSTEMS – 2

This is chapter begins by exploring different ways of charging for computer systems. It then provides a summary of background knowledge required regarding computer hardware and software.

Objectives

By the time you have finished this chapter you should be able to:

- briefly describe the types of cost incurred in delivering information systems

- describe how the costs of the information systems function may be distributed between customer departments

- explain the principles, benefits and drawbacks of cross-charging costs

- discuss the issues raised by establishing the information systems function as a cost or profit centre

- describe the advantages and disadvantages of establishing the information systems function as a separate company

- explain the problems of accounting for shared infrastructure costs

- describe the typical hardware, software, data and communications infrastructures found within information systems functions

- discuss the meaning and need for contingency planning

1   Accounting for IS costs

1.1   Costs incurred in delivering information systems

An organisation can incur many different costs in delivering information to its directors, employees, customers and suppliers. These costs can be summarised as follows.

One-off capital costs
These will include:
- hardware and software purchase
- specialist accommodation for computers
- wiring for networks
- installation costs such as new desks for employees
- new rooms/premises.

One-off revenue costs
These will include:
- systems development costs including programmers' salaries, systems analyst fees, costs of system testing , cost of converting files.
- redundancy payments (if any)
- hiring of new specialist staff
- staff training.

On-going costs

These will include:

- IS staff wages

- help desk and information centre salaries

- subscriptions to external information providers such as news services

- data transmission costs (telephone line rental, Internet access fees)

- consumable materials such as floppy disks, CDs, paper

- power for computers, VDUs

- any rental costs for hardware not initially purchased

- hardware maintenance and support contracts

- software maintenance and support contracts

- standby and backup arrangements

- regular staff training.

All of these costs have to be accounted for within the organisation.

Although IS costs could be treated as a non-rechargeable cost centre, there are a number of good reasons for establish a charging mechanism.

1 **Improved financial control for the IS and other user departments**. Charging for the service provides an incentive for the IS department to give good customer service.

2 **Encourage effective use of IT**. Charging forces users to assess their use of IT. Departments will only subscribe to services that repay their costs in terms of business benefits rather than making indiscriminate use of a free service.

3 **Improved systems development.** Charging encourages users to assess their demands for new systems. Any new system will increase IS costs to a user department and will therefore have to demonstrate positive benefits before it is commissioned.

During the development and operation of information systems, there are many costs incurred. List the intangible costs that might result.

There is no feedback to this activity.

1.2 Accounting for information system costs

The costs of an information system can be accounted for in three main ways:

- IS is treated as a non-recharged cost centre

- IS is recharged at cost

- IS is recharged above cost, to make a profit.

The advantages and disadvantages of these methods are discussed below.

1.3 Non-recharged cost centre

IS and IT costs are charged to an IS cost centre, and treated as a period cost. Costs are then charged directly to the profit and loss account without being apportioned to user cost centres.

Advantages

- Simple and cheap. No apportionment of IT costs is needed.

- Might encourage customer-driven demand for innovation. Users might demand better systems knowing that these will have no cost effect on their departments.

- Users can concentrate on the main activities of their departments, as they do not have to worry about IT costs.

Disadvantages

- There is no incentive for users to moderate their demands for IS services or to consider the business benefits of their demands

- The IT department has little incentive to control costs.

- Users have little control over the operation of the IS service and is difficult for users to complain about poor quality systems or service.

- The true cost of departmental activities is underestimated due to the exclusion of IT costs.

1.4   Recharged at cost

In this approach IS costs are recharged to user departments. Recharge mechanisms vary but might involve time-based or user-based approaches. Charge out rates are set at a level sufficient to recover costs but not to generate a surplus.

Advantages

- Non-controversial as users are charged at cost

- Users are made aware of the link between IT use and cost

- Empowerment of users to demand system improvements and provision of a high quality service

- Effective cost control as users will complain if costs rise excessively.

Disadvantages

- The IS department may be able to pass on cost over runs by inflating its charge out rates, reducing the incentive for internal cost control

- Users may feel that a particular mechanism for recharge penalises them unfairly. Not all users utilise IS systems to the same degree so charge out mechanisms based on user numbers may be particularly unfair. Departments may also feel that they are subsidising systems developments elsewhere in an organisation.

1.5   Recharged at a mark-up

Under this approach IS services are charged out at a commercial rate to generate a surplus for the IS department. If this approach is developed user departments are free to seek IS/IT services from outside the organisation if they can be obtained at a cheaper rate.

Advantages

- The IT department should be able to make a surplus. This can then be reinvested in service development

- Making a profit depends on being efficient with costs and offering services that users want to buy and which are competitively priced. The IT department should therefore develop a more commercial outlook

- Users drive provision of IS/IT services. In a commercial environment only services for which there is a demand will be provided

- Arguably, providing services at commercial cost gives a better indicator of business cost.

Disadvantages

- If there is no suitable outside supplier, it can be difficult to decide on charge-out rates that should be used.

- Total cost can be increased. In addition to funding partial outsourcing of IS/IT by some departments, an organisation will still have to meet the costs of its in-house provision for users groups still dependent on internal provision.

1.6 Cross-charging of costs including shared infrastructure costs

Charging systems can become more complicated when parts of an IT system are shared between departments. To provide an estimate of usage prior to charging, some or all of the following activities should take place:

- review of network traffic to establish either the number of messages or amount of data being transferred over the shared resource by each department
- checking the number of users of each shared resource and allocating charges based on these figures
- checking the amount of disk space used on network servers and then allocating charges based on this measure
- logging the number of telephone calls made to the help desk and using these as a rough guide to use of resources.

Whatever method of charging is chosen it must be seen to be fair. It follows that charging should be based on a measure of actual usage rather than on some form of arbitrary split.

1.7 Establishing information systems function as a separate entity

A logical development from commercial charging for services is to set up an IS department as a separate company. It is then free both to bid for service contracts from its parent company, together with seeking business with third parties.

The benefits to user departments include:

- only paying for IS resources and staff when they need them, rather than supporting them internally as a fixed overhead.

- increased management time. Senior management's time (and cost) does not have to be spent on organising, motivating and training employees who are not delivering the core business activities of the company.

- access to a larger pool of experienced and motivated staff. The company no longer has to develop, maintain and support such a pool.

Setting up the IS department as a separate company is not without risks, however. If the IS department cannot survive commercially, an organisation may find itself unable to obtain the services it requires. It is also a difficult process to reverse if in the future it is decided to take IS provision back in-house.

2 Computer hardware

This section introduces common hardware and software that are found in most information systems.

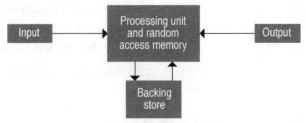

Fundamentally, all computer systems require some form of input. This is then stored and processed and then output for use by users.

2.1 Servers

A server, in a hardware sense, is simply a computer with a powerful processor and lots of random access memory. As the name suggests a server provides computing services to other computers (and hence users) on a network.

2.2 Mainframe computers or enterprise servers

Much of the computer processing in large organisations is carried out on powerful mainframe computers. They are designed to support multiple processing tasks and multiple concurrent users. Mainframes are often used to store and manage access to corporate databases and for systems requiring remote and multiple access to data e.g. stock control and electronic point of sale (EPOS) systems. Given that mainframes can be used to provide computing resources for a whole organisation they can be referred to as enterprise servers. Mainframe computers require specialist support and are therefore normally managed by the IS department.

2.3 Minicomputers or mid-range servers

Minicomputers are, like mainframes, designed to support multiple processing and multiple concurrent users. However they are generally less powerful and costly than mainframes. Given their lower specification, they are sometimes referred to as mid-range servers. Mini-computers represent a cost effective way of providing networked computer resources at the corporate level for small organisations or at the divisional level for larger organisations.

2.4 Personal computers

As their name suggests personal computers (PCs) are designed for use by one individual at a time. Their low cost and increasing power allows users to perform data processing tasks at their desk, which would have formerly required a mainframe computer. In addition to providing personal computer resources, PCs can act as terminals linking the user to centralised hardware and information resources.

2.5 Laptop PCs

Laptop computers have similar capabilities to PCs. Improvements in technology have reduced the weight and size of laptops, increasing their portability. In addition new battery technology has increased the duration of use between charges.

Most modern laptops have network cards built into them, allowing easy connection to corporate networks.

Handheld PCs (also known as pocket PCs, palmtops or personal digital assistants (PDAs)) are increasingly common, and may also be used for specialist applications such as carrying out market research surveys.

2.6 Peripherals

These are hardware devices other than processors. The term peripherals refers to input, output and communications hardware. Some of these devices are covered below.

2.7 Data storage

Internal storage

Data and programs can be stored in the internal RAM of the computer or on a hard disk.

KEY POINT

A server, in a hardware sense, is simply a computer with a powerful processor and lots of random access memory.

KEY POINT

Mainframe computers are designed to support multiple processing tasks and multiple concurrent users.

KEY POINT

Mid-range servers may act as the main computing resource in small or medium sized organisations, or may be used as departmental servers within large organisations.

KEY POINT

PCs are the most commonly used computer.

They can be stand-alone or networked.

KEY POINT

Laptop computers can be used by business people while travelling.

KEY POINT

Data and programs can be stored in the internal RAM of the computer, or on a hard disk.

DEFINITIONS

RAM (random access memory) is volatile memory accessible directly by the computer.

Hard disks provide permanent storage in a computer.

KEY POINT

The function of external storage is to maintain files of data and programs in a form intelligible to the computer.

KEY POINT

Magnetic tape is still very widely used as a back-up storage device.

KEY POINT

Floppy disks are convenient for taking copies of small amounts of data but they are slow and easily damaged.

KEY POINT

Hard disks stay permanently in PCs and typically hold several gigabytes (GB).

KEY POINT

Compact disks hold about 650MB of data.

KEY POINT

Digital versatile disks store up to 3.5 gigabytes.

RAM (random access memory) is volatile memory (the contents are lost when the computer is turned off) but it is accessible directly by the computer. It is used to store software instructions and data currently being used by the processor.

Hard disks provide permanent storage in a computer. They are not volatile so that data are retained when a computer is switched off.

External storage

The function of external storage is to maintain files of data and programs in a form intelligible to the computer. The principal requirements of external storage are that:

- sufficient storage capacity exists for the system to function adequately
- stored data can be quickly input to the computer when required
- stored data can be quickly and accurately amended when necessary.

2.8 Computer storage

Magnetic tape

Magnetic tape is still very widely used as a back-up storage device because of its low cost, reusability and reliability. Tape drives have quite high data capacity and can be used to back up both individual PCs and data/programs stored on a server.

Magnetic disks

The main types of magnetic disks are:

Floppy disks

Floppy disks are a convenient and cheap way to back up small amounts of data. They are also highly portable because of their size and weight. However, they are quite slow to use and are very easily damaged. Each floppy disk can store about 1.4MB of data.

Internal hard disks

These stay permanently in PCs and typically hold up to 120 gigabytes (GB). They are fast and reliable and are used to hold both data and programs. A server will typically have at least two internal hard disks.

Compact disks

These disks look like ordinary audio CDs and are similarly robust. They are very cheap and can hold about 650MB of data. In smaller systems they are now the most widely used back-up medium. They are also used to distribute new software packages. Re-writeable CD storage (CD-RW) is also available.

Digital versatile disks (DVD)

Digital versatile disks (DVDs) are now used as storage on many computer systems. DVDs offer enhanced capacity (from 3.5 GB up to 18 GB of data), which makes them ideal for multimedia applications containing large video and audio files.

3 Architectures

The term **architecture** is used to describe the physical appearance of a system and the way in which its component parts relate to one another. The choice over which architecture to adopt is a difficult one, but recent developments in operating software have simplified this task.

Until about 1990, it was impossible to fully interconnect PC hardware with mainframe or minicomputer processors. This was due to incompatibilities between the operating systems used, as most mainframes and minicomputers had their own operating systems that were specific to each manufacturer, and often to each model of equipment!

In 1990, the first operating systems capable of working on different types of hardware were developed. These **multi-platform operating systems** allowed full interconnection of PCs and centralised hardware, so the users could instruct processing to be carried out on their own workstation, or on any of the shared hardware devices.

This allows users to choose the most appropriate tool to perform the various applications, depending on the organisation's needs and the hardware available.

Many modern systems use a client-server approach to provision of IT resources. Clients (normally PCs) provide local processing and data storage facilities. However, also part of the system are a series of servers that support specialist tasks required by clients such as printing or access to the Internet. Servers also execute data processing tasks beyond the capacity of clients.

The different hardware elements of a client-server system are summarised below:

Client workstations	These are normally PCs used by individual users. Clients require tasks to be completed on their behalf e.g. printing of a document or extraction of data from a database.
Local or departmental servers	These are shared by a few users with the same computing needs. Departmental servers meet the needs of clients e.g. a local print server would manage all of the printing for a group of PCs.
A central or corporate server	This is shared by all users throughout the organisation. Corporate servers meet the needs of client computers throughout the organisation e.g. extracting data form a centralised corporate database on behalf of client PCs.

4 Computer software

Computer software is a collection of instructions used to control the operation of computer hardware.

4.1 Types of software

- There are five principal types of software:

- operating systems
- middleware
- applications (bespoke or off-the-shelf)
- utilities packages
- programming tools

Operating systems

Operating systems are dealt with in detail later.

Middleware

Middleware is software that acts as a bridge between two or more software types. For example, PHP, a web-based scripting language, manages the input of data captured on web pages into on-line databases.

Utilities packages

Utilities packages are software tools designed to improve the way in which the operating system works. These might automate routine operations such as file management or backup (as with 'Norton Utilities'), or might make the whole operating system easier to use (as with 'Windows' when used with a conventional operating system such as DOS).

Programming tools

Programming tools include the programming language itself, the tools to allow programs to be executed (such as compilers or assemblers) or more advanced tools such as computer-aided software engineering (CASE) packages.

4.2 Operating systems

Without an operating system a computer will not function. Example of operating systems are Windows XP, Mac OSX and Linux. Modern operating systems carry out the following functions:

- communication between the operator and the computer
- control of the processor and storage hardware
- management of files
- use of peripherals such as printers and modems
- management of communications with other computers on networked systems

Operating systems can generally be used in two modes.

- Command-driven mode. In this mode users enter commands line by line.
- Graphical user interface (GUI)-based mode. In this mode users do not need to enter commands line by line as the operating system is controlled by selecting from drop down menus in windows using a mouse. This type of user-friendly interface is commonly referred to a WIMP environment (Windows, Icons, Mouse and Pointer).

Modern operating systems often have networking facilities built into them. This allows the operating system to manage communications with other computers on a network, both clients and servers, together with managing the transmission of email. In many cases it is also possible to manage exchange of data with remote corporate databases.

4.3 Bespoke applications

Bespoke (tailor-made or purpose-written) applications are software that has been written to meet the specific needs of an organisation. It is not normally offered for sale to other organisations.

Advantages of bespoke software

- it precisely fits an organisation's information capture and processing needs
- the organisation has complete control over its functionality
- it can be integrated with other applications within the organisation
- its unique nature may offer competitive advantage
- it can be modified to fit changing needs.

KEY POINT

Operating systems enable:

- communication between the operator and computer
- control of the processor and storage hardware
- management of files
- use of peripherals such as printers and modems.

KEY POINT

Operating system modes:

- command-driven
- GUI-based.

KEY POINT

Bespoke applications are written to meet the specific needs of an organisation.

Disadvantages of bespoke software

- development takes a long time, which delays implementation

- bespoke software is costly to develop and test

- many bespoke software packages are started but not completed

- support of a bespoke system will be expensive as there is no user community or software vendor with which to share the costs.

4.4 Off-the-shelf applications

This is software that can be purchased and used immediately. Whilst off-the-shelf software has a particular purpose, it is designed to be flexible to meet the needs of a wide variety of organisations e.g. Sage is specifically an accounts package but it is very flexible and can be configured to meet individual user needs.

Examples of off-the-shelf applications include the following.

- spreadsheets

- word processing

- databases

- accounting

- communications.

Advantages of off-the-shelf packages:
- generally cheaper to buy than bespoke packages are to develop

- available almost immediately

- many supported by training programmes and documentation

- updated versions of software available on a regular basis

- the experience of a great number of users with similar needs to those in the organisation has been incorporated into the design of the package

- community of user for ideas and technical support.

Disadvantages of off-the-shelf packages:
- they do not fit precisely the needs of the organisation – users may need to accept reduced functionality

- software development is not controlled by users, possibly leading to loss of functionality in new versions

- users forced to purchase upgrades to ensure on-going technical support from the supplier.

- difficulty of integrating different software packages purchased from different suppliers

- Lack of competitive edge as the same software is available to all businesses.

5 Computer communications

It is quite rare today for an organisation to use individual computers in isolation (standalone). Most systems involve some form of connection (network) between computer hardware. Any system that requires computers to communicate with each other will need specialised hardware and software such as:

- modems

- communication programs

- network cards, hubs, bridges and routers and networking software.

5.1 Modems

The modem (MOdulator/DEModulator) is the interface between electronic pulses used to transfer data within the computer system and the signals needed for transmission through the telephone system. It is controlled by communications software running on the computer and provides an input and output link with the telephone system. With appropriate software, intelligent modems (those with built-in control circuitry) can handle communications with minimum manual intervention, allowing redialling of engaged numbers and call answering to be performed automatically. Many models are also capable of adjusting their information reception rate to match the transmission rate of the calling modem.

5.2 Communications software

Despite the sophistication achieved by modems, special software is still needed to handle the communications process itself, and the software used by the transmitter and the receiver must be compatible. To achieve this, certain standard protocols (agreed communications formats) have been developed so that systems can signal to each other the start and finish of transmission and reception and any problems experienced with data. Modern operating systems often include this software as part of their core functionality.

5.3 Local area networks (LANs)

Local Area Networks (LANs) link together computers and other hardware to allow sharing of hardware resources, software and data. In the case of a LAN the entire network is owned and controlled by one organisation i.e. the network does not involve use of public networks such as the Internet or telephone network.

Advantages of local area networks:

- data can be shared by users as can software applications
- LANs are very easy to extend to meet the growing needs of an organisation
- users can share expensive hardware such as high quality printers
- LANs are technically robust. Failure of a single item of hardware should not deny all users access to data and computing resources
- cost effective for large numbers of users
- members of the network can send electronic mail to one another thus reducing the amount of paperwork.

The distance over which a LAN can be set up is limited by the efficiency of the cables connecting the machines, and they are typically used within relatively small areas. Within these limits they provide an efficient means to communicate and to share hardware and software resources.

5.4 Wide area networks (WANs)

Wide area networks (WANs) contrast with LANs as at least part of the network involves use of shared communications such as the telephone system.

A modem is often used to gain access to a WAN, though other devices such as routers may be used. Any device that gives access to a WAN is known as a **gateway**. Given that WANs involve use of shared networks additional security precautions are advisable including use of data encryption.

6 Disaster recovery strategies (contingency planning)

Information systems are of growing importance to the operation of many businesses and the information they contain is a key business resource. Even temporary loss of a system can lead to major disruption, loss of business and increased cost.

Contingency planning for IS systems involves putting in place plans to deal with partial or total loss of an organisation's information systems. Fundamentally, contingency planning has two objectives:

- Ensuring that the data resources of an organisation cannot be lost regardless of the nature of a disaster

- Ensuring that replacement information systems are available as soon as possible to minimise business disruption

There are four steps in drawing up any contingency plan. These are:

- management commitment
- selection of the planning team
- selection of the standby option
- detailed planning

Management commitment

Without commitment from senior management contingency planning is unlikely to receive the input of time or resources needed for success. Further, major decisions have to be made regarding acquisition of back-up resources which require senior management input and approval.

Selection of the planning team

The planning team should be a mix of business and technical experts, together with representatives from senior management. Technical input is needed to determine the best way of backing up data and sourcing replacement systems. Equally, business input is needed to plan how to manage transition to replacement systems to minimise business disruption.

Selection of the standby plan

There are a number of different ways organisations can obtain back-up systems. The choice of option depends on the size of the organisation and the importance of the information systems involved. Below are some possible options.

1   Creation of multiple data processing facilities on separate sites, with the smallest site being capable of supporting the crucial work of at least one other site during the calculated recovery time. This strategy requires hardware and software compatibility and spare capacity.

2   Reciprocal agreement with another company. Although a popular option, few companies can guarantee free capacity, or continuing capability, which attaches a high risk to this option.

3   Pay a retainer to a disaster recovery company to maintain a duplicate system. Though this is expensive, it does allow very quick recovery as operations can be switched within a few hours to an alternative system.

4   Hot and cold systems. This involves an organisation setting up and maintaining a duplicate facility itself. This is an expensive but secure option.

The effectiveness of the contingency plan is dependent on comprehensive back-up procedures for both data and software.

Detailed planning

Once standby options have been identified a detailed contingency plan has to be developed. Issues covered here, include:

- Who has management responsibility for installation of the back-up data?

- Who is to manage the activation of back-up IT resources, possibly involving liaison with a third party provider?

- Who is to manage and communicate with the company' staff during the recovery period?

- Who is to liase with a company's customers and suppliers?

Once a plan has been developed, it should as far as possible be tested. Particular attention should be paid to data and software back-up procedures. Are all the necessary data being backed up and is it possible to restore an operational system from the back up?

The greater the effort invested in the preparation of a contingency plan, the more effectively the organisation will be able to mitigate the effects of a disaster.

Conclusion

This chapter has introduced some important issues such as risk management and how to charge for Information System services, as well as a long list of information about computer hardware and software. Remember in an examination question you will need to apply this background knowledge to the specific circumstances of the question, so please ensure that you understand all the terms mentioned in the chapter.

SELF-TEST QUESTIONS

Accounting for IS costs

1   List the main ways of re-charging the costs of the IS department. (1.2)

2   What are the benefits to the user department of establishing the IS function as a separate entity? (1.7)

Architectures

3   What are the arguments for decentralised systems? (3.1)

Computer software

4   What are the main types of computer software? (4.1)

Computer communications

5   List the advantages of using LANs within an organisation. (5.3)

Disaster recovery strategies

6   What is a contingency plan? (6)

EXAM-TYPE QUESTION

National Counties Hotels plc

National Counties Hotels plc ('National') runs a chain of 40 major hotels. Most of the hotels are in major cities, but some are located in areas of natural beauty and away from towns. Each hotel has a general manager and separate managers for its restaurant, conferences and group bookings. The housekeeper, chef, and senior barman also have some management responsibility.

The company's head office is in London. Each week head office receives a report from every hotel in the chain; this is used for planning and evaluation purposes. Head office also has a reservations section that can take bookings for all the hotels; alternatively, guests can ring up specific hotels. Guests who are touring will often ask the receptionist to make a booking for them at another of the group's hotels in an area they hope to travel to next.

The company is reviewing its information systems, as there have been some problems of late in several of the company's hotels or at head office. These have included:

- Arrangements made by a group bookings manager had not been properly recorded and individual bookings were subsequently accepted when no rooms were available.

- The kitchens did not pick up conference booking information and lunches that had been arranged could not be provided.

- A general manager wanted to review room occupancy by week and profitability. The analysis had to be performed by hand.

- At year-end, head office prepared accounts and it was discovered that an advert that had been placed in a travel magazine had been inadvertently allowed to appear every month. Invoices had been received and paid each month and the cost overrun was in the order of £9,000.

- There has been some revenue lost because room numbers have not been correctly recorded when services to guests have been provided. For example, in the restaurant or bar, guests can charge purchases to their rooms. So far guests have merely had to quote their room numbers without having to show any proof of identity.

You have been asked to advise the company on certain matters and have had a preliminary meeting with a head office official. In response to these problems, the official has said, "What the company needs is a proper operating system. If we had that we would be assured that we would be supplied with the proper information that would allow the company to operate more efficiently".

Required:

Produce a memorandum to the head office official that covers the following:

(a) Describe the major components of National in terms of their activities and explain the linkages that may exist between these various activities. **(10 marks)**

(b) Suggest a data capture method that would improve the accuracy of charging for services. Justify your choice in terms of fulfilling the requirements of National and in terms of guest convenience. **(5 marks)**

(Total: 15 marks)

For the answer to this question, see the 'Answers' section at the end of the book.

Chapter 4
FEASIBILITY STUDIES

Once an organisation has identified the need for a new information system, it can begin to set up a project to develop and deliver that system. The first stage of this process is to define more clearly the system that is required, together with key constraints that have to be taken into account. A written document covering the objectives and scope of the project is produced (a project initiation document). A feasibility study can then be completed to explore the practicality and business case for the system more thoroughly.

Objectives

By the time you have finished this chapter you should be able to:

- explain the purpose and objectives of a project initiation document and a feasibility study

- evaluate the technical, operational, social and economic feasibility of the proposed project

- describe and categorise the costs and benefits of the proposed project

- apply appropriate investment appraisal techniques to determine the economic feasibility of a project

- define the typical content and structure of a feasibility study report.

1   Project initiation and terms of reference

Once a preliminary decision has been made to go ahead with development of an information system, a project initiation document should be produced. This should outline system purpose and functionality, together with the scope of the proposed development. This project initiation document acts as the terms of reference for the project as a whole.

This document is developed by the project sponsor (normally the board or similar decision-making group in an organisation), the project manager and other key people involved in the project.

The project initiation document should contain the following information:

- **Statement of the purpose of the system**. Why is the system being developed?

- **Scope statement**. This establishes the **boundaries** of the new system and what it is trying to achieve. It specifies the major **business** activities that the system will support. A clear statement of scope is critical to maintaining project focus. Without this, there is tendency for projects to expand uncontrollably, slowing development and increasing costs.

- **Objectives**. To help retain project focus there should be a clearly defined set of project objectives and critical success factors against which to measure project progress.

- **Milestones.** Milestones identify key points in the project development process and are critical in monitoring project progress.

- **Cost and time estimates.** Although it can be difficult to specify costs and completion times accurately, it is important to set targets. These can then be kept under review as project development work progresses.

- **Constraints and resources**. If there are any constraints on project development, these should be stated. In particular, there might be a requirement to develop a new system by a specified target date or the system should be developed within a specific budget. Possible constraints imposed by existing systems should also be identified here. Resources critical to system development should also be outlined.

- **Stakeholders**. Groups of people that have an interest in the system should be defined here. These can include senior management, users, customers, suppliers and the project development team itself. The nature and importance of their interest should also be defined.

- **Management structure**. The relationship between the board of directors, the IT steering committee and the project team should be defined. Clear lines of reporting and management responsibility are essential if the project is to be a success.

1.1   Controlling the project

During development of a project initiation document and execution of a feasibility study, there may not yet be a clearly defined project team. Responsibility for a project at this early stage may be divided between two groups of staff.

The IT steering committee

The IT steering committee oversees and controls development of information systems within an organisation. The committee is responsible for project initiation and for approving project initiation documents. It is also responsible for acting on feasibility study reports, recommending projects be progressed or closed down to the board of directors.

Study group

A study group normally contains middle managers from different departments in an organisation. This group is responsible for the production of project initiation documents and the completion of subsequent feasibility studies.

2   The feasibility study

Although strategic planning identifies the need for new or modified information systems, and the project initiation document provides a roadmap for systems development, a detailed business case has to be made before development actually begins.

Before committing resources to a project an organisation has to be able to answer the following questions:

- What is required of the system?

- How can the requirements be satisfied?

- Is it technically feasible?

- Is it worth doing?

- Will the organisation have to change its way of doing business?

The feasibility study is carried out to help provide the answers to these questions.

The purpose of a feasibility study is not to carry out an in-depth study of new system requirements. It is designed to gather and present just enough information to enable management to reach a well-informed judgement on whether to proceed with developing a new system. Detailed system investigation and specification only begins once a successful feasibility study has been completed.

2.1 Stages of the feasibility study

Assuming that an organisation already has an IT steering committee and has completed a project initiation document, setting up and executing a feasibility study involves the following stages.

Formation of the study group

A successful study group requires individuals having different skills and backgrounds. Different business areas should be represented and there should be at least one member with financial skills. Members should also have technical skills. It is also quite common to find external consultants with specific skills and experience being brought into such groups.

Planning the study

The project team will now draw up a programme of work, with clearly defined timescales and lines of responsibility. Such plans have to be flexible to allow for the uncertain and dynamic nature of feasibility studies.

Problem definition and information gathering

The next stage is to produce an expanded version of the system and project requirements identified in the project initiation document. In many organisations requirements and system structure will be captured using specific diagrammatic models. These tools are discussed in a later chapter.

The list of problems and requirements is likely to cover the following areas:

- data inputs

- information outputs (contents, level of detail, timing, etc)

- predicted future volumes of transactions and data to be processed

- key business processes to be supported

- organisational structure of user departments and their support staff

- operational costs of the current system

- hardware and software currently available, together with a list of the applications using the hardware and software.

At the end of this stage it will be possible to produce a set of documents defining system requirements.

Project identification and evaluation

In this stage various system options are identified and evaluated. Project feasibility is assessed in a number of ways using criteria established in the project initiation document and subsequently refined in the problem definition and information gathering stage of the process.

Producing a feasibility study report

A report is produced and presented to the steering committee.

The report will include the following aspects:

- the original terms of reference
- description of the business area/department/processes under investigation
- the objectives to be satisfied by the new system
- description of the present system and the problem areas
- new system requirements
- description(s) of proposed solution(s).

For each proposed system option information on the following should be provided:

- development and running costs
- implementation timescale
- resources to develop and run the new system
- impact on staff and the organisation
- benefits, both tangible and intangible.

3 Assessing project feasibility – categories and techniques

To be feasible, a project should be justified on the following grounds:

- economic (costs and benefits)
- technical
- operational
- social.

3.1 Economic feasibility

Economic feasibility focuses on the balance between expected costs and benefits of a proposed system. Although non-financial benefits can be considered, economic feasibility should assess costs and benefits in financial terms.

Costs

Tangible costs associated with developing and running information systems were discussed earlier and were classified into one-off and on-going. Tangible costs are easy to quantify and can be related directly to development and operation of a system. However, information systems often incur intangible costs that are much harder to quantify or to relate back to specific systems. Examples of intangible costs include:

- staff dissatisfaction if systems are poorly specified or implemented
- the cost of increased staff mistakes and reduced performance during the learning period after a new system is implemented

- opportunity costs. Whenever money is invested in one area of the company, the opportunity to invest in another area is foregone

- lock-in costs. Purchasing a particular solution can bind a company to a particular supplier, reducing its ability to take advantage of future developments from other providers.

For practical purposes during a feasibility study, costs may be classified according to cause e.g. hardware related, software related and staff related. A specimen classification is shown below.

A specimen summary of costs

	Year					
	1	2	3	4	5	etc
Costs						
Hardware						
Purchase						
Installation						
Software						
Purchase						
Development						
Implementation						
Staff[1]						
Operation[2]						
Changeover						
Other						
Information[3]	___	___	___	___	___	___
Yearly totals	___	___	___	___	___	___

Notes

1   Including redundancy, recruitment and training costs.

2   The net difference in operating costs between the existing and the proposed system.

3   A quantification of changes in quality and timeliness of existing information and the value of new information provided by the proposed system.

Benefits

Benefits can classified into direct benefits/cost savings and indirect (intangible) benefits. A selection of the benefits in each category is given below.

Direct benefits

- Savings resulting from an old system no longer operating. These include savings in staff salaries, maintenance costs and consumables.

- Greater efficiency. A new system should process data more efficiently and reduce response times.

- Business benefits gained through improved management information e.g. reduced stock levels due to improved inventory control.

Indirect benefits

- More informed decision making.

- Improved customer service, resulting in increased customer satisfaction.

- Freedom from routine decisions and activities, resulting in more time being available for strategic planning and innovation.

- Better understanding of customer needs through improved analysis of data.

- Gaining competitive advantage. A fully integrated ordering and delivery system, for example, could reduce costs, generating the ability to price competitively.

3.2 Cost-benefit analysis

Once information on project costs and benefits is available it becomes possible to carry out a cost-benefit analysis. Results should be interpreted with care, however, as analysis is based on estimates of future cash flows, and on assumptions regarding likely costs and benefits.

3.3 Payback

Payback calculates the time taken for project cash inflows to equal project cash outflows. The decision rule is to accept the project that pays back most quickly. Whilst projects that payback quickly may be inherently less risky, the overall return on a project is not considered, as cash flows occurring after payback are ignored.

Payback is often used as initial project selection tool, to exclude projects that payback too slowly to be acceptable. The remaining projects are then appraised using more sophisticated tools.

Example

		Project 1	Project 2
Cost		(£100,000)	(£150,000)
Net savings			
Year	1	£50,000	£20,000
	2	£50,000	£70,000
	3	£50,000	£70,000
	4	£50,000	£70,000
	5	£0	£70,000

Project 1 has paid back by the end of year two. Project 2, however, does not recover its investment until near the end of Year 3. Using payback Project 1 would be selected, even though total return is greater for Project 2.

3.4 Accounting Rate of Return (ARR)

Accounting rate of return (ARR) calculates the return on capital employed in a project. It can be calculated using either average annual capital investment or initial capital investment.

Example

Two projects have the following cash flows:

Initial investment	£90,000	£100,000
Value after 5 years	£20,000	£20,000

	Profits (before depreciation)	
	Project 1	Project 2
Year 1	£5,000	£0
Year 2	£20,000	£40,000
Year 3	£25,000	£40,000
Year 4	£25,000	£40,000
Year 5	£25,000	£40,000
Total	£100,000	£160,000

ARR can be calculated using:

$$\text{ARR} = \frac{\text{average annual profit after depreciation}}{\text{Average investment}} \times 100\%$$

Average annual profit

For Project 1, average annual profit $= \dfrac{\text{£}100,000}{5} = \text{£}20,000$

For Project 1, average annual depreciation $= \dfrac{\text{£}90,000 - \text{£}20,000}{5} = \text{£}14,000$

Average annual profit after depreciation for project 1 = £20,000 - £14,000 = £6,000

For Project 2, average annual profit $= \dfrac{\text{£}160,000}{5} = \text{£}32,000$

For Project 2, average annual depreciation $= \dfrac{\text{£}100,000 - \text{£}20,000}{5} = \text{£}16,000$

Average annual profit after depreciation for project 2 = £32,000 - £16,000 = £16,000

Assuming straight-line depreciation, average capital investment can be calculated as:

For Project 1, Average investment $= \dfrac{\text{£}90,000 - \text{£}20,000}{2} = \text{£}55,000$

For Project 2, Average investment $= \dfrac{\text{£}100,000 + \text{£}20,000}{2} = \text{£}60,000$

ARR can then be calculated as:

For Project 1, ARR $= \dfrac{\text{£}6,000}{\text{£}55,000} \times 100 = 11\%$

For Project 2, ARR $= \dfrac{\text{£}16,000}{\text{£}60,000} \times 100 = 27\%$

On this basis Project 2 is a better investment. ARR is easy to calculate but it ignores the timing of cash flows. Early income is seen as being less risky and can be reinvested, whereas later income is devalued by the rate of inflation.

3.5 Discounted cash flow methods

Discounted cash flow (DCF) methods take into consideration the time value of money.

Net present value (NPV)

This method calculates the net present value of all the project cash flows. If NPV is equal to, or greater than, zero the project should be considered, as its return is at least equal to the discount rate used.

Internal rate of return (IRR)

The IRR is the discount rate at which the NPV of a project is zero and it represents the actual return of the project. This can then be compared against the rate of return expected by a company.

3.6 Technical feasibility

Technical feasibility is concerned with assessing whether a proposed project option can meet technical specifications mapped out during the problem definition and information gathering stage of the feasibility study.

Typical technical specifications may relate to:

- system response time

- transaction volumes

- user volumes

- data volumes

- integration with existing systems

- levels of security

- levels of reliability and backup.

3.7   Operational feasibility

Operational feasibility is concerned with the business 'fit' of a system i.e. does the system support the way an organisation works and/or intends to work in the future? Example issues here, include:

- Does the system support the management structure of an organisation? If, for example, an organisation is decentralised, does the system provide users with the information needed to make decentralised decisions?

- Does the system support the information culture of the organisation? If an organisation has an information on demand culture, for instance, does the new systems have data extraction and manipulation tools necessary to support this approach?

Even if a system is economically and technically viable, a poor business fit will threaten its success, as users will be unable or reluctant to exploit the system to its full potential.

3.8   Social feasibility

The system must be compatible with the social organisation of a company, and the company must be sufficiently sophisticated to be able to deal with the complexity of the system being suggested.

Social feasibility can be split into three broad areas:

- the suggested system should not threaten industrial and personnel relations and motivation

- the system must not conflict with the corporate ethos and way of doing business

- skills and experience within the organisation must be of a high enough level to cope with the complexities of the system.

3.9   The feasibility study report

The output from a feasibility study will be a feasibility study report. This is presented to the steering committee that will then recommend continuation or termination of the systems development project to the board. A feasibility report typically contains the following sections.

- Introduction.
- Terms of reference.
- **Description of the existing system**. The existing system should be described.
- **System requirements**. A clear statement of new system requirements should be made, drawing contrast with the specification and capabilities of current systems.
- **Outline of the proposed system**. This section should describe the system proposed to meet the requirements outlined above. The economic, technical, operational and social feasibility of the system should be demonstrated at this point. This should include the results of any cost-benefit analysis completed as part of the feasibility study.
- **Development plan**. A description of how the new system will be implemented. This should include an outline of the resources required, their cost, together with a preliminary development timetable.
- **Alternative systems considered**, and the reasons for rejecting them.
- **Conclusions and recommendations**.

Conclusion

This chapter has looked at the purpose of feasibility studies, together with exploring how they are completed. Once a feasibility study report has been accepted by the steering committee, and ultimately the board of directors, it becomes possible to commence the detailed process of development, the first step of which is to set up a project team.

<table>
<tr><td>SELF-TEST QUESTIONS</td><td>

The feasibility study

1   What role does the IT steering committee play? (1.1)

The main features to be examined in assessing project feasibility

2   List the four areas of feasibility that a project must satisfy to be acceptable. (3.0)

3   In a feasibility study what items may be investigated under the three aspects of Economic, Technical and Operational Feasibility? (3.1-3.7)

Cost-benefit analysis

4   Name two measures of investment that can be used together, and explain in what circumstances they can be used. (3.4)

6   What are the contents of a typical feasibility study report? (3.9)

</td></tr>
<tr><td>EXAM-TYPE QUESTION 1</td><td>

Cost-benefit analysis

A project feasibility study presented to senior management must always contain a detailed cost justification for any proposed computer system.

Categorise and give examples of the costs and benefits that would appear in such a report, including those that might indicate why a project showing a positive net present value is not necessarily of greatest benefit to the company.   **(20 marks)**

</td></tr>
<tr><td>EXAM-TYPE QUESTION 2</td><td>

Feasibility report

(a)   Outline the main sections of a feasibility report and briefly explain the purpose of the typical contents of each section.

An important part of any feasibility report is a section giving a financial justification for the proposed system.

(b)   Describe in detail the costs dealt with in this section.   **(20 marks)**

</td></tr>
</table>

For the answers to these questions, see the 'Answers' section at the end of the book.

Chapter 5
PROJECT PLANNING AND CONTROL

Once a system has successfully passed through a feasibility study the next stage is to begin the detailed process of project planning. This chapter deals with both project planning and the set up of project teams.

Objectives

By the time you have finished this chapter you should be able to:

- describe the typical contents of a Project Quality Plan and explain the need for such a plan
- define in detail the role and responsibilities of the project manager
- identify the roles and responsibilities of other team members
- explain the concept of a flat management structure and its application to project-based systems development.

1   Project characteristics

A project is a collection of linked activities with a clearly defined start and finish point, carried out in an organised manner, to achieve some specific result.

In the examination you may come across a range of projects. An individual examination paper may focus on a project for the development or redevelopment of an Information System.

In some examination questions, you may be placed in the role of project manager, project finance manager, project team member, project sponsor or external advisor. Whatever context is given to you in the examination, you will need to demonstrate understanding of the project management process.

DEFINITION

A **project** is a collection of linked activities with a clearly defined start and finish point, carried out in an organised manner, to achieve some specific result.

1.1   Sources of projects

As the result of strategic business and information systems planning, an organisation will identify a series of possible information systems projects. The link between business strategy and information system projects is shown in the diagram below.

Whilst an organisation many be carrying out several projects at once, it is often the case that they are interrelated and this should be taken into account during the project planning and management process.

1.2 Characteristics of a project

The following are the characteristics of a project according to Trevor Young in his book *The Handbook of Project Management*.

A project:

- has a **specific purpose** which can be readily defined

- is **unique**, because it is most unlikely to be repeated in exactly the same way by the same group of people to give the same results

- is **focused on the customer** and customer expectations

- is **not usually routine** work but may contain some routine-type tasks

- is made up of a **series of activities** that are linked together, all contributing to the desired result

- has clearly defined **time constraints** – a date when the results are required

- is frequently **complex** because the work may involve people in different departments, and even on different sites

- has **cost constraints** which must be clearly defined and understood to ensure the project remains viable.

These characteristics make project management complex. Inherently projects often involve development of unique solutions to difficult problems whilst working under strict constraints of time and cost. The uncertainty involved in many projects also makes precise planning difficult.

1.3 The project lifecycle

All projects have a lifecycle i.e. they are started, progressed and completed. A typical project lifecycle is shown in the diagram below:

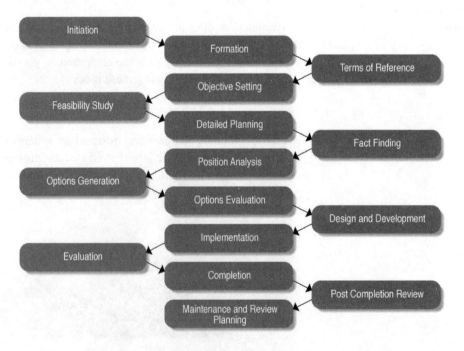

Small projects may miss out or combine stages shown in the diagram above. In some cases, technical constraints may mean that there is only one option available for a system if it is to integrate successfully with existing information systems. Some of the key stages in this lifecycle are examined in more detail in the following sections of this chapter.

1.4 Project constraints

Successful management of a project often requires project managers to balance a series of interrelated constraints. These are shown in the diagram below.

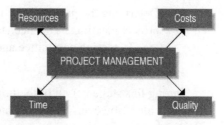

Maintaining quality, for instance, may slow down a project and at the same time increase costs as additional resources are used in the project. Conversely, in order to meet budget constraints a project manager may have to accept slower progress and/or lower quality.

Identification of these key constraints in the early stages of project planning, together with their active management during project execution, is one of the keys to successful project management. Effective communication and co-ordination of project activities is also critical to successful project completion.

2 Project planning and implementation

Whilst some preliminary planning will have been completed as part of the feasibility study, project managers need to undertake further outline planning, followed by detailed planning.

2.1 Outline planning and objective setting

Outline planning builds on planning started in the feasibility study by:

- refining the objectives and targets for the system
- setting a timescale for completion of particular phases
- estimating development cost and setting budgets
- dividing the project into identifiable activities and using this as a basis to prepare an outline plan of major development stages
- identifying a timescale and establishing resource needs and budgets for each development stage.

Outline planning may be quite time consuming. It is possible that several versions of the plan will be completed before it is accepted and it is possible to move onto the next stage of the process.

2.2 Detailed planning

During this phase, outline plans are developed further to produce a workable action plan to ensure completion of the projection on time, to specification and to budget. Detailed planning is normally undertaken by the project manager and their team. Typical activities involved in detailed planning are given below.

- Identification of specific project activities and their sequence of completion. Network analysis techniques may be used at this stage.

- Identification of resources (human and technical) needed to complete project activities. From this is possible to identify which resources are already available and which need to be procured.

- Preparing a schedule detailing purchases of equipment, software and services required for the system.

- Preparing detailed budgets.

- Developing a system for monitoring and controlling project progress in respect of time, resource utilisation, costs and quality.

- Determine the project reporting structure, including the nature and frequency of project meetings. The mechanism for reporting project progress and problems to the IT steering committee and the organisation as a whole should also be established.

During this stage not all of the information needed to complete a detailed plan may be available. However, the more planning that can be completed at this stage the greater the chance of project success.

2.3 Implementation

Project implementation involves carrying out and completing project activities identified in the project plan. During the implementation stage progress is monitored closely by the project manager to ensure that the project meets its specifications and remains within its constraints of budget, time and quality.

2.4 Progress monitoring and evaluation

The process of monitoring and review takes place at varying time intervals and at different stages of the project. Common to all reviews is comparison of actual against planned performance, with particular reference to time, resources, costs and quality. Each of these aspects is considered in more detail below.

Monitoring time performance

This is achieved by comparing actual completion dates against planned ones. Management should be supplied with progress reports to enable them to determine whether or not each activity is on or behind schedule.

Monitoring resource performance

Project resources are both human and technical.

Key issues addressed here are:

- have adequate resources been made available to the project?

- have resources been used in a way to achieve project objectives?

- • have resources been used in an efficient way?

Monitoring cost performance

The monitoring and review process involves comparing actual against planned expenditure. The effectiveness of this process depends to a large degree on the quality of the costing system in place within an organisation. It should be possible to identify and quantify costs directly attributable to project activities.

Monitoring quality performance

Measuring the quality of both the project development process itself and the system under construction can be difficult. However, production of a project quality plan (see below), together with a set of quality standards will provide a framework against which performance can be measured.

Progress monitoring may identify a number of areas where a project is failing to progress satisfactorily. It is then necessary to:

- assess the implications of poor project progress and performance for future project activities and the ultimate success of the project. This should focus on the implications for the key constraints of time, resources, cost and quality

- devising a range of remedial actions to be taken to resolve current or potential future problems

2.5 Control activities

The need for control activities arises from problems identified during the monitoring and review stage. They are designed to bring actual project progress and performance back to that planned.

More specifically control activities aim to:

- prevent deviations from the planned activities, unless changes are required

- correct any deviations from the plan identified in the previous reporting period

- prevent any future deviations by revising plans, targets, performance standards and monitoring systems

- implement any other conclusions resulting from the process of monitoring and review.

Most control activities are undertaken by the project manager and the project team. However, those activities involving significant changes in timescale, project cost or specification will require approval from the IT steering committee.

2.6 Post implementation review

Once a project has been completed and the system involved implemented, it is usual to carry out a post implementation review. Broadly this has two objectives:

- to assess the extent to which the system meets its specifications and the extent to which it is generating the expected business benefits

- to review the whole process of project selection and implementation to improve the process for future systems projects.

More specifically, aspects assessed during this process include:

- the extent to which required quality has been achieved

- the efficiency of the system during operation compared with the agreed performance standards

- actual development costs compared to planned costs

- the time taken to develop the system compared with the targeted date for completion, and reasons for a variance identified

- the effectiveness of management processes and structures

- the significance of any problems encountered, and the effectiveness of the solutions generated to deal with them.

The primary benefit derived from this process is to augment the organisation's experience and knowledge.

3 Project quality plan

The purpose of a Project Quality Plan is to specify all the relevant organisational procedures and standards for making sure that the project is completed to the required level of quality. It should be prepared alongside the project plan.

A Project Quality Plan covers a wide range of issues, but it is not necessarily a long document. This is because it refers to other documents where relevant organisational standards are set out, and it only describes quality issues in detail when there are no such documents to cross-reference to. This means that a Project Quality Plan is essentially an 'exception document', setting out only exceptions or additions to established organisational procedures and standards.

3.1 Contents of a project quality plan

A Project Quality Plan might contain the following items.

Content item	Comments
Introduction	This should explain how the plan applies to the systems development project. Where the need for a plan has been specified by the system user, as a contractual requirement, this should be stated.
Project overview	This provides a broad description of the project, including its objectives, its main deliverables and the identity of the client/customer. This overview can be extracted from the Project Initiation Document.
Glossary of terms	A glossary of definitions for key terms should be provided.
Product requirement	This section of the plan provides a description of the work to be carried out, project milestones, and what has to be delivered to reach each successive milestone. Timescales for achievement of each milestone and to complete the project should be specified. References should be made to relevant formal project specifications. This section might also specify security requirements, performance criteria, legal requirements and client standards.
Project organisation	This should set out the organisation and management specifications for project development. Each management role should be specified, and the individual filling each role should be named. Where management roles are standard, this might be presented simply as a list of roles and associated managers' names.
Monitoring and reporting procedures	This section specifies the procedures for planning, monitoring and controlling the project. If computer software such as Microsoft Project is to be used for planning, estimating, monitoring and reporting project progress, this should be stated.
Development life cycle	This section specifies the main phases of the systems development life cycle. For example, these might be systems analysis, systems design, programming, program testing, system testing, user testing and implementation. For each phase, the plan should specify: • start criteria for the phase • methods and procedures to be used in the phase, and standards to be applied • procedures for testing and review • phase completion criteria.

Quality Assurance	Quality Assurance (QA) is about reviewing the project work *as it progresses*. The aim is to identify errors as early as possible, and put them right. QA checks can be carried out in a variety of ways, and the methods applicable to the project should be stated in the plan. QA checking methods are: • self-checking • peer review (checking by colleagues) • formal review by an internal review team • formal external review.
Testing	This section of the plan should specify the testing phases to be undertaken (program testing or unit testing, system testing, user testing and so on).
Quality documentation	The results of quality assurance and testing should be documented to verify that the checks and tests have been carried out, and what the outcomes were. This section of the plan should state how the QA checks and tests should be documented. The organisation might use a standard form, with each check or test documented on a separate form.
Procurement	When there is a requirement to purchase hardware or software items externally for the project, there should be established procurement procedures and standards. The plan will probably provide a cross-reference to the organisation's established procurement procedures.
Sub-contractors	When project development work will involve sub-contracting some of the work, the plan should specify which work will be put out to a sub-contractor, and what the procedures should be for evaluating and selecting a suitable sub-contractor in each case. There should also be procedures for monitoring the work of the sub-contractor as it progresses, and for acceptance procedures for checking the work when it has been completed.
Changes to the scope of the project	If the scope of the project is changed during development, there should be procedures for authorising and documenting these changes. This section of the plan should specify what those procedures should be.
System version/configuration management	During development of a new system, it is very common for different versions of work to exist at the same time. To avoid confusion, it is important to know which version is current. This section of the plan should set out version control systems.
Risk management	Risk management involves identifying potential risks and then taking measures either to eliminate or reduce them. Risk assessment should take place throughout a project. Each significant risk should be identified, and a decision taken about how it should be eliminated or reduced (or whether the risk is in fact tolerable). Risk management procedures (and documentation requirements) should be set out in the plan.
Delivery	This section of the Plan should set out the arrangements for installing and delivering the completed system to the user.

4   Role of the project manager

Being an effective project manager requires an individual to have a broad range of skills. Some of these skills are developed as a result of experience but increasingly managers undertake formal training in project management. The Project Management Institute (PMI), for instance, has a certification examination leading to a Project Management Professional (PMP) qualification.

Adair identifies three overlapping groups of skills for effective leadership. These are shown in the following diagram and described below.

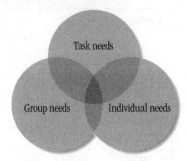

The tasks that a leader carries out to meet **team needs** are as follows:

- building the team and maintaining team spirit
- developing work methods so the team functions cohesively
- setting standards and maintaining discipline
- setting up systems for communication within the team
- training the team
- appointing subordinate leaders.

The tasks that a leader carries out to meet **task needs** are as follows:

- achieving team objectives
- defining tasks
- planning work
- allocating resources
- assigning responsibilities
- monitoring progress and checking performance
- controlling quality.

The tasks that a leader carries out to meet **individual needs** are as follows:

- developing the individual
- balancing group needs and individual needs
- rewarding good performance
- helping with personal problems.

Being able to perform all of these tasks would be a good starting point for any project manager!

4.1 Core skills

According to Yeates and Cadle, a project manager requires the following core skills in order to be effective.

- **Leadership.** Project managers should be able to stimulate action, progress and change.

- **Technological understanding.** Project managers need to be able to translate business needs into their corresponding technical needs.

- **Evaluation and decision making.** Project managers should have the ability to evaluate alternatives and to make effective and appropriate decisions.

- **People management.** Project managers should be able to motivate, co-ordinate and control their teams to ensure a productive and harmonious environment in which project objectives can be achieved.

- **Systems design and maintenance.** Project managers should be able to demonstrate their individual competence with systems design and development techniques.

- **Planning and control.** Project managers should have good planning skills, together with being able to set up and exploit systems of monitoring and control.

- **Financial awareness.** Project managers should be proficient in budgeting and financial appraisal techniques.

- **Procurement and contractual skills.** Project managers should understand the basics of procurement and be able to develop the procurement strategy for their project. This includes a working knowledge of contract law.

- **Communication.** Project managers should be able to express themselves clearly and be able to do this in a wide range of situations with a wide range of people.

- **Negotiation.** Project managers have to be able to negotiate with their own team, users, senior managers and external contractors.

5 Project team selection

As a project manager, one of the most important steps is the selection and recruitment of a project team.

In some projects managers may have a team 'forced' on them, or may inherit a team from a previous project manager. If this is the case, little can be done to change team membership. However, if a project manager is able to select a team, this can be a major determinant of the success of a project.

5.1 Selection

Simply accepting a team member because of their functional specialism and availability is not sufficient. Team members should view being part of a project team as a privilege. A formal set of recruitment interviews will help to reinforce this view.

At the recruitment stage, the project manager should consider asking candidates the following:

- What is your relevant technical experience?
- Have you any specialised knowledge relevant to the project?
- Have you worked in project teams before?
- Have you other departmental or project commitments?
- When do these commitments end?
- Can you commit to the project full-time?
- Do you get on well with others?

- Do you like working alone?
- What do you seek to gain from the project?
- Is your line manager in agreement with you joining the team?

On the basis of these questions, and others relevant to the specific project, it should be possible for the project manager to select the right team.

5.2 Induction

Once the team is selected, the project manager might decide to run an induction programme for the group. This is an opportunity to discuss project objectives, organisational structure, and other key issues. Induction will also be an opportunity for team members to identify their role in the team.

5.3 Managing and communicating

Once the project is under way, one of the project managers major responsibilities is to develop and manage the work of the project team.

One of the keys to success in project management is creating and maintaining a communication structure within the project team. There are a number of communication tools that the project manager can use. These are described below.

Job/task descriptions

Each team member should have a written statement of their roles and responsibilities. This provides focus for their activities and a framework for performance review.

Checkpoint meetings and reports

Regular meetings should be held (perhaps weekly) to discuss project progress and problems.

Notice boards

If the project team have an office, a notice board can be used for team-related correspondence. If the organisation has an intranet, an electronic bulletin board can be established.

Appraisals

Team members should undergo regular appraisals to provide feedback on personal performance and progress.

Newsletters

The project team can publish and distribute a weekly or monthly newsletter, either in hard copy form or by e-mail.

5.4 Co-ordination and motivation

Successful teams share a common purpose and have a sense of shared ownership of the project, its problems and outcomes. Successful teams are also characterised by collaborative working to solve project issues effectively.

Teambuilding events, such as training courses and social events, particularly at the start of a project, will help to foster a team spirit and project culture. Part of the project manager's role is to motivate and focus staff attention on the project. A project manager must take the time to get to know each of the team member's needs and work with them to ensure that their project role fulfils these. Motivation during long projects can become particularly important as team members become frustrated and bored with dealing with the same issues and problems.

6 Team members

The skills and experience required for a successful project team will be depend on the nature of the system being developed, but typically a project team may consist of individuals selected from the following groups:

- specialist IT staff (systems analysts, system designers programmers)
- specialist functional staff (e.g. a seconded accountant to manage a finance project)
- user representatives
- human resource development and training specialists
- external specialists or consultants

6.1 Team leaders

It is not uncommon, in the case of large development projects, for there to be several leaders, each with responsibility for a specific area of the project.

The team leader will typically be responsible for:

- planning and organising the work of the team members on a regular basis (daily/weekly)
- constantly supervising the activities of each individual team member
- providing advice or taking appropriate decisions in the case of technical difficulties
- co-ordinating and overseeing intercommunication between user departments and other project teams
- reporting to the project manager and/or user group and, where problems have been encountered, providing advice on feasible solutions
- reporting back to the team members any modifications to the project resulting from decisions made at a more senior level
- supervising the implementation of any changes to the planned activities or schedules resulting from control activities.

6.2 Team roles

In addition to the project manager and team leaders it is often possible to identify other groupings and roles within a team.

Systems analysts

Systems analysts have a number of responsibilities. These include defining the current system (if any) together with capturing user needs for the new system. Analysts are responsible for producing much of the systems specification documentation that is then used to inform systems design and implementation.

Systems designers and developers

Members of this group have responsibility for practical realisation of the system design provided by the systems analysts. The complexity of this role and the exact composition of the group depends on the type of system being developed. If the system largely involves off-the-shelf hardware and software, their role will focus on supplier selection and ensuring that the chosen option meets the system specification and is capable of integration with existing systems. In the case of bespoke systems development, hardware engineers and programmers will have a much greater role to play. This group will play a very significant role in the testing of any hardware and software acquired.

Implementation team

Members of this group have a wide range of responsibilities. Typical responsibilities include managing installation of the new system, conversion of data, system testing, changeover and training of users. In many cases systems analysts and designers are also involved in these tasks.

Members of each group may be employees of the company. However, in many cases external specialists will be bought in at different times in the project to meet specific project needs. System security experts, for instance, may be called in to assist the design team to ensure development of a secure system.

6.3 Project management structures

Members of a project team are often highly creative and skilled individuals with diverse backgrounds and experiences. Managing a group of this type is quite difficult.

Creative and skilled staff normally do not respond well to strict hierarchical line management in which there is a clearly defined superior- subordinate relationship or to management structures where there are many layers of responsibility. Project staff often respond best when management structures are loosely defined and staff are able to communicate freely with others without the need to pass through a management hierarchy. This type of environment is created when a project has a flat management structure i.e. one in which there are very few levels of management. In consequence most project teams only have two levels of management – the project manager and team leaders. Whilst project staff will report to a specific team leader, they should be encouraged to communicate directly with other team members and leaders without the need for management authorisation.

Conclusion

This chapter has introduced the concept of projects and project management. A key element in the success of any project is the extent to which planning occurs. Absent or inadequate planning greatly increases the risk of cost overruns, time delays and poor quality systems. It also significantly increases the risk of project failure.

SELF-TEST QUESTIONS

Phases of a project

1   What are the distinct phases of a project management plan? (1.3)

Role of the project manager

2   What are the three main needs that the project manager should consider in running a project? (4)

Project team selection

3   What factors would you take into account when choosing a project team? (5)

Structures for project teams

4   Who will normally be a member of a project team? (6)

EXAM-TYPE
QUESTION **1**

Squiggy

The Board of the Squiggy organisation are about to authorise their first systems project to upgrade an old and failing computer system. Unfortunately, no member of the Board has any recent project management experience. The Board has recognised this as being an issue and asked the Finance Director to produce a list of requirements for the project. These requirements will be given to a systems analyst in preparation for a full feasibility study later in the year. The report from the Finance Director includes the following comments. The project will update the current systems of the company.

'The focus of the project is to provide the Board with the necessary information to run the organisation.

We expect the project to take about 12 weeks. During this changeover phase, we will use manual accounting to continue order processing and maintain the customer ledgers.

As we are a small company, the project is unlikely to be complex; so one systems analyst will carry out the work.

An initial budget of £24,000 has been set aside for the project.

As discussed, I will be in charge of the day-to-day running of the project.'

Required:

Evaluate the comments made by the FD, showing any weaknesses in those comments.

(18 marks)

EXAM-TYPE
QUESTION **2**

Skills of a project manager

Project managers require a broad range of skills to be effective.

Identify these skills and briefly explain how they apply to a project manager.

(15 marks)

For the answers to these questions, see the 'Answers' section at the end of the book.

Chapter 6
PROJECT MANAGEMENT TOOLS

This chapter begins by exploring the importance of project planning and control in information systems development. It then goes on to examine some of the tools project managers can use to assist in the planning and management process.

Objectives

By the time you have finished this chapter you should be able to:

- understand how and why projects are broken down into smaller work-based or product-based packages

- draw and interpret network diagrams and Gantt charts

- understand the role of project management software in the project planning process and the benefits its use brings

- understand the importance of risk identification and management during project planning

- appreciate the importance of change control during project management.

1   Project planning and control

Project planning identifies activities necessary for project completion, together with their sequence of completion and the resources required.

Project control ensures that resources are utilised in a way that is compatible with the plan to ensure project completion on time, to budget and specification.

Three major activities occur during planning and control. These are:

- **a plan is prepared** specifying project requirements, activities, responsibilities, schedules and budgets

- **the plan is compared** to actual project performance, time and cost during the development process

- **corrective action is taken** if there are differences between actual and planned performance.

A fourth action is also possible. Plans may require updating in the light of changed system specifications made at the request of users or because of unforeseen technical difficulties.

2   Project planning and management tools

Project managers have a range of tools available to assist with planning and control of systems projects. If applied correctly, these tools should speed up and improve the quality of the planning process.

Project management tools available include:

- work breakdown structures

- network analysis

- Gantt charts

- resource histograms

- budgets.

2.1 Work Breakdown Structures

Even small projects can require a host of activities to be completed. Effective project management requires these activities to be identified and analysed in order to identify practical packages of work and their logical sequence of completion.

Work breakdown structures (WBSs) are one way of breaking a project down into manageable packages of activity that can then be allocated to team members for completion.

Creating a WBS involves breaking project work down into smaller and smaller parts that can be managed by an individual or part of the project team. These **work packages** form the basis of project activities used in network analysis.

A step-by-step is often taken to WBS production. The first step is often to breakdown the project on the basis of its lifecycle stages. This is illustrated below.

Top-level WBS

The second step involves breaking each of these lifecycle stages into a series of tasks. This is illustrated below.

Second level WBS

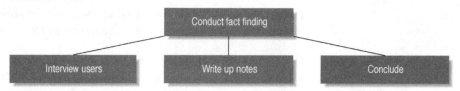

If tasks still require a significant amount of work they can be further sub-divided into a series of smaller tasks. This is shown below.

Third level WBS

Once a series of manageable and coherent work packages have been identified, they can then be allocated to members of the project team in accordance with their skill and ability.

2.2 PRINCE2 – Product Breakdown Structures

PRINCE2, a project planning and management methodology, uses a different approach to breaking down a project. It focuses on the outputs required to complete a project, rather than the activities required to produce those outputs. The end result is a series of product breakdown structures (PBSs) rather than a series of work breakdown structures. A step-by-step approach is again adopted, but in every case the same starting PBS is used. This is shown below.

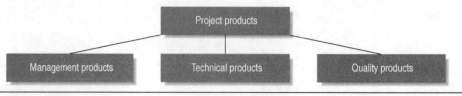

Management products are those products associated with the planning and control of the project. They include the project initiation document (PID) and other project planning documents. **Technical products** are those outputs the project has been set up to create i.e. the system itself. **Quality products** are outputs associated with the definition and control of quality e.g. the project quality plan.

This top level view would then be broken down into a series of more detailed PBS diagrams, such as the one shown here for technical products.

PBS for technical products

The next level would further analyse each type of technical product. This is shown below.

PBS for hardware products

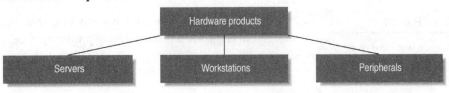

The end result of this process is a very clear identification of the outputs needed to complete a project. Responsibility for each of these outputs can then be allocated to team members.

2.3   Planning the sequence and timing of activities

Once a project has been broken down into a set of distinct activities, it becomes possible to consider the sequence in which these activities have to be completed. From this the timescale of a project can be determined. If the resources needed are known for each activity it also possible to determine the timing and quantity of resources needed at different stages of a project.

There are a number of tools available to assist project managers in this process.

Network analysis

A project network diagram displays the inter-relationship between project networks and hence the sequence in which they have to be completed. Using network analysis it is possible to determine:

- the shortest time in which a project can be completed (the critical path)

- activities which, if delayed, will delay the whole project

- activities which can be completed more slowly without impacting on project timing.

Gantt charts

Gantt charts display project activities in the form of a horizontal bar chart. They allow project managers to clearly identify changing demand for resources as a project progresses.

Resource histograms

This is a stacked bar chart showing resources required over the duration of a project. They are most commonly used to show staff numbers but they can be used with other types of resource.

Budget

Typical project budgets show planned expenditure for a project on a month-by-month basis. As the project progresses actual data will be used to produce variance reports.

Most project planning and management tools are now computerised which increases their value to project managers; computerised as tools are much quicker and easier to use. It is also much more straightforward to update information in the event of project changes.

Students should have the practical skills necessary to draw and interpret project networks and Gantt charts using information provided in exam questions.

2.4 Network analysis

Network analysis is a very effective way of displaying the sequence of activities required to complete a project. Using project networks it is also possible to identify the shortest time to complete a project, together with activities that must be completed on time if the project itself is to be competed on time.

The longest sequence of consecutive activities in a network is known as the *critical path* and represents the shortest time for project completion. Remember that time to complete is governed by the slowest activities rather than the quickest.

Activities that lie on the critical path are known as *critical activities* and if delayed will delay the whole of the project.

The duration of the critical path is sometimes known as the *elapsed time*.

Activities that do not form part of the critical path have some degree of flexibility in their timing and duration – this is known as a *float*.

Network analysis involves breaking down a project into its constituent activities, together with identifying the sequence in which they have to take place. This information is then displayed in the form of a network diagram.

Network analysis involves a number of steps.

Analyse the project

This involves identification of project activities and the sequence in which they must occur. WBSs can be used here to help identify project activities. The duration of each activity should also be estimated, together with the resources required for completion.

Draw the network

The sequence of activities can then be displayed in diagrammatic form.

Locate the critical path

This represents the longest sequence of consecutive activities in the network. Activities that make up this path should be given special attention, as any delay in their completion will delay the whole *project.*

Optimise the project

Activities not on the critical path have a degree of flexibility in their timing and duration. This can be exploited to optimise resource utilisation during a project.

Monitor and control the progress of the project

A completed network diagram provides a benchmark against which actual project progress can be compared. The impact of delays and change in project structure can also be assessed by redrawing the network.

2.5 Drawing a network diagram

Learning to draw network diagrams from information presented in exam questions takes practice. It is important to adopt the correct notation for networks and to make sure that any network drawn follows some simple rules but accurately reflects the information given on a project.

Any network diagram fundamentally has two components:

- *events*, which describe the state of the project at a particular point in time

- *activities*, which progress the project and consume time and other resources.

There are two types of network diagram notation. **Activity on arrow** diagrams show activities as arrows and events as circles. **Activity on node** diagrams show activities as boxes. Throughout this textbook an activity on arrow approach is adopted. However, the examiner will accept answers that use either approach.

A very simple activity on arrow diagram is shown below, depicting a simple project of moving from one side of a room to another.

This network has two events and one activity. Event 1 describes the starting state of the project (person standing on the left of a room) and event B the finishing state of the project (person standing on the right of the room). Activity A describes the person walking from one side of the room to the other, which consumes time and resources.

2.6 Rules for drawing a network

1   A network must begin with a single event and end with a single event.

2   Two activities cannot begin and end with the same pair of events. The connection shown below is not allowed.

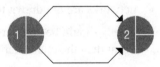

3   Instead, a dummy activity is used, shown by a dashed arrow, so the correct version of the above would be either of the following two diagrams:

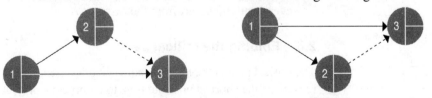

4   Events do not exist until all activities feeding into them are complete. In the network below event 3 only exists when activities B and C are complete.

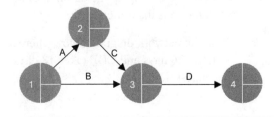

5   **Loops** are not allowed. You cannot have a series of activities leading from an event that lead back to the same event. The essence of drawing a network is that it represents a series of activities moving on in time. **Neither of the two following diagrams is allowed:**

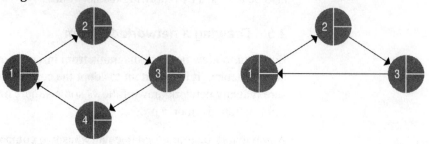

6   **Danglers** are events that do not represent project completion but that have no further activities leading from them. These are not allowed. If left they create a network with two end points. This is illustrated below.

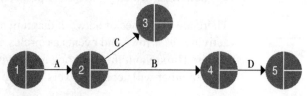

A dangling event should be connected to the final event by using a dummy activity.

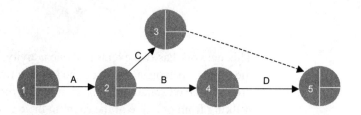

2.7   Conventions for drawing networks

In addition to the rules described above, certain conventions are followed for the sake of clarity and conformity.

• networks are normally drawn from left to right

• networks are not drawn to scale

• events should be numbered so that an activity always finishes at a higher numbered event than the one it started at

• lines that cross should be avoided

• the starting event may be represented as a line instead of a circle, particularly when several activities start from the event.

2.8   Finding the critical path

The critical path is the longest sequence of consecutive activities in a network and represents the shortest possible time to complete a project.

Finding the critical path is straightforward. Follow all possible routes through a network, adding up the duration of activities on each route. The route with the longest duration is the critical path.

In the network diagram below, there are two routes through the network. Route ABE takes 26 days and CDE takes 18 days. Route ABE is the critical path as it takes the longest time.

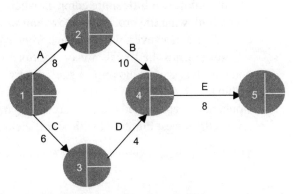

2.9 Earliest event times (EETs) latest event times (LETs)

In the network diagram above activities A, B and E are critical activities i.e. any delay in starting them or an increase in their duration will delay the overall project. However, activities C and D are not on the critical path so there is a degree of flexibility in their timing and duration. This flexibility is a known as a float. Floats are calculated using EETs and LETs for events on either side of a non-critical activity.

Earliest event time (EET) is the earliest time that an event can exist which is determined by the slowest activities that feed into it. Remember an event only exists when all of the activities feeding into it have been completed.

Latest event time (LET) is the latest time that an event can come into existence without delaying the project as a whole.

EETs are straightforward to calculate for events that only have one activity leading into them. To calculate an EET simply add up the duration of activities on the route leading into the event. For event 2 the EET is 8 days and for event 3 the EET is 6 days.

For events with more than one activity leading into them the procedure is a little more complex. Work out the duration of each route leading into the event. The route with the **longest** duration is the EET. Again, remember that an event only comes into existence when all of the activities leading it into are complete which will only occur once the slowest route has been completed.

There are two routes into event 4. Route AB takes 18 days and route CD takes 10 days. The EET is therefore 18 days. Since event 4 only comes into existence at 18 days the earliest time activity E can start is after 18 days. Given that it takes 8 days to complete the EET for event 5 is 26 days. These EETs are shown on the diagram below.

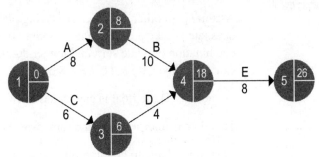

Calculation of LETs involves working from right to left through a network i.e. working backwards from the final event. They are straightforward to work out if there is only one route back into an event. Working from the final event, subtract the duration of each activity from the duration of the critical path to calculate the LET.

Starting from event 5 which must be reached by 26 days, subtract the duration of activity E to get the LET of event 4 i.e. 26 – 8 = 18 days. In other words event 4 must be achieved by 18 days to complete the project on time. To calculate the LETs for events 2 and 3 take the LET of event 4 and subtract the duration of activities B and D respectively. This gives an LET of 8 hours for event 2 and 14 hours for event 3.

The procedure is a little more complex where there is more than one route back into an event. Following the procedure above and working back from event 2 to event 1 gives an LET of 0. However, working back from event 3 to event 1 gives an LET of 8 hours. In cases like this the LET is always the *lowest* time, in this case 0 days. If no work was done for 8 days after the project started activities C and D could be still be completed within the 18 days allowed. However, if activities A and B were similarly delayed they would not be completed until 26 days, delaying the project by 8 days. The LET is always the lowest duration to allow sufficient time for the slowest route to be

The diagram below shows both the EETs and LETs for the network.

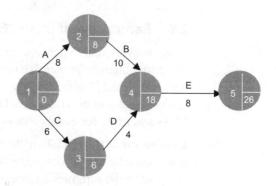

It is worth noting that each event on the critical path has the same pair of numbers for its EET and LET i.e. there is no flexibility in timing for these events if the project is to be completed on time.

2.10 Calculating the float

Floats only arise for activities not on the critical path of a network and represent the amount of spare time there is for the completion of the activity involved.

For the network that has been used as example so far this means that floats are only occur for activities C and D, neither of which lie on the critical path.

The total float time of an activity can be calculated by using the following expression:

Total float = LET for ending event – EET for starting event – activity duration

For activity C the float is calculated as $14 - 0 - 6 = 8$ days.

Assuming all other activities are taking place on time, activity C can either start up to 8 days late or take 8 days longer without affecting the project completion time. A combination of a late start and longer duration is also possible as long as the delay and extra time taken do not exceed 8 days

For activity D the float is calculated as $18 - 6 - 4 = 8$ days.

This float is interpreted in the same way as the float for C.

Total floats have to be interpreted care. The calculations above suggest that activities C and D both have a float of 8 days. This is not the case as the activities share the float. If, for instance, activity C was only completed after 14 days, activity D would have to start immediately and be completed within 4 days if the project was not to be delayed. In this case, the entire float has been consumed by delays in activity C.

2.11 Benefits of network analysis

Network analysis enhances the quality of project planning and management in a number of ways.

1   *Project overview.* Network diagrams have a high visual impact and very clearly illustrate project activities and their inter-relationships.

2   *More effective planning.* Network analysis forces management to think a project through thoroughly. It requires careful and detailed planning to identify individual activities and their sequence. The discipline this imposes justifies use of networks even without any other benefits.

3   *Identification of critical activities.* Simply by understanding which activities have the capability to delay a project allows management to focus its attention on these areas to ensure that they are completed as smoothly as possible.

4   *Improved resource allocation.* Resources can be allocated to critical activities first to ensure they do not delay a project.

5   *Exploration of options.* A network diagram can be used to explore the impact of changes in project activities on project duration and resourcing.

7   *Improved project monitoring.* Networks provide a clear benchmark against which actual performance can be monitored.

2.12 Gantt charts

A Gantt chart can be used to display information on project activities in a different way to a network diagram. A Gantt chart is a form of horizontal bar chart with each bar representing a project activity. The horizontal position of a bar is determined by the EET of the event from which the activity leaves. The width of the bar is determined by its duration. Floats can also be marked on the chart.

A Gantt chart is initially drawn using expected EETs and durations. As a project progresses actual event times and durations are used to draw on a second set of activities that can be used for monitoring and control purposes.

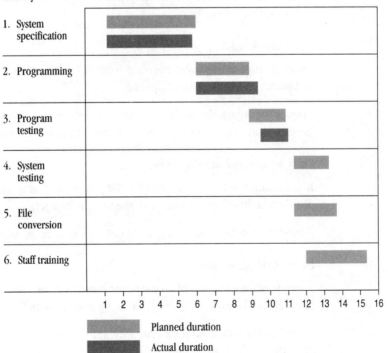

3 Risk management

To be successful a project must be completed on time, to budget and to specification. Anything that threatens achievement of this represents a risk to a project. Effective project management involves identifying such risks in advance and then developing strategies either to reduce or remove the risks.

Risk management consists of the following steps:

1 risk identification

2 estimating the impact on the project

3 estimating the probability of risks arising

4 deciding how to manage the risk

Risks can be managed in the ways detailed below.

- Do nothing. This is appropriate where the effect is small or the chance of occurrence very remote.
- Remove the risk by completing the threatened activities in a different way.
- Reduce the risk e.g. by increasing resources in known areas of project complexity.
- Transfer the risk e.g. seek guarantees and penalty clauses for non-performance from suppliers and third parties.

3.1 Sources of risk

There are many sources of risk to a project, some of which are explored below.

Poor management

Information system project managers often have a technical rather than a managerial background and may lack skills necessary to control and co-ordinate large projects.

Project leaders should be properly trained so that they have managerial skills as well as technical skills.

Poor planning

Initial planning may have been inadequate leading to an under-estimate of project complexity and resources required.

Project managers should be skilled in project planning techniques and should be familiar with computer software that can be used to support this process.

Lack of control mechanisms

It is essential to be able to monitor the progress of projects otherwise it is impossible to decide whether they will meet cost and time budgets.

Reporting mechanisms and review dates should be set out in advance.

Unrealistic deadlines

There is often pressure from users for projects to be completed quickly. Project teams, in order to win a contract, may have suggested times that are unrealistic.

Project managers must look critically at the deadlines. They should identify the critical activities of the project and ensure that these do not slip.

Insufficient budget

An organisation may seek to minimise cost to the detriment of project quality. This can lead to under-resourcing of a project, increasing the likelihood of delays. Organisations have to be realistic about cost and what is affordable to them. Project managers should also have sufficient authority to challenge cost estimates at an early stage, particularly if they feel them to be unrealistic.

Moving targets

The project specification keeps changing as the project progresses. This will certainly add costs and delay to the project.

Accurate capture of user needs at the start of a project will help to reduce constant change in specification. Users should also be made aware of the cost and time consequences of any requested change.

4 Project change procedure

Some change in specification is almost inevitable during a project of any complexity. A project manager should put in place formal mechanisms to manage this change.

This will involve developing mechanisms to:

- capture details of the changes required
- assess the impact of the change on project timescale, resourcing and cost
- make decisions regarding acceptance or rejection of a proposed change
- communicate accepted changes to the project team and key users.

More specifically a change management procedure for a project will normally involve the following activities.

Identifying the need for change

This may arise from many sources including user requests, technical difficulties or resourcing problems.

Definition of change
Once the need for a change has been identified it should be defined formally in a change document. This should include details of the change itself, why it required, together with its costs and benefits.

Assess feasibility of change

The project manager and senior members of the project team will assess the feasibility of the change, with particular attention being paid to technical feasibility and the impact of the change on overall system operation. The change document is then updated with this information.

IT Steering committee approval

For significant changes IT steering committee approval will have to be sought. For more minor changes decisions can be made by the project manager themselves.

Project sponsor approval

Major changes will have to be authorised by the project sponsor and possibly the board.

Amend project plan

The project plan will be amended to take account of the change. Deadlines and costs will be revised.

Make change

The change is actually carried out and tested to ensure that there are no conflicts with other sections of the project.

5 Project management software

Software to construct networks, Gantt charts and resource histograms is widely available. In order to use this type of software, the following information is needed:

- the start date of each activity
- the duration of each activity
- dependencies between activities
- the resources available
- when resources will become available.

The input screen for such software is often similar to a spreadsheet. Users are normally presented with a grid of cells in which to enter the data to be converted into a schedule. The software will convert the input data into a Gantt chart or a network diagram as requested. Another screen may ask for resources that are to be allocated to each of the activities, and produce a resource scheduling diagram or table for the manager.

5.1 Advantages of using project management software

- The use of project management software allows a manager to achieve tedious, clerical tasks quickly and efficiently. The challenge for a project manager is not to draw the diagrams, but to identify dependencies, and manage the resources available.

- The software is able to perform the calculations for deriving critical paths and floats available much faster than humans can. It is also very quick to update documentation in a consistent way when changes occur.

- The software can help to track resources used across multiple projects.

- Having the plans available on software makes maintenance and adjustments easier.

- Billing complications, arising from cross-project allocation, can be handled more simply by the software.

- Project management software should also handle the configuration management (version control) of all project documentation.

- Document management: all documents produced for the project can be stored, and their quality criteria set and checked, using the software.

Conclusion

This chapter has introduced you to the range of project management software tools available to the project manager, and provided guidance on the production of networks and Gantt charts.

SELF-TEST QUESTIONS	**Project planning and control**
	1 Identify the most commonly used project management tools. (2)
	Project management tools
	2 What is the critical path in a network? (2.4)
	3 Explain purpose and structure of a Gantt chart. (2.12)
	Risk management
	4 What factors may cause project deadlines to slip? (3)

EXAM-TYPE QUESTION 1	**Drawing networks**

(a)   Identify the errors of logic and the departures from convention in the following diagram:

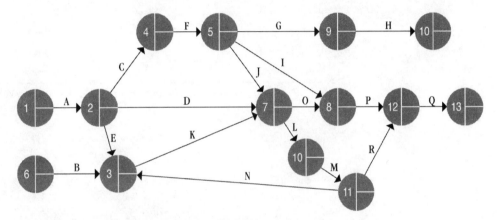

(b)   Draw a network diagram from the following information:

Activity	Immediately preceding activity
A	-
B	-
C	A
D	A, B
E	C, D
F	D
G	E, F

(15 marks)

EXAM-TYPE QUESTION 2	**Finding the critical path**

Draw networks and find the critical paths for the following projects:

(a)

Activity	Preceding activity	Duration
A	-	5 days
B	A	5 days
C	B, D	5 days
D	-	15 days

E	B, D	10 days
F	E	5 days

(b)

Activity	Preceding activity	Duration
A	-	4 days
B	A	2 days
C	B	10 days
D	A	2 days
E	D	5 days
F	A	2 days
G	F	4 days
H	G	3 days
J	C	6 days
K	C, E	6 days
L	H	3 days

(15 marks)

For the answers to these questions, see the 'Answers' section at the end of the book.

Chapter 7

DEVELOPING AN INFORMATION SYSTEM

Effective development of complex information systems cannot be undertaken in an ad-hoc manner. In order to meet design specifications in an effective and efficient way development should be guided by some form of methodology. This chapter explores some of commonly used approaches to systems development.

Objectives

By the time you have finished this chapter you should be able to:

- define participants in the systems development process – managers, users, analysts, data designers and programmers

- understand the Systems Development Lifecycle and key activities undertaken at each stage of the cycle

- describe the waterfall and spiral approaches to systems development

- understand the concept of Structured Systems and Design Methodology (SSADM) and Rapid Applications (Development (RAD).

1 Participants in the systems development process

Most information systems development projects have a number of different participants.

Project Manager

The Project Manager has overall responsibility for managing a project to ensure that it is delivered to specification, on time and to budget. The roles and responsibilities of a project manager were discussed in an earlier chapter.

System Users

Users can provide information on both current systems and on new system requirements. Users can also provide on-going feedback on proposed designs and systems solutions. Selected users may also be involved in the testing and implementation stages of a new system.

Systems Analysts

Systems analysts are responsible for detailing how any existing system operates, together with capturing information on new system requirements. A wide range of fact-finding techniques can be used here. Analysts will then consolidate this information into a requirements specification, which details the functionality and performance required from the new system. These documents will then be used as the framework to guide subsequent development of the system. Systems analysts also play an important role in the testing and implementation stages of a project.

Data Analysts

Data Analysts can be employed to refine and expand the requirements specification produced by systems analysts. Typical tasks here included detailed analysis of data to be included in the new system, leading to design of file and database structures. Data analysts also help to refine understanding of processes carried out on data in a system.

Programmer

In cases where a bespoke application is being produced or where standard software is being modified, programmers play a key role in the development process. Programmers are responsible for writing the computer code that converts the requirements and design specifications into a working piece of software.

2 The systems development lifecycle (SDLC)

In response to growing use of computer systems, the National Computer Centre (NCC) developed a structured approach to systems development – the Systems Development Life Cycle (SDLC). The objective was to provide a formal structure to the development process to improve systems quality.

2.1 Stages in the systems development life cycle (SDLC)

The SDLC identifies five stages in the development of an information system. These are:

• planning

• analysis

• design

• development

• implementation.

The initial letters of these stages spell PADDI which is useful pneumonic for remembering the SDLC. Each stage of the SDLC can be broken down into three sub-stages. These are detailed below.

Planning

Recognise	The first stage is to recognise that a problem exists and to identify its symptoms. This will involve some preliminary investigation.
Diagnose	Preliminary investigation should go beyond simply identifying the symptoms of a problem to the point where the underlying cause can be identified.
Define	Once recognised and diagnosed the problem can then be defined.
Summary	The need for a new or replacement system is identified by users or as the result of a strategic business review. A feasibility study is then carried out to explore possible system options to meet the identified needs. If a system successfully passes the feasibility stage the project moves into the analysis stage of the lifecycle.

Analysis

Review	A review of the existing system needs to be undertaken.
Gather	Information on existing and proposed system functionality should be collected.
Measure	The performance achieved by the existing system should be measured for effectiveness. This provides a benchmark for the new system.
Summary	Whilst some analysis of needs and system specification would have taken place as part of the feasibility study, it is during this phase of the lifecycle that details of current and new system operation are gathered. Information will be recorded in a series of dataflow diagrams and entity-relationship diagrams so that the system can be designed.

Design

Consider	Using information collected in the analysis stage it becomes possible to define and consider options for the new system.
Select	Once the alternatives have been considered then a selection must be made.
Design	Once the selection is made then the design of the new system can begin.
Summary	Information collected during the analysis stage can be used to produce a detailed design proposal. Typical components of such a proposal include:

- data inputs, processes and outputs
- file structures
- program specifications for each program in the system
- a test schedule for each program
- a test schedule for the overall system
- the method of implementation
- a detailed time schedule for hardware/software acquisition or creation
- operating instructions
- training schedule for users
- system performance measurement.

Development

Develop	The new system must be developed either in-house or externally, depending on the option chosen.
Purchase	Appropriate hardware and software resources must be procured and tested individually.
Test	The system should be tested to ensure that it works and that it meets the needs of the users.
Summary	As hardware and software resources are obtained they should be tested. It is particularly important with bespoke software to test that it functions correctly and meets its design specification. Once all the components have been individually tested they should be tested together as a system to check for their compatibility and the extent to which they meet design specification.

Implementation

Document	User and technical documentation must be produced.
Changeover	The new system must be brought into operation.
Review	The system and project must be reviewed.
Summary	Many key activities take place in this stage of the life cycle, including:

- production of documentation
- conversion of data between systems
- system installation
- user training
- user acceptance testing
- system changeover.

Once a system has been implemented there should be a post completion review to assess the extent to which the system is meeting expectations and to learn any lessons from the development process itself.

3 The waterfall model

The waterfall model of systems development was published in 1970 by W Royce.

In the waterfall model, systems development is broken down into a number of sequential stages. Each stage is interlinked as the output from one stage is input to the subsequent stage. In this way all activities at each stage have to be competed before development can progress.

The model has eight different stages which can be represented by the following figure.

The waterfall model of the system development life cycle

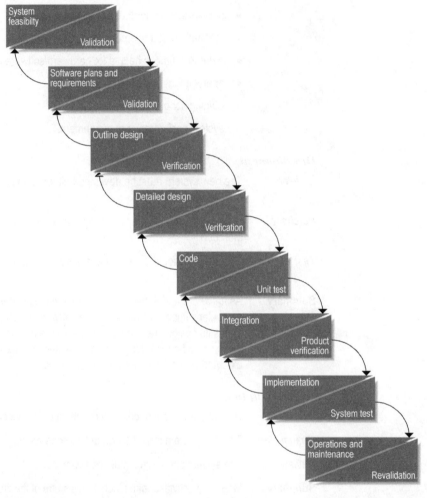

Each stage is divided into two parts. The first part covers actual work to be carried out. The second part is the validation or verification procedures to be carried out on that work. Within this model the terms verification and validation have specific meanings:

Verification means checking that the specified product is being delivered.

Validation means checking whether the product is fit for its operational purpose i.e. was the right product been specified in the first place?

The processes of validation and verification, together with the interlinked nature of the stages, are designed to create a linear development process in which significant reversal of the process or rework is not necessary.

3.1 Advantages and disadvantages of the waterfall model

The advantages of the waterfall model can be summarised as follows:

- it provides a clear and easy to follow sequence of activities

- issues of quality management are addressed through the verification and validation sections in each stage of the model

- project management and control is facilitated by the need to complete each stage before moving on the next.

The disadvantages of the waterfall model include:

- systems development may not be linear and it may be necessary to revisit the work of past stages in the light of changed requirements

- estimating times and costs are difficult for each stage

- users are only involved at the start and end of the process and do not have an opportunity to feedback on progress during development.

- The life cycle can take so long that the original requirements may no longer be valid by the time the system is implemented.

The waterfall model works best when a stable design specification can be established early on in the development process.

4 The spiral model

The spiral model is another approach to systems development, first devised in the 1980s. It differs from the waterfall model as it develops an iterative/repetitive approach to systems development.

A diagram of the spiral model is shown below:

The spiral model of the system development

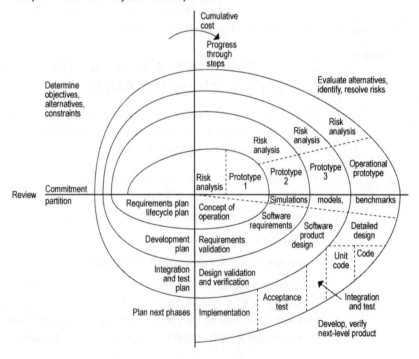

The model is divided into four quadrants. The purpose of each quadrant is:

- **top-left** – the objectives of the project are determined and any alternatives and constraints identified

- **top-right** – the different alternatives are evaluated and the risks of each alternative are evaluated and resolved

- **bottom-right** – the development of the system takes place. This is the linear phase of development not dissimilar to the waterfall model

- **bottom-left** – the next phase or iteration of the model is planned (if necessary).

Whilst quadrants of the model should be completed in sequence, there is allowance for the need to return to previous work to allow review and rework. The same activities may be repeated in order to clarify issues or provide a precise definition of requirements. The development process may therefore be repeated a number of times for the same project. After each iteration, understanding of needs, system functionality and system specification have been improved and the system developed is that much closer to what is required.

The essence of the spiral model is as follows:

- User requirements are not fully specified when systems development work begins.

- The project goes through a series of iterative cycles of development. Each cycle produces a new **prototype** (working model) of the system.

- After each cycle the prototype more closely approaches user requirements until the prototype and the required system become indistinguishable.

The spiral model is more flexible than the waterfall model and is a closer reflection of the reality of systems development where it often necessary to visit and revisit areas of work until they are perfected.

Regular production of system prototypes encourages user feedback. Users often find it easier to comment on a tangible system rather than a paper-based design specification.

There is a danger of slow progress with the spiral model, particularly if the degree of change between each iteration is quite small. There is also a temptation to seek a perfect system though excessive iteration, rather than to accept a workable solution that can be delivered on time and to budget.

5 Structured Systems Analysis and Design Methodology (SSADM)

Structured Systems Analysis and Design Methodology (SSADM) was originally developed in conjunction with the UK government's Central Computer and Telecommunications Agency (CCTA).

SSADM represents a data–oriented approach to systems development and approaches systems development from three angles:

- **data**, modelled with entity relationship models
- **function**, modelled with dataflow diagrams
- **events**, modelled with entity life histories.

SSADM is a highly structured and quite complex methodology. It divides development of a system into modules, which are further broken down into stages, then into steps, and finally into tasks. Each task produces a deliverable, helping the project manager plan a project and monitor progress and quality.

The ethos of SSADM can be expressed in three statements:

- an accurate understanding of the system being examined can be obtained from looking at it in three ways – its processes, its data and its events

---

- the logical design of the system is separated from physical design and implementation; this allows analysts to focus on business need and functionality free from the constraints imposed by technical constraints.

- user involvement and client liaison at significant points in the process, in order to ensure that the development always meets business needs.

SSADM has a number of advantages over other approaches to systems development. These include the following.

1 **User involvement** in the development process. Users are involved with reviewing products throughout the design process and in formally accepting or rejecting products as development progresses.

2 **Separate logical and physical designs**. There is a separation between *what* is to be achieved and *how* it is to be implemented. Initial focus is therefore on achieving maximum business benefit, free from the constraints of technical development and implementation.

3 **Emphasis on data**. There is a focus on system data rather than system process. Data tend to change less than processes over time so emphasis is on developing a data structure that is flexible enough to cope with changing process without the need for complete system redesign.

4 **Easily understood documentation**. Documentation tends to be diagrammatic. This increases its ease of use.

5 **Integration of project management and systems development.** There is a close integration between structured methods and project management. Successive breakdown of stages to reach individual tasks is very similar to the production of work breakdown structures used to develop project networks.

Structured Systems and Design Methodology has become a generic term that can be applied to a variety of development methodologies, all of which has characteristics similar to those described above.

5.1 Stages in SSADM

SSADM covers the early parts of the life cycle, from feasibility study through to physical design, and expresses them in seven stages.

Stage 0: Feasibility study

This is called Stage 0 because it is not compulsory in SSADM projects. The feasibility study assesses the case for undertaking a particular project in terms of its technical, operational and economic feasibility.

This stage has four steps.
- prepare for the feasibility study
- prepare a problem definition statement
- select feasibility options
- prepare a feasibility study report.

Stage 1: Investigation of current environment

The current system is investigated and analysed using fact finding techniques, and documented using dataflow diagrams and entity-relationship models.

Stage 2: Business system options

At this stage user needs are defined in detail. These are used to formulate a series of business system options i.e. different ways of meeting the needs. Users are then involved in the evaluation and selection of an option.

Stage 3: Requirements specification

This stage takes the results of the previous stage and draws up a requirements specification, as follows:

- the chosen option is defined more precisely

- detailed dataflow diagrams are drawn up

- specifications for input and output are prepared

- A relational data analysis is performed

- Entity life histories are drawn up

Stage 4: Technical system options

Users are presented with a series of technical options for systems implementation. Examples are shown below:

- hardware configuration (e.g. centralised or distributed processing, peer-to-peer networking vs. client server and PCs vs. Apple Macs.)

- software options (e.g. Windows or Unix for the server, choice of accounting packages).

Users are then involved in the assessment and selection of an option.

Stage 5: Logical design

This stage involves design of data and file structures for the entire system. It includes specification of output formats, and the style of user interface to be developed.

Stage 6: Physical design

Finally the logical system specification and technical system specification are used to create a physical system design and a set of program specifications. Physical design involves:

- further defining the processing required, for instance considering the requirements for audit, security and control.

- creating program specifications, showing in detail exactly what a particular program is supposed to achieve.

- assessing programs for their performance, for instance estimating the time that programs will take to run and making sure this is acceptable.

- detailed file and database specification e.g. typical contents, record size, and format.

- preparing user documentation e.g. manuals

SSADM has some structural similarities to the waterfall model, as both are made up from a series of interlinked and self-checking stages. However, built into the structure of SSAM there is provision for iteration and prototyping, which are both structural features of the spiral model.

6 Rapid Application Development (RAD)

Rapid Application Development (RAD) is based on an iterative (spiral) life cycle model. Its philosophy is to capture user requirements through workshops and to further involve users in the development effort through use of prototyping. The objective is delivery systems quickly.

DEFINITIONS

RAD development teams include users and IS specialists. Extensive use is made of rapid development software tools and prototyping.

A **time box** is a period, say three months, agreed by users and developers.

RAD teams are made up of developers and users. Among the developers is someone known as a SWAT (skilled with advanced tools). The team should not be larger than four or five strong. All members should be treated as equals, i.e. users are genuine team members and not guests who are tolerated by developers. To be successful RAD teams have to be made up from highly motivated people.

During RAD extensive use is made of rapid development software tools and prototyping. A staged approach to systems development is often adopted.

RAD divides the development process into time boxes. Each time box contains a complete lifecycle for a piece of functionality. The objective is to produce usable elements of the system early on in the development process.

6.1 RAD and the spiral model

RAD fits quite well into the spiral model of system development. It is possible to map stages in RAD to stages in the spiral model.

Determine objectives, alternatives, and constraints. As part of RAD, analysts spend a lot of time with system users to capture their requirements. Given the speed of RAD it is very difficult and costly to make changes once each time box has been completed.

Evaluate alternatives, identify and resolve risks. As with any approach to systems development RAD considers possible risks to the project and considers different ways of developing and implementing a required system.

Develop and verify. Development of each time box can involve extensive use of prototypes with users providing input at each stage of the process.

Plan next phase. Planning the next means checking that the prototype meets user requirements, and then ensuring that any amendments or changes to requirements are included in the next iteration of the spiral.

If all goes to plan, then the final software will be available in a matter of months, rather than a year or so.

6.2 Strengths of RAD

RAD has a number of strengths:

- user workshops and prototyping helps clarify user needs
- RAD can commence without a detailed specification. The process of investigation will itself lead to a specification being developed
- it encourages user participation at all levels
- timescale for delivery can be very quick.

6.3 Weaknesses of RAD

RAD has a number of weaknesses:

- RAD is highly dependent on motivated and enthusiastic users
- RAD does not offer sufficient control for large and complex projects
- It may not be practical to break a system into a series of time boxes or to deliver output in a staged manner.

Conclusion

Different approaches to systems development exist. Some are highly structured and linear (the waterfall model), whilst others are more flexible and iterative (RAD and the spiral model). All, however, have the same purpose as they all aim to contribute to the development of effective systems in a cost-efficient and timely manner.

SELF-TEST
QUESTIONS

The evolution of the systems development life cycle

1   What are the main stages of the SDLC? (2.1)

The waterfall model

2   Explain the waterfall model of systems development. (4)

The spiral model

3   What are the four quadrants of the spiral model? (4)

SSADM

4   What are the three views of the system adopted in SSADM? (5)

RAD

5   What is a time box? (6)

EXAM-TYPE
QUESTION

WRF Inc

WRF Inc trades in a dynamic environment where it is essential that information is presented quickly and clearly to its staff. The information can come from the company's database or from other staff members. Significant processing of the information is also required on each individual's personal computer (PC) before effective decisions can be made.

WRF Inc intends to upgrade its computer system to improve speed and clarity of information. Each member of staff will have a PC linked to a local area network (LAN). Each PC will run the latest version of Windows® and a word processor and spreadsheet on its local hard disk. The network will be used for centralised backup, access to a central database, and storage of data files. The LAN will also be used for communication within the office by e-mail.

The systems analyst in charge of the project thinks that users will require a Pentium processor running at 2.6MHerz with 512 megabytes of RAM. The network will incorporate a central file server. He is pleased that the system will cost only £2,000 per user). The systems analyst is on a fixed-term contract that terminates when the system installation is complete.

Users have broadly welcomed the move although they have not been formally told of the systems change. The requisitioning department of WRF Inc has now questioned the order for the computer hardware and software because of lack of authorisation from the Board.

Required:

Write a report to the Board:

(a)   briefly explaining the systems development life cycle (SDLC); and   **(8 marks)**

(b)   explaining why it is preferred to the situation outlined above as a means of providing a systems changeover for WRF Inc.   **(12 marks)**

(Total: 20 marks)

For the answer to this question, see the 'Answers' section at the end of the book.

Chapter 8
USER REQUIREMENTS

Capturing user requirements is an essential part of the systems development process. Without a comprehensive and detailed knowledge of requirements it is impossible to develop an effective and appropriate information system. This chapter explores different methods of capturing user requirements.

Objectives

By the time you have finished this chapter you should be able to:

- define the tasks of planning, undertaking and documenting a user interview

- identify the potential role of document review, questionnaires and special purpose surveys in the definition of requirements

- describe the purpose, conduct and recording of a facilitated user workshop

- explain the potential use of prototyping in requirements definition

- explain how requirements can be collected from current computerised information systems

- discuss the problems users have in defining, agreeing and prioritising requirements.

1   Obtaining user requirements

1.1   Gathering requirements from the current system

Effective capture of user requirements involves use of a range of fact finding techniques. Each technique provides a different insight into the needs of users and the system that should be developed.

There are five main ways of collecting information:

- asking questions, through interviews, surveys and email questionnaires

- observational studies, including formal observation of a task, shadowing a user through their working day, ethnographic studies, participating within the user environment

- prototyping requirements that have already been identified at a high level, and prototyping the interface for usability requirements

- formal sessions, including group discussions, focus groups and facilitated workshops

- document review involving study of systems development notes for the current system, user guides and procedures, together with any systems review notes.

Information on user needs collected during fact finding is used to develop a systems requirements specification. This then forms the foundation for subsequent development work by programmers and systems engineers. Techniques used to present information in a format usable during systems development are discussed in a later chapter.

1.2 The role of the analyst

Systems analysts play a key role in the information gathering phase of systems development. In addition to planning and managing the information gathering process, analysts will also carry out much of the work themselves. They are also responsible for collating and presenting information in a form useful to the development team.

During the fact finding process, analysts will seek information on:

- current processes
- data and documents currently used
- problems with the current way of working
- user requirements

1.3 Interviews

A face-to-face interview is an excellent way to obtain detailed information. It is a major investigative method and requires good communication skills from the analyst. Interviews can be formal, informal, structured or unstructured. Irrespective of format, however, every interview should be planned if it is to be effective.

User interviews are not always easy to complete. Many users can find it quite hard to communicate their needs clearly. Further, users can be unwilling participants, viewing the systems development process as either unnecessary or a threat to their employment. Good communication skills are essential here and it helps if the analyst has been trained in effective interviewing techniques.

The interviewer needs to plan:

- **whom to interview**: unless a project is of very narrow scope it is not possible to interview all users. The analyst needs to identify key users to interview and should ensure that all major interest groups are represented.
- **when to interview**: interviews should be schedule to minimise disruption to the working day.
- **what to ask**: a clear idea of purpose will help to identify key questions for the interview and ensure that the process is effective.
- **where to interview**: if a user is required to demonstrate their job or use of a system then interviews should take place in the office environment itself. This can be a noisy and disruptive environment and many interviews are better completed in a training room or spare office.
- **how to begin and end the interview**: thought has to be given to how to start the interview in a way that gains the confidence of the interviewee, together with closing the interview in an effective way.
- **information analysis and feedback:** information collected in the interview should be analysed and feed into the systems specification. Users should also be given the opportunity to confirm the accuracy of information recorded during the interview.

When planning an interview, an analyst could do worse than prepare a set of questions based on Rudyard Kipling's 'six honest serving men':

- What?
- Why?
- When?
- How?
- Where?
- Who?

KEY POINT

Thorough planning and good communication are critical to successful interviews.

These key words guide formulation of questions to be used during the interview. Effective interviews will use a mix of both open and closed question. The analyst should have a list of pre-prepared questions and some form of reporting template so that answers can be placed in the appropriate section of the form for later analysis and comparison to other responses.

During an interview, detailed notes should be taken. These can be written but it may be more effective to record the interview for later analysis. Recording an interview can create problems, however, as some users are inhibited by the presence of a tape machine. A copy of interview notes can be given to the interviewee to allow verification of the information recorded.

1.4 Facilitated user workshop

KEY POINT

Information concerning user requirements can also be obtained in a facilitated user workshop.

Information concerning user requirements can also be obtained in a facilitated user workshop. During these workshops groups of users present their requirements guided by a trained facilitator. Whilst these workshops provide useful information on individual user requirements, they also provide key information on how different requirements fit together. They particularly highlight incompatibility between requirements and offer the chance to negotiate a workable solution.

Workshops usually involve participants from a range of user departments, though they can focus on individual areas of a system if required. The facilitator plays an important role in these meetings. The facilitator has to encourage participation by all members of the group to ensure that all requirements are identified and fairly discussed. They should also try to encourage the group to reach consensus without actually imposing an agreement on the users.

KEY POINT

Workshop agenda includes:

- information requirements of users

- developing compatible and consistent specifications..

Working with groups of users can be a very effective way of capturing requirements. Individuals all have different perspectives on a system, proposed functionality and structure. With a group of users, an analyst can very quickly develop an understanding of requirements. Group meetings also highlight contrasting and conflicting needs quickly which can then be addressed and a solution developed. Group meetings are also a very effective way of testing the consistency and compatibility of the needs identified to that point in the process.

Workshops can be recorded in a number of ways. Flipcharts and paper notes are often used. However, increasing use is made of workgroup software in which networked users can work collaboratively on documents to develop a shared view of the system.

At the end of the workshop, detailed minutes will be produced and circulated to all participants to ensure that information concerning the workshop has been recorded correctly. Any amendments can be sent to the workshop administrator. The analyst will use the workshop information to update the systems notes and ensure that logical design of any new system takes into account the information obtained from users.

1.5 Document review

KEY POINT

Useful information can be gained from a review of current system documentation.

Useful information can be gained through a review of documentation on the current system. This provides an insight into the thinking behind the current system, its implementation and any problems experienced during its operation. Documentation available to users can include:

- systems specification
- development notes
- post-implementation review reports
- user guides
- procedure manuals
- maintenance logs.

1.6 Observation

Direct observation can yield useful insights into the effectiveness of a current system, how it integrates with other information systems and the degree of business fit. Obtaining meaningful results can be difficult, however, as the presence of an observer disrupts system operation. Some users will react to be being observed, for instance, by working faster as they feel their performance is being assessed. It is important for observers to stress that they are observing process rather than people.

Observation can yield useful information on:

- the degree of system use by users

- patterns of system use during the working day

- the extent to which users have developed informal systems to by-pass company systems

- the extent to which input documents and screens match

- the competence of users in systems operation.

1.7 Questionnaires

Questionnaires are a cost effective way of collecting information from a large number of users. Increasingly, questionnaires are delivered and returned via email, allowing users over a wide geographical area to participate in the information gathering process. Questionnaires can also be completed on-line, allowing data to be entered immediately into a database for analysis.

Effective questionnaire design requires consideration of:

- questionnaire objectives

- questionnaire tone and style

- question format

- statistical methods to be used in data analysis

- the need for a pilot

- the timescale for return and analysis.

Using questionnaires it is difficult to obtain highly detailed information or reasoned argument. However, they are an excellent way to obtain background information and to test user opinion on a range of issues.

1.8 Prototyping

Prototypes are models of a proposed system. They vary greatly in complexity. A simple prototype may be little more than a series of non-functional screens to illustrate interface design and system structure. A more complex prototype may allow users to enter data and execute business processes.

Irrespective of its complexity, a prototype has two main purposes:

- to capture unknown user requirements through feedback on the prototype

- to validate the analyst's understanding of known user requirements

Many users respond well to prototypes. Providing a tangible system on which to comment and criticise often increases the quality and volume of user input.

1.9 Special purpose surveys

Special purpose surveys are used when an analyst requires highly detailed information about a specific aspect of a system. An accounts clerk could, for instance, be asked to log their use of a system over a period of week. Using information collected in this way, the analyst can determine:

- overall use of the system

- detailed patterns of system use

- types and volumes of transactions

- types and volumes of data

2 Recording information

2.1 Types of documentation

Fact finding can create an enormous volume of information. To make effective use of this, systems analysts need to produce a structured set of documents. These can then be used to develop the system specification and to prepare documentation that can be used by developers.

Typical documentation produced as a result of fact finding includes:

- sources of information (people interviewed, documents studied)

- a narrative description of the system

- comments on the system, with particular attention to any weaknesses, eg errors, delays, excessive costs, bottlenecks

- recommendations for improvements

- system flowcharts and process dataflows

- specimen documents, both blank and completed

- organisation charts

- tables giving staff numbers, work volumes, costs

- graphs, bar charts and diagrams, where appropriate.

2.2 Evaluating fact finding techniques

The following table lists the main advantages and disadvantages of different methods of fact finding.

Method	Advantages	Disadvantages
Interview	• personal contact	• time consuming
	• good relationships can be established	• interviewee may be unco-operative
	• follow-up questions can be asked at once	• interviewee may ramble or be incoherent
	• analyst can assess quality of staff and work	• interviewee may describe what he *should* do, not what he *does* do
		• delay may occur in arranging appointment

Method	Advantages	Disadvantages
Observation	• cross checks information obtained by interview	• time consuming
	• gives in-depth knowledge of system	• exceptional items may be missed
	• reveals quality of work	
Questionnaire	• time saving	• difficult to design
	• saves cost if information needed from remote points	• unpopular
	• suitable for small amounts of specific information	• may not be returned
		• not suitable for large amounts of information
		• non-reactive to unexpected responses
Study of other documents	• saves interview time	• may be out of date
	• gives useful background information	• may describe what should be done, not what is done
Prototyping		• expensive to produce
	• can prompt the user to identify other requirements	• may not be representative
	• can allow the user to explain how they wish to perform a task	

2.3 Verifying and validating requirements

KEY POINT

After information about requirements has been obtained, it must be verified and validated.

Information on requirements must be verified and validated.

Verification ensures that information supplied by different users is consistent and complete. Checking consistency can be carried out by comparing information obtained from different users or documents. Conflicting information can then be investigated through further analysis and questioning of users. Completeness of information is much harder to ascertain, as a master list of all relevant information on a particular system will not exist.

The process of validation ensures that a requirements specification is an accurate reflection of user needs. A requirements specification can be reviewed in a number of ways:

• comparison with information captured from users to ensure consistency and completeness of coverage

• user workshops in which users are taken through the specification in detail and are then invited to comment

• use of a prototype system to visualise the specification.

2.4   User communication problems

Users involved in fact finding commonly face two types of problem:

* inability to communicate requirements clearly to systems analysts

* difficulties in providing meaningful feedback to system specifications produced by analysts.

To overcome this users should be given opportunities to communicate needs and feedback on proposals in a variety of ways e.g. in meetings, on paper and through the use of prototypes.

Specific problems faced by users during fact finding are discussed below.

1   **Uncertainty over system boundaries**. Users may be uncertain of the scope of a new system. As a result, they may withhold relevant information as they feel it is outside of the project remit. Alternatively, analysts can be swamped with information that is of only peripheral interest to the project.

2   **Failure to appreciate the potential of technology.** Users may not request particular functionality as they feel it is beyond the capability of the technology involved.

3   **Omitting obvious needs.** As regular users of a system, individuals may feel certain functions are obvious or intrinsic. These may not be apparent to the analyst and may not be mentioned in meetings.

4   **Evolving requirements**. As users realise the potential of the system, new opportunities for its use become apparent. Users can therefore begin to identify more and more requirements, losing focus on the original purpose of the system.

5   **Untestable requirements**. Some user requirements are simply not testable or possible to include within a requirements specification. Requests for a user-friendly system, for instance, are perfectly reasonable. However, it is quite hard to define this in precise terms that are acceptable to all users.

6   **Not obtaining all the requirements**. Even if a range of fact finding techniques are used it is still possible to miss user requirements. This is particularly the case for large and complex systems.

2.5   Prioritising requirements

A successful information gathering phase will often identify more requirements than it is possible to meet within the budget and timescale of a project. There is, therefore, a need to prioritise requirements to ensure efficient use of project resources and development of a system that maximises business benefits.

A commonly used approach to prioritisation is known as the MoSCoW rules. This classifies each requirement as:

Must have

Should have

Could have

or

Won't have this time (but maybe in the next stage)

Conclusion

This chapter has investigated how user requirements are obtained, and looked at the various methods available to the analyst.

Obtaining user requirements

1   What is the role of the analyst in fact finding?? (1.2)

2   How can prototypes be used in fact finding? (1.8)

Recording information

3   What are the main advantages of different methods used for fact-finding? (2.2)

Analyst

Analysts are responsible for identifying and defining user requirements. This is usually carried out as part of the feasibility study and during the detailed investigation stage. During these stages, an analyst will use a number of fact finding techniques to obtain information.

Required:

Briefly explain the following fact finding techniques available to the analyst in their investigation:

(a)   Interviews   **(4 marks)**

(b)   Observation   **(4 marks)**

(c)   Questionnaires   **(4 marks)**

(d)   Prototypes   **(3 marks)**

                                                                                        (Total: 15 marks)

For the answer to this question, see the 'Answers' section at the end of the book.

Chapter 9
DOCUMENTING AND MODELLING USER REQUIREMENTS – 1

The current syllabus includes a number of **'either/or'** options regarding documentation and modelling of user requirements, two chapters are presented on this topic.

You should read **both Chapters 9 and 10 at least once.** You should then revise the topics that you are most comfortable with.

Objectives

By the time you have finished this chapter you should be able to:

- describe the need for building business process, business structure and business event models of user requirements

- describe in detail the notation of a dataflow diagram

- describe in detail the notation of an entity-relationship model

- describe in detail the notation of an entity life history

- construct business process, business structure and business event models of user requirements using dataflow diagrams, entity-relationship models and entity life histories

- explain the role of process, structure and event models in the systems development process

1   Building models of user requirements

1.1   User requirements

Developing a requirements specification involves a number of stages. These are:

- **acquisition** or capture of information from users

- **expression** of this information in a way that describes those requirements

- **analysis of requirements** to ensure that they are consistent with each other and expressed to a suitable level of detail

- **specifying each requirement** in a definitive statement.

Once information concerning a proposed system has been captured, it has to be expressed in a way that is useful to the systems development process.

This can be done in several ways.

Business process models define how data enters a system, how they are processed and stored, and ultimately how they are output or transferred to another system. Dataflow diagrams are an example of business process models.

Business structure models define the relationships that exists between different elements of a system e.g. how are customers related to accounts and how do accounts relate to orders? Entity relationship models are a good example of a business structure model.

Business event models portray actions within a system that lead to changes in data stored within a system e.g. under what circumstances is a new customer account created or an existing one modified or deleted? Entity life histories are a good example of this type of model.

Development of an information system requires production of all three types of documentation as each one deals with a different aspect of system structure or operation. A combined approach allows development of a comprehensive understanding of the system required.

1.2 Requirements notation

Documentation produced as part of a requirements specification generally uses some form of notation.

Notation normally has two elements:

• a set of symbols used in the diagrams themselves

• a series of rules that govern how each symbol is used.

Using a standardised notation has a number of advantages:

• standardised documents are easily understood by staff joining an existing project

• notation rules ensure diagrams are easy to compare

• specifications produced by different analysts can easily be combined

• notation rules enforce discipline on the documentation process

• notation and its rules enforce a form of quality control over the process of specification.

Notation does have a number of disadvantages:

• without knowledge of the notation a specification becomes difficult to understand

• it is difficult for users to provide effective feedback on this form of specification

• the need to learn a notation limits active user involvement in the completion of documentation.

2 Business process models: dataflow diagrams (DFDs)

Business process models depict the flow of data into a business process, their transformation, storage and output. As such they contain key information for the development of an information system at both a functional and technical level.

Dataflow diagrams are a commonly used form of process model. They are also important in the context of the exam. Past exam questions have required students to assess and comment on a dataflow diagram, both in terms of its notation and fit with business process. Guidance from the ACCA states that 'questions may be set that describe a short scenario that has to be modelled using a DFD …' (or the alternative described in Chapter 10).

The June 1994 exam notes state that in the case of a DFD 'it is important to stress the rules of construction which prevent the DFD from just being a picture (e.g. prohibiting the connection of data store to data store). Candidates should understand how the dataflow diagram is decomposed into lower-level dataflow diagrams but they will not be expected to undertake such a decomposition.'

2.1 Dataflow diagrams (DFDs)

Dataflow diagrams (DFDs) are used to depict how data enters a system, are transformed by processes, stored and then output from the system.

DFDs can be drawn at different levels of detail. Top level context diagrams give an overview of system structure, describing key system components and data flows. Successive detail is added at subsequent levels until individual processes, data flows and data stores are being described, together with their inter-relationships. As the level of detail increases, the scope of a dataflow diagram decreases e.g. a level 1 diagram might depict the whole of the sales order processing system, whilst a level 2 diagram may just depict the process of order acceptance.

2.2 DFD notation

Different forms of notation can be used in DFDs. The notation used here is part of the Structured Systems and Design Methodology, and is accepted by the examiner. Details of the notation are given below.

External entities Entities are something about which data are stored e.g. a customer is an entity as is an order or a product. External entities interact with processes but are not part of them i.e. they make inputs into process and/or receive outputs from them. The notation for an entity is shown to the right. If the same entity has to be shown on a DFD more than once then a diagonal line is added to the top left of the symbol.	Customer Duplicated entity
Process A process involves accessing or manipulating data in some way. Fundamentally, processes can lead to new data being stored, old data being deleted or existing data being updated or moved.. The notation used for processes is shown to the right. Each process should have a unique ID number (top left of symbol). Process IDs do not indicate sequence – they are purely for identification. The name of the process is used to identify the processor executor or owner and the location of the process. Each process also has a description that states what the process involves..	1 Telesales Take customer order
Dataflow Arrows depict dataflows, with the arrowhead showing the direction of the dataflow. The label describes the data that are moving.	Order form →

Data stores

These are places that data comes to rest. They may be manual (M), such as folders; temporary (T), such as in-trays/out-trays; or digital (D), such as an entry in a spreadsheet or a database. The number given to each store is simply an identifier and does not imply sequence. Remember, arrows are used to show how data move.

If a data store has to be shown more than once, an extra bar is added at the left.

M1	Order form folder
T1	Out-tray
D1	Order database

Dataflows are used to connect the components of a dataflow diagram. Rules for connecting components are very simple:

- every dataflow must either begin or end with a process

- dataflows can both begin and end with a process.

It follows that it is not possible to make a direct connection between two stores or two entities using a dataflow, nor is it possible to join a store and an entity directly using a dataflow.

It is also convention to begin a DFD with an external entity (source entity) and to terminate the DFD with an entity (sink entity).

2.3 Context diagram

The highest level of DFD is a **context diagram**. This depicts a system as a rectangular box and puts it in the context of its external environment, showing the major information flows into and out of the system.

The example below shows the context diagram for a Sales Order Processing (SOP) system.

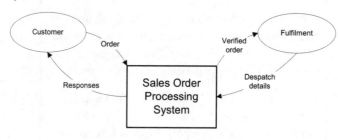

2.4 Level 1 DFDs

The next level dataflow diagram breaks down (decomposes) the context diagram into more detail. In this example, it involves identifying major processes within the sales order processing system, together with key data stores.

Level 1 Dataflow Diagram: Example

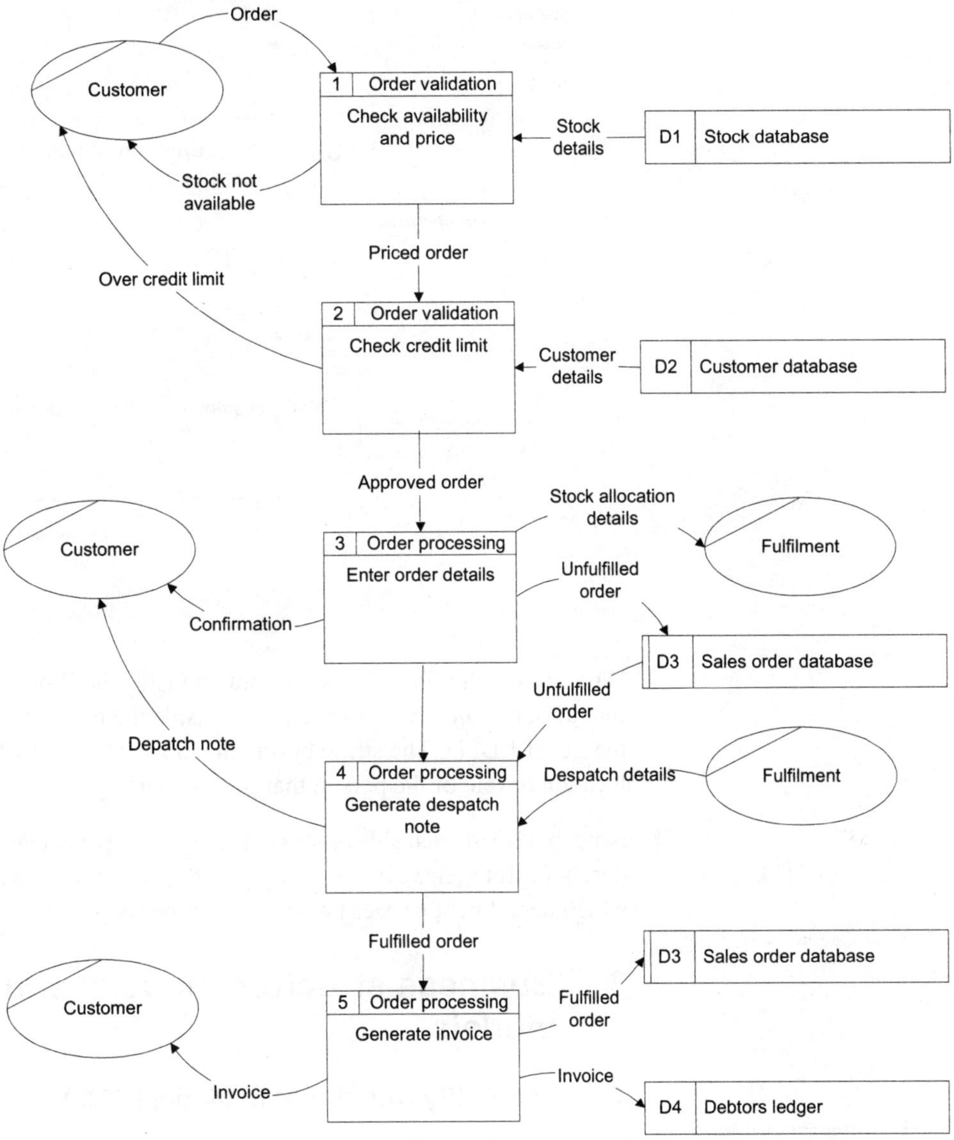

2.5   Level 2 DFDs

Level 2 DFDs expand on processes shown in the Level 1 DFD. Process 3 is shown below.

Level 2 Dataflow Diagram: Example

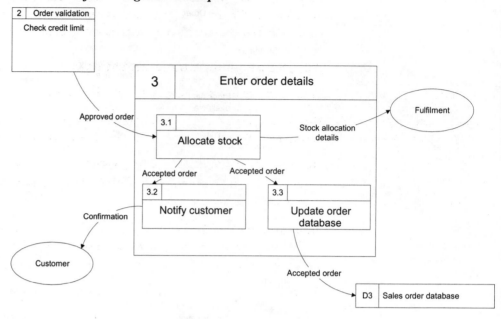

Dataflows within the process are drawn inside the Process 3 box and any dataflows into or out of the process are shown outside the box. Inputs and outputs should match the Level 1 DFD. The stripe beside the id has the name of the process rather than the location or role of the person that performs it.

Note that ID of each sub-process does **not** imply sequence or dependency – they are purely for reference . At Level 1and 2, the box at the top of each process identifies which department or user performs the process.

3 Business structure models: entity-relationship models

3.1 The Entity Relationship Model (ERM)

Entities are things about which data must be stored in a system. Customers, orders, and products are all examples of entities. Invoices, deliveries and customer accounts are also entities.

An important part of documenting system requirements involves establishing the exact relationship that exists between different entities. This helps to define the data structure within a system. Entity Relationship Models (ERMs) or Logical Data Structures (LDSs) can be used to show these relationships.

An ERM is a **static** view of the relationship between different entities i.e. it does not show how entities can change over time. This latter aspect is covered in event models.

3.2 Entities, attributes and relationships

Entity Relationship Models have three components:

Entities. Entities are something about which data has to be stored in the system e.g. a customer. An entity occurrence is a specific example of an entity e.g. Mr Smith and Mrs Jones are two occurrences of the entity type customer.

Attributes. These are items of information stored about a particular entity. Customer name, address and phone number are three possible attributes for the customer entity.

Relationships. These are used to link entities together.

DEFINITION

An **entity** is something of significance to a system about which data must be held.

KEY POINT

An **entity relationship model** reflects a static view of the relationship between different entities.

KEY POINT

An **attribute** is an individual piece of information about an entity.

A **relationship** describes the link between two entities.

ERMs are a very important item of systems documentation as they define the structure of data to be stored in a system. This is particularly important for database systems as each entity represents a possible data table and each attribute a field.

3.3 Relationships between entities

DEFINITION

Entities can be related to each other in a number of ways:

- one to one
- one to many
- many to many

Entities can be related to each other in different ways.

One to one (1:1). In this case one occurrence of an entity is related to only one occurrence of another entity e.g. one customer has only one account.

One to many (1:M). In this case one entity occurrence is related to one or more occurrences of another entity e.g. one customer has many orders in a system but each order relates to only one customer

Many to many (M:M). In this case one entity occurrence is related to one or more occurrences of another entity and vice versa e.g. an order can relate to many products and each product can relate to many orders.

Notation

Represents an entity

Entities normally have many occurrences e.g. a system can contains many customer or many orders.

Represents a one to one (1:1) relationship

One occurrence of entity A is related to only one of B. The reverse is also true in that one occurrence of B is related to only one occurrence of A.

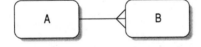

Represents a one to many (1:M) relationship

One occurrence of entity A can be related to one or more occurrences of entity B but each occurrence of entity B is related to only one occurrence of entity A.

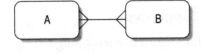

Represents a many to many (M:M) relationship
One occurrence of entity A is related to one or more occurrence of entity B and vice versa for entity B.

3.4 Resolving complex relationships

Many to many relationships quite commonly exist between entities. However, from a practical design perspective it is difficult to incorporate them efficiently into a system. If they are left unchanged, the same data many have to be stored several times in a system and the data structure may lack flexibility.

If a many to many relationship is identified it is common practice to split it into two one to many relationships by using an **association** or link entity.

The entities *Employee* and *Project* could have a many to many relationship. This can be shown as follows:

In this case one employee can be assigned to many projects. Equally, one project can have many employees.

This relationship can be simplified by breaking it down into two one to many relationships by adding the associate entity assignment. This is shown below:

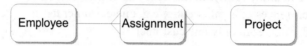

One employee now has many assignments but each assignment only relates to one employee. Equally, each project can have many assignments but each assignment only refers to one project.

Although this may seem like a small change in the ERM, removing many to many relationships greatly improves the efficiency and flexibility of data storage in a system.

3.5 Attributes

Attributes are items of information stored about entities. Each entity may have many attributes. The entity type employee, for instance, could have the following attributes:

Employee Number

Name

Address

Telephone Number

Date of Birth

Grade

Department ID

Each entity will have an attribute that is used to identify each of its occurrences uniquely. In the employee example, each staff member would be given a unique employee number. In some cases, a combination of attributes is used to provide a unique identity.

3.6 Sub-types and super-types

Some approaches to entity relationship modelling distinguish between **super-type** and **sub-type** entities. For instance, employee could be a super-type entity for the sub-type entities permanent and contract employees. Sub-type entities inherit all of the attributes of their super-type but also have attributes unique to themselves. For instance, a contract employee could have the attribute contract duration that is not present in employee super-type entity.

Use of sub-type entities can be a very efficient way of portraying data structure, as it avoids the need to repeat shared attributes.

3.7　Showing optional relationships

Some relationships may be conditional, whereas others are mandatory. Conditional relationships are normally shown using broken or partially broken connecting lines.

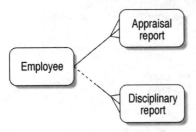

This shows that a fully established employee *must* have one or more appraisal reports, but *may* have one or more disciplinary reports. If a disciplinary report exists it can only refer to one employee. Using entity relationship models in this way not only portrays data structure but it also helps to demonstrate the rules governing entry of data into a system.

3.8　Validation of an ERM

Entity relationship models are normally quite straightforward to validate. Once a model has been constructed it can be tested against different scenarios and/or actual data. For instance, can the entity relationship model accommodate data required to enter a new customer, add several multi-product orders to a customer and so on. This process of validation is best completed with the help of users as they have the best knowledge of individual business processes.

4　Business event models: entity life histories

4.1　Events

Entity relationship models are *static* diagrams i.e. they depict the relationship between entities but do not demonstrate how these entities can change over time. Changes to data stored about entities are triggered by *events*.

There are three types of event:

- External events, such as a customer placing an order
- Time-based events, such as calculation of interest on late payments
- Internal events, such as modification of an existing product's details.

Entity life histories are **event** models i.e. they display how an entity occurrence can come into existence, how it can be modified and ultimately deleted from a system. This is in contrast to static DFDs and ERMs.

4.2　Entity life history (ELH)

Fundamentally, three things can happen to an entity occurrence:

- it can be created
- it can be modified
- it can be deleted.

For instance a new customer can be added to a system. Over time that customer's details may be updated e.g. changes in address. Ultimately, the customer may be removed from the system.

Entity life histories display these three events, together with some of the rules governing what happens e.g. can a customer's details be updated more than once and what are the conditions that determine deletion of an entity occurrence?

The diagram below shows the entity life history for a bank account. It begins with the entity itself and then branches into the three main lifecycle events for the entity.

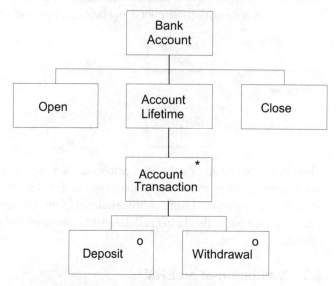

The section under account lifetime illustrates how an entity can be updated over time. The asterisk in the account transaction box indicates that update can occur many times i.e. many transactions can take place on the account. Circles in the deposit and withdrawal boxes denote mutually exclusive events and as such display the rules for updating the entity i.e. an individual transaction must either be a withdrawal or a deposit but not both.

4.3 Operations

The entity life history of the bank account is produced at a high level and lacks detail. To be useful in the systems development process each event, and the rules governing its execution, would need to be displayed in more detail.

A detailed life history for a purchase order is shown below.

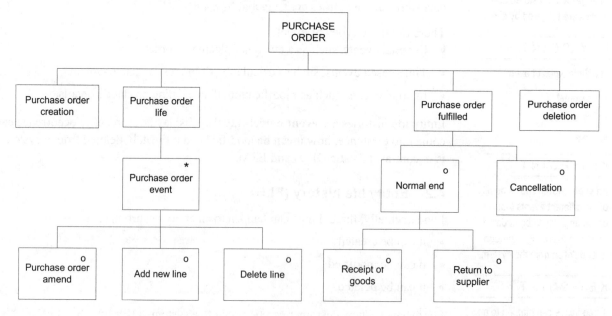

For each of the events it is then possible to identify a series of operations. Possible operations are listed below.

1 Create purchase order
2 Select supplier account
3 Create one or more order lines
4 Set purchase order status to 'open'
5 Set purchase order issue date
6 Set purchase order due date
7 Update purchase order due date
8 Amend one or more existing lines
9 Add one or more order lines
10 Delete one or more order lines
11 Update purchase order status to 'complete'
12 Update purchase order status to 'open'.
13 Update purchase order status to 'cancelled'
14 Update purchase order cancellation date
15 Delete each order line
16 Delete purchase order from supplier account
17 Delete purchase order

Each of these operations can then be added to the entity life history, providing additional detail on what happens during an event. The numbering of actions is significant as it does denote sequence.

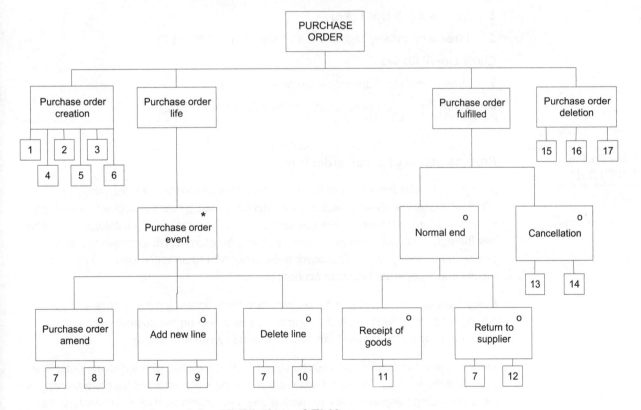

4.4 Validation of ELH

The entity life history should be cross-referenced to both the DFD (or other process model) and the ERM. Each event on the ELH should correspond to a process on a DFD. This type of comparison often highlights inconsistencies, where events are present in the ELH but have been missed off the DFD.

4.5 The value of an ELH

The ELH diagram provides a pictorial representation of what happens to an entity occurance. By constructing ELHs the analyst begins to understand the processes involved in the capture and transforation of data in a system.

ELHs also describe the sequence in which operations occur, together with some of the logical rules governing their execution. All of this information is needed during the development phase if a system is to support business processes effectively and in a way that does not break current business rules.

Conclusion

Effective system specification requires definition of system structure, data structure and business processes. This chapter has explored some of the modelling techniques that can be used to build an effective system specification.

SELF-TEST
QUESTIONS

Dataflow Diagrams

1   Why are the characteristics of processes? (2)

2   What symbols are normally used to produce dataflow diagrams? (2.2)

3   What is decomposition? (2.4)

Entity-Relationship Models

4   What do the terms entity, attribute and relationship mean? (3.2)

5   What is a sub-type? (3.6)

6   What is optionality and how is it shown on an ERM? (3.7)

Entity Life Histories

7   Why might an event model be needed (4.1)

8   What do the terms iteration and selection mean? (4.2)

EXAM-TYPE
QUESTION

Process model of a mail order firm

A large mail order firm operates through several thousand local agents, who sell mainly to close friends and relatives. An agent receives a new catalogue every spring, summer, autumn and winter. Friends select goods from the current catalogue and then pay the agent the appropriate amount, receiving in return a receipt detailing goods ordered and moneys paid. The agent adds their order to an order form and pays their money into a separate business account.

Every Saturday the agent posts the order form (now containing items ordered by a number of people) together with a single cheque drawn on the business account, retaining a copy of the order form, which is kept in a red ring binder.

The company sends items ordered by return of post together with a delivery note. The agent checks the items received against both the delivery note and his/her own copy of the order, using telephone calls to resolve any discrepancies. If all is satisfactory, the agent then throws away the order form but retains the delivery note in a blue ring binder.

At the end of every quarter the agent receives, along with the new season's catalogue, a statement of all items ordered in the quarter, together with a commission cheque for 10% of their total value. After checking the details against the delivery notes in the blue ring binder, the agent pays the commission into his/her own personal bank account.

Required:

(a)   Draw a suitable process model depicting the above procedure.   **(14 marks)**

(b)   With reference to dataflow diagrams, explain the meaning of the following terms:

    (i)   external entity   **(1 mark)**

    (ii)   context level   **(1 mark)**

    (iii)   decomposing   **(2 marks)**

    (iv)   top-down approach.   **(2 marks)**

(Total: 20 marks)

For the answer to this question, see the 'Answers' section at the end of the book.

Chapter 10

DOCUMENTING AND MODELLING USER REQUIREMENTS – 2

Chapter 9 described a structured approach to documenting and modelling user requirements. However, in the exam there is the option to display knowledge of more up to date techniques.

You should read **both Chapters 9 and 10 at least once.** You can then revise the methods that you are most comfortable with.

Objectives

By the time you have finished this chapter you should be able to:

- describe the need for building business process, business structure and business event models of user requirements

- describe in detail the notation of a flowchart and an activity diagram

- describe in detail the notation of a class model

- describe in detail the notation of a statechart diagram (state transition diagram)

- construct business process, business structure and business event models of user requirements using activity diagrams, class models and statechart diagrams

- explain the role of process, structure and event models in the systems development process.

1   Unified Modelling Language (UML) and object-oriented analysis and design

1.1   Unified Modelling Language (UML)

Unified Modelling Language (UML) is a system of notation in use since the mid 1990s. It has become the standard for modelling information systems in a modern 'object-oriented' programming environment. UML is supported by most major companies in the IT industry including Microsoft, Oracle and Hewlett-Packard.

Though the latest version of UML has twelve kinds of modelling diagrams, three are relevant to the exam syllabus. Most of this chapter is devoted to describing the UML approach to modelling business **processes, events** and **structures**.

1.2   Object orientation

Object-Oriented (OO) technology has its origins in the late 1960s/early 1970s, but it only really began to have an impact in the mid 1980s when OO programming languages such as C++ emerged. Today many new systems are created using OO analysis and design methods and OO programming languages. It is interesting to note that Excel macros are written using an OO approach.

1.3   Object orientation versus structured methods

The OO approach differs significantly from the structured approach described in Chapter 9.

Structure analysis and design techniques adopt a top-down approach, beginning with a system overview and then progressively breaking it down (decomposing) into more detail. Since all levels are interlinked, small changes in detail can lead to major redesign. Under an **object-oriented** approach the design of a system can be modelled at a much higher level. Any potential problems can be fixed at this higher level minimising the need for rework.

The principal difference between structured programming and OO programming relates to the way **data and functions** are stored.

In structured programming, data and functions are kept **separately**. In OO programming, related data and functions are **placed together** within one unit called an **object**.

Key OO concepts relevant to the syllabus are: objects, encapsulation, messages, classes, and inheritance.

1.4 Objects and encapsulation

Objects are things about which data exists and have parallels to entities described in Chapter 9. Objects can be a person, item, or concept.

- Objects have **attributes**. For instance, name and address are attributes for a customer.

- Objects take different **state**s eg an account can be in good order or have an overdue balance.

- State changes reflect the behaviour of an object which defines how it acts and reacts. Behaviour is determined by the set of **operations** (or methods or functions) the object can perform. For example, if a printer is an object, then its behaviour or function is to print whatever it receives.

An object's attributes and their values make up the data of an object. Access to the data is only provided via the object's operations. This shielding of data by the operations is referred to as **encapsulation**.

If this all sounds rather abstract, think of a television. A *Viewer_Object* (eg you) typically has no idea how the *Television_Object* actually works. The *Viewer_Object* only knows how to send requests to the *Television_Object*, using the on/off button and the remote control buttons. Equally the *Television_Object* knows how to display television programmes, but it has no need to know whether the *Viewer_Object* is enjoying the programmes and it does not 'enjoy' the programmes it displays itself: enjoyment or lack of it are states of the *Viewer_Object*.

1.5 Messages

Objects interact and communicate with each other via messages. A message is a request for the receiver object to carry out the indicated method or behaviour and return the result of that action to the sender object.

A message contains the name of the object to which it is addressed, the name of the method that should be performed, and the information the method requires to perform its task properly. No other information or context is required.

To: Television Object
Method: Display TV programme
Information required by the receiving object: Channel 4

1.6 Classes and inheritance

A class is a generic definition for a set of similar objects. A class provides the specifications for the data and operations of the objects it contains. In effect a class acts as a template.

Creating an object from a class is known as **instantiating** an object. Each time an object is created it inherits the default class attributes class definition provides the initial values for the variables in each object. During the lifetime of the object these variables may change because of messages the object receives from other objects or from internal processing.

In an accounting package, for example, there might be a **class** called 'SalesInvoice'. Every instance of that class would have the same attributes eg. an invoice number, an invoice total, a sales ledger account, all with initial values of 'nil' or 'none').

Inheritance is one of the most powerful features of object-orientated design. Rather than creating a new class from scratch it is possible to clone an existing class and then modify it.

1.7 Identifying classes

A class acts as the template for an **object.** Creating classes involves trying to find related items in a system with similar attributes and then grouping them together. Skidmore suggests grouping all data items in a system into potential classes to find related groups (for example Invoices/Credit Notes/Statements). Alternatively, organisational functions can be broken down into classes by considering what objects are needed to perform the tasks they involve.

The most popular method – and by far the most practical in an exam – is to search for nouns in the description of system requirements.

Noun searching

This approach has two steps:

- identify candidate classes by picking up all the nouns and noun phrases out of a requirements specification

- discard candidates which are inappropriate for any reason, renaming the remaining classes if necessary.

Inappropriate classes are those that are redundant (the same class given more than one name), vague, an event or an operation (if the noun refers to something which is done to, by or in the system), outside the scope of the system, or if they refer to an attribute (eg' colour'). Meta-language (language for defining other languages) is also inappropriate eg if the noun or noun phrase is something like 'system' or 'business rule'.

Example

Here is a description of a college library system.

The library contains books and journals. It may have several copies of a given book. Some of the books are for short-term loan only. All other books may be borrowed by any library member for three weeks. Members of the library can normally borrow up to six items at a time, but members of staff may borrow up to 12 items at one time. Only members of staff may borrow journals. The system must keep track of when books and journals are borrowed and returned, enforcing the rules described above.

Step 1: Here it is the paragraph again with nouns and noun phrases underlined.

The <u>library</u> contains <u>books</u> and <u>journals</u>. It may have several <u>copies of a given book</u>. Some of the books are for <u>short-term loan</u> only. All other books may be borrowed by any library member for three weeks. Members of the library can normally borrow up to six items at a time, but members of staff may borrow up to 12 items at one time. Only members of staff may borrow journals. The system must keep track of when books and journals are borrowed and returned, enforcing the rules described above.

Step 2: Analysis of candidates.

Library	Outside the scope of the system
Books	Potential class
Journals	Potential class
Copy of a given book	Potential class
Short-term loan	An event of lending a book
Library member	Potential class
Week	A measure of time not a thing
Members of library	The same as library member
Item	Vague (book or journal?)
Time	Vague
Members of staff	Potential class
System	Meta-language
Rule	Meta-language

Note that the library is beyond the scope of the system because it is the library itself that contains all the classes that are being modelled.

Summary

Potential classes are:

Book
Journal
CopyOfBook
LibraryMember
MemberOfStaff

2 Business process models: flowcharts and activity diagrams

The purpose of business process modelling was introduced in Chapter 9.

2.1 Flowcharts

Flowcharts are a modelling technique introduced in the 1940/50s and popularised for structured development as well as business modelling in the 1970s.

The June 2004 exam notes tell us that: "Flowcharts are well-established process models. They usually have symbols for showing processes, decisions, data stores, documents and flows. The symbols used in Microsoft Word templates for flowcharts, together with arrow-headed lines for flows, should be sufficient for examination purposes".

Here are the symbols used in Word (and very widely elsewhere).

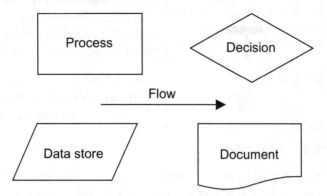

Flow charts are typically used to describe the detailed logic of a business process or business rule.

2.2 Activity diagrams

UML activity diagrams are the object-oriented equivalent of dataflow diagrams used in structured development. They may be used to document the logic of complex operations, business rules and processes.

2.3 Notation

As the June 2004 exam notes state: "This notation has symbols for initial and final states, action states, branches and concurrency. It is an acceptable alternative to the traditional flowchart. There is no requirement to show sub-activity states. Like most flowcharts, activity diagrams allow the symbols to be organised in 'swimlanes' to show who is handling the information. Swimlanes may be organised horizontally or vertically".

●	**Initial state**. A filled circle represents the initial action state.
⟶	**Action flow** arrows illustrate the relationships among action states.
Check credit status	**Action states** represent the actions of objects. They are drawn as a rectangle with rounded corners.
[condition] [condition]	**Branching**. A diamond represents a decision with alternate paths. The outgoing alternatives should be labelled within square brackets.
	A **fork transition** represents the forking of one action state into multiple parallel states; in other words activities that can (or must) occur in parallel (concurrently).

	A **join transition** represents the synchronisation of multiple action states into one state; in other words it shows that concurrent activities must be completed before the next activity can occur.
	Final state. A filled circle nested inside another circle represents the final action state.

2.4 Example

Here is an example of an activity diagram. This shows how **swimlanes** are used to group related activities into one column. This activity diagram models the same information as the level 1 dataflow example in Chapter 9. Unlike dataflow diagrams, however, activity diagrams do not show dataflows or data stores. As their name suggests, activity diagrams model activities.

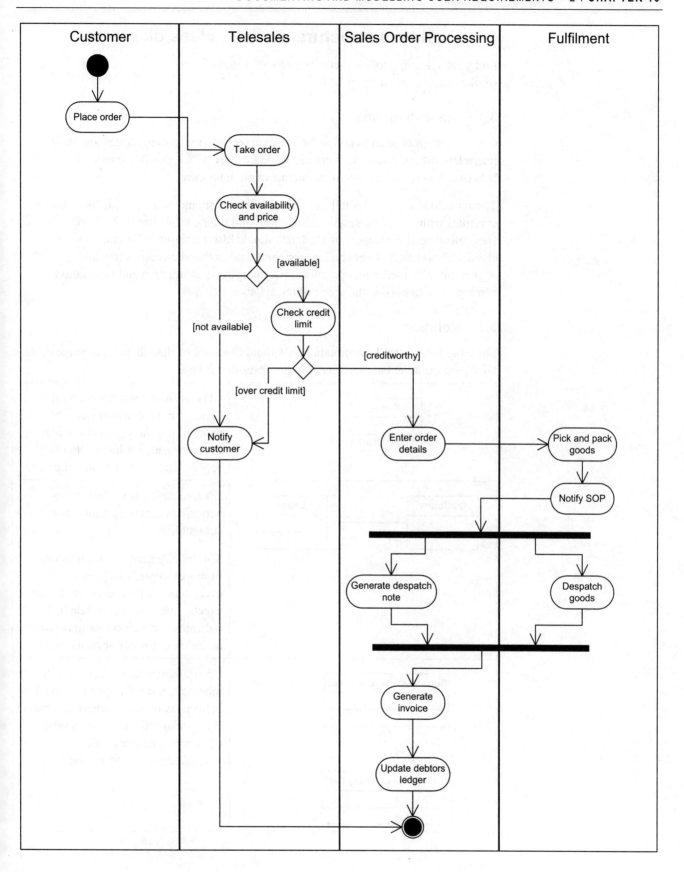

3   Business structure models: class diagrams

Entity relationship models model the data structure of a system. Class models serve a similar purpose when using UML.

3.1   Class diagrams

Class diagrams give an overview of a system by showing system classes and their interrelationships. Class diagrams are static i.e. they define possible interactions between classes but not how they interact or what happens.

The June 2004 exam notes tell us that: "Candidates should be able to identify classes, attributes within classes, simple associations and their cardinalities (i.e. multiplicities). Generalisation (inheritance) of attributes should also be learnt, as should association classes. However, it is unnecessary for candidates to handle composition and aggregation. Furthermore, operations, polymorphism, abstraction and association naming are also outside the scope of the syllabus".

3.2   Notation

The table below details the notation that should be used in class diagrams. Some of the points are explained in more detail in the notes that follow.

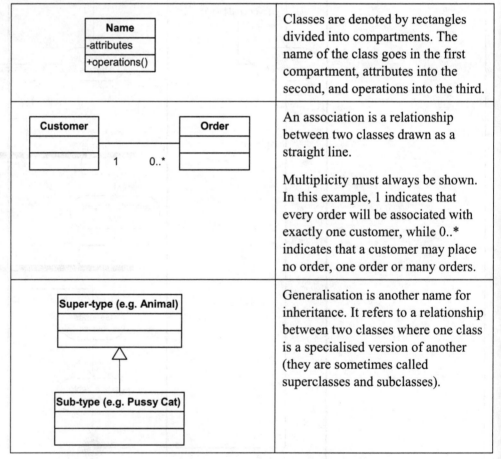

Notation	Description
Name / -attributes / +operations()	Classes are denoted by rectangles divided into compartments. The name of the class goes in the first compartment, attributes into the second, and operations into the third.
Customer 1 — 0..* Order	An association is a relationship between two classes drawn as a straight line. Multiplicity must always be shown. In this example, 1 indicates that every order will be associated with exactly one customer, while 0..* indicates that a customer may place no order, one order or many orders.
Super-type (e.g. Animal) △ Sub-type (e.g. Pussy Cat)	Generalisation is another name for inheritance. It refers to a relationship between two classes where one class is a specialised version of another (they are sometimes called superclasses and subclasses).

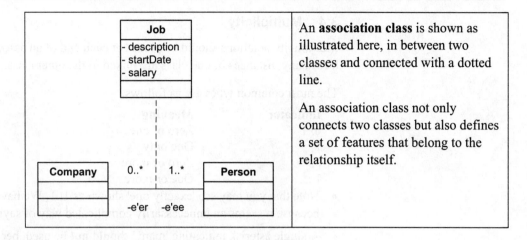

An **association class** is shown as illustrated here, in between two classes and connected with a dotted line.

An association class not only connects two classes but also defines a set of features that belong to the relationship itself.

3.3 Naming conventions

Symbols used to describe classes should always be broken into three compartments. Use of these compartments is described below.

Top compartment

Class names are nouns with an initial capital. If there is more than one word in the name each is capitalised but there are no spaces.

DespatchNote

OrderLine

This is for programming purposes: a name of "Despatch Note" could be interpreted as two separate things.

Middle compartment

Attributes are nouns describing the data items contained within the class. They are shown in lower case, but subsequent words are capitalised, not spaced.

–dateStarted

–productSize

The **minus sign** indicates that the attributes are **hidden** (private) from other classes (the principle of encapsulation, explained earlier).

Bottom compartment

Operations are verbs that describe what the class can do. The naming style is again initial lowercase with subsequent words capitalised and the name ends with round brackets (for programming reasons).

+calculateTotal()

+createAccount()

The name is usually the same as the message that is sent to the class requesting the operation to be performed. The **plus sign** indicates that the operations are accessible to other classes (public).

As noted above, operations are outside the syllabus. They are only mentioned to complete the description of the notation.

Associations are sometimes named but the relationship is often self-evident. For example you might write 'places' above the association between customer and order, but this is probably not necessary. In any case, the exam notes indicate that it is not in the syllabus.

3.4 Multiplicity

Multiplicity notations should be placed at each end of an association line to indicate how many instances of one class are linked to the other class.

The most common types are as follows.

Indicator	Meaning
0..1	Zero or one
1	One only
0..*	Zero or more
1..*	One or more

- Note that you may see 'exactly one' shown as 1..1. We have not used this notation because it seems an unnecessarily complicated way of saying 'exactly 1'.

- A single asterisk indicating 'many' should **not** be used, because it is not clear whether this means 'zero or more' or 'one or more'.

- Sometimes a specific number may be used. For example, if an ordering system allows a customer to provide details of up to three credit cards this might be shown as follows.

Customer		CreditCard
	1 1..3	

However, if the system is built to reflect this it may be difficult to change it later on, for instance if you want to allow customers to use more than 3 different credit cards. It would be better to express the multiplicity as 1..*.

3.5 Example

Shown below is a class model for a customer order. The central class is the Order itself. Associated with it is the Customer making the purchase and the Payment. A Payment is one of three kinds: CreditCard, Cash, or Cheque, shown as sub-types (generalisation): they all inherit an amount attribute, but also have unique attributes of their own. Each order contains OrderDetails (in other words one or more separate lines), each with its associated Item.

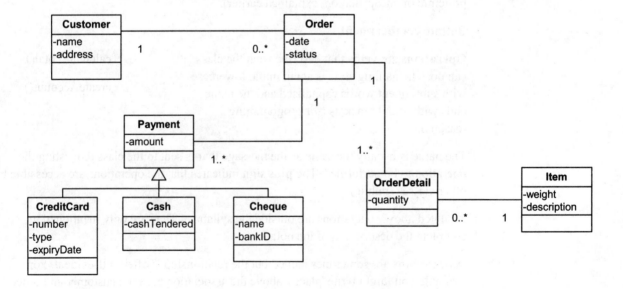

4 Business event models: statechart diagrams

State chart diagrams serve a similar purpose as entity life histories.

4.1 Statechart diagrams

The state of an object depends on its current activity or condition. A statechart diagram shows the possible states of an object and the transitions that cause a change in its state. In other words statechart diagrams describe the dynamic behaviour of a system in response to external stimuli.

The June 2004 exam notes tell us that: "the UML statechart diagram has symbols for initial state, final state, states, transitions, events and actions. The nesting of states should be learnt but there is no requirement for showing decomposition of states or the modelling of guards".

This type of diagram is called a 'state machine diagram' in the latest version of UML, but we will stick to the term used by the examiner. It can also be called a 'state diagram' or a 'state transition diagram'.

4.2 Notation

The object itself is not actually named in the diagram, therefore the diagram needs a heading.

Some of the notation will be familiar from activity diagrams.

●	**Initial state**. A filled circle represents the object's initial state.
event/action →	**Transition** arrows represent the path between different states of an object. The transition is labelled with the event that triggered it and the action that results from it.
State1	**States** represent situations during the life of an object. They are shown as a rectangle with rounded corners and are labelled with a description of the state.
◉	**Final state.** A filled circle nested inside another circle represents the object's final state.

An **event** is something that happens outside the object under consideration, possibly requiring some action to be taken. Events may be caused by the arrival of data, or some simple stimulus which may be due to human activity or some other part of the system. Events may also be caused by the passage of time. Event names are normally verbs or verbal phrases.

Actions are what is done by the object being modelled in response to an event. Action names are also usually short active verb phrases.

Here is the transition between two possible states for a Television object with the event that causes it and the action that results.

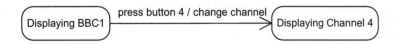

In fact events and actions can often be represented by the same word when modelling business systems. For instance an order might initially be in a 'received' state and when it has been checked it would be in a 'validated' state. The event is the validation of the order and the action is that the order becomes validated. In this case the simple word 'validate' would be used as the transition label.

A **state** is a condition in which the thing being modelled stays for some period of time, during which it behaves in the same way. When dealing with physical objects names of states are usually adjectives such as 'idle', 'busy', 'full', but when dealing with objects in a business system such as a customer order, states may include words such as 'validated', 'cancelled', 'despatched' and so on.

4.3 Example

Here is an example of a statechart diagram for a **SupplierInvoice** object.

Statechart diagram — SupplierInvoice

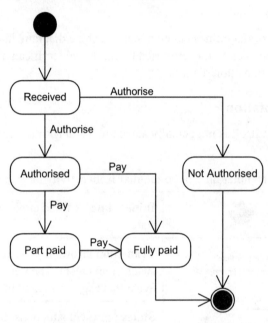

4.4 Nesting of states

For all but the simplest systems, the number of states and transitions in a statechart may become unmanageable. This problem can be addressed by allowing nesting of states, introducing a hierarchy into diagrams, and allowing system behaviour to be understood at different levels.

For example the authorisation of a supplier invoice is likely to involve a number of steps not shown above – checking to the original order, checking to the Goods Received Note and so on.

This can be modelled by showing the events to do with authorising in a separate box with the two possible outcomes shown outside the nested part.

Statechart diagram — SupplierInvoice

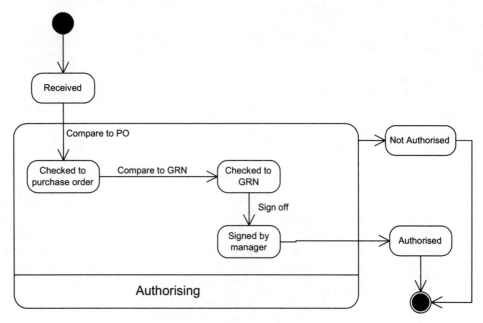

Conclusion

This chapter has explored methods of documenting system requirements. Activity diagrams focus on business processes taking place whereas class models show static data structures. Finally, statechart diagrams portray events that cause changes in data.

SELF-TEST QUESTIONS

Unified Modelling Language (UML) and object–oriented analysis and design

1 What is the principal difference between structured programming and OO programming? (1.3)

2 Explain the terms object, encapsulation, message, class and inheritance (1.4 -1.6)

Business process models: flowcharts and activity diagrams

3 What symbols are used in a flowchart? (2.1)

4 What does an action state symbol represent? (2.3)

Business structure models: class diagrams

5 What is a swimlane? (2.4)

6 How is an association shown on a class diagram? (3.2)

7 What does multiplicity represent and what are the most common types? (3.4)

Business event models: statechart diagrams

8 How is a transition shown on a statechart diagram (4.2)

9 Why might nesting of states be necessary? (4.4)

Chapter 11
EXTERNAL DESIGN

This chapter explores different methods of data input, the human-computer interface and system outputs. Inappropriate input methods, a hard to use interface and poor output reports can all greatly reduce the business value of an information system.

Objectives

By the time you have finished this chapter you should be able to:

- define the characteristics of a user-friendly system

- describe the task of external design and distinguish it from internal design

- design effective output documents and reports

- select appropriate technology to support the output design

- design effective inputs

- select appropriate technology to support input design

- describe how the user interface may be structured for ease of use

- explain how prototyping may be used in defining an external design.

1   External and internal design

External design concerns the design of the interface between a computer system and users. This does not only include the layout and style of screens but also includes:

- methods of data input

- methods of validating data input

- method of data output

- format of data output

- screen design and layout

- screen sequences and navigation

- user dialogue with the system.

This chapter explores these issues of external design in detail. Users are often heavily involved in specifying and testing different elements of the external design. Internal design in contrast does not involve users. It is concerned with the technical aspects of design eg database and program design.

2   Input devices

Any information system requires input of data. A wide variety of input methods are available, each having its own strengths and weaknesses. These are explored below.

2.1   Data collection and input

Before a computer can process data, that data must be input to the computer in a machine-intelligible form. The term data collection is used to cover the following activities.

KEY POINT

External design concerns the interface between users and the system.

Internal design does not involve users, but is concerned with the technical aspects of a system.

KEY POINT

Before a computer can process data, that data must be input to the computer in a machine-intelligible form.

Originating the data

Historically, the source of most data was a paper document. Increasingly, however, data are entered directly into a computer system through use of scanners and other sensors.

Data transmission

This is transfer of data from its original location to the site where it is processed and stored. In some cases data transmission may involve telephone links between the input and processing locations eg a PIN number entered into a cash machine is transmitted to a central computer for authorisation.

Data preparation

In some cases, particularly in large corporate server operations, data must be prepared before it is input to the computer, eg. collation of branch returns on sales.

Data input

Data are read by an input device and transferred to the internal storage of the computer where it is processed.

2.2 Choice of data input method

Choice of data input method involves consideration of the following:

- the nature of data to be entered

- the volume of data to be entered

- the importance of accuracy

- the speed of data input required

- who is to enter the data

- the cost and benefits associated with different input methods.

Selecting an appropriate input method ie one with appropriate flexibility, speed, reliability and cost, is critical to successful design and implementation of an information system.

2.3 Keyboard input (and visual display unit)

KEY POINT

Keyboards are still the most commonly used method of data input.

Keyboards are still the most commonly used method for data input. In addition to alphanumeric keys, most keyboards have special function keys, the purpose of which is often software-defined.

Although keyboard input is very common many users have poor keyboarding skills. This slows down data entry and increases the level of errors made. Keyboards are also largely limited to entry of alphanumeric data. The accuracy and speed of data input can be improved by offering users predefined options and through use of default values.

2.4 Mouse and tracker ball input

KEY POINT

Computer mice and tracker balls are extensively used as input devices on PCs, particularly if graphical user interfaces (GUIs) are used.

Computer mice and similar devices such as tracker balls or touch-sensitive pads are extensively used as input devices on PCs, particularly if graphical user interfaces (GUIs) are used. A mouse is a particularly effective way to enter data if users are offered predefined options on-screen or in drop down menus. System navigation is also very efficient if it is mouse driven, using clickable icons or buttons to move quickly between screens.

2.5 Optical mark recognition (OMR)

In Optical Mark Recognition (OMR), pre-printed documents are scanned into the computer. The position of marks made by users on these documents is then translated into a value. The grid below for instance shows a pre-printed document that allows entry of values between 0 and 9.

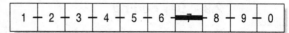

OMR has been used for sometime as a method of quickly marking multiple-choice exams. It is also used by the National Lottery to read in numbers selected by players.

OMR has a number of advantages:

- its speed

- its low unit cost at high data volumes

- its ease of use by non-experts

- a high degree of accuracy.

However, OMR has a number of disadvantages:

- cumbersome to record large volumes of data on a OMR grid

- a limited range of data can be captured

- inflexibility of pre-printed documents

- high unit cost for low data volumes.

2.6 Optical character recognition (OCR)

Optical Character Recognition (OCR) is more advanced than OMR. As the name suggest characters rather than marks are recognised. This allows tidy handwritten text to be read into a computer system directly and stored as an editable text document. Modern OMR scanners are capable of scanning several pages of text per minute.

OCR is much more flexible than OMR as there is no requirement for a pre-printed document. It is also much easier for users to prepare data for input. However, it is far less accurate than OMR, requiring visual checking of input once a scan has been completed. Poorly written text will not scan well, for instance, and will require checking before use, slowing down the input process considerably and increasing its cost.

2.7 Magnetic ink character recognition (MICR)

Magnetic ink character recognition uses highly stylised characters printed onto documents using inks that contain iron oxide. The document is then passed through a special reader. Input speeds are up to 2,400 documents per minute.

This method is used mainly for **banking applications** and is used on cheques and paying-in slips. Processing checks now involves passing them through a scanner which will then read the account number, check number and sort code automatically. MICR has a very high level of accuracy but the equipment for printing and reading magnetic text is expensive. As a result it is only cost effective for high volume applications.

2.8 Swipe cards

Swipe cards have a machine-readable magnetic strip attached to them. Applications include debit and credit cards, phone cards and security passes.

Historically, the amount of information stored on swipe cards has been quite small due to the capacity of the magnetic strip. More modern swipe cards have a small microchip embedded in them and have an enormous capacity. In addition to a security code, for instance, a new generation credit card has the capacity to store all of the transactions ever carried out on the account.

2.9 Bar coding

Bar codes are patterns of black and white lines. Using a reader these can be decoded. They are very widely used, particularly in the retail sector. Most stores now use EPOS systems (Electronic Point of Sale Systems) where items selected by a customer are scanned into a till. The following are typical examples of bar codes:

This input method is extremely quick, taking only as long as the 'beep' to confirm that the code has been read and verified against the stock master file. In such systems the code is used to provide continuous stock recording and re-ordering, as well as providing the customer with a detailed receipt. Bar coding reduces user input error, and saves time and money.

2.10 Scanners

In addition to capturing the position of marks or recognising individual characters, scanners can be used to input images into a computer. Colour scanners are now widely available at low cost for both business and domestic use.

2.11 Voice recognition and other input methods

Voice recognition/voice data entry

Voice recognition is growing in importance as a method of data input. As the sophistication of software increases less time is needed to calibrate a system to a user's voice and the accuracy of input is increasing.

Once set up, voice recognition software can be a very fast, flexible and cost effective method of entering data, particularly large volumes of text. Voice recognition is also a good way of automating system commands. Many mobile phone systems, for instance, now use voice recognition as a way of speed dialling and retrieving messages.

Touch screen/light pen

If light-sensitive or touch-sensitive devices are connected to a VDU, then the screen can act as an input device. By touching the screen with a finger or the light pen the user can select menu options. Many train stations now use this technology, allowing fast and easy purchase of tickets.

Stylus and tablet

A stylus device is often used to input technical drawings or graphic designs to a computer. The stylus looks like a pen with a small ball bearing in its tip. A graphic artist or technical drawing expert can trace a drawing on a drawing board called a tablet, with the image being reproduced on-screen.

3　Input data validation

The quality of data input into a computer system is dependent on two things:

- the accuracy of the original data source
- the accuracy of input.

Computer software can validate data input through a series of different validation checks. Common types of data validation check are as follows.

Format checks

At their most simple this type of check ensures that text is not entered into a numerical field and vice versa. More complex format checks ensure that dates are entered in the correct predetermined format. Data that do not comply with the format will be rejected.

Valid value and range checks

Range checks ensure that only data that lie inside an acceptable range are accepted eg only product codes within a range of 1,000 to 4,999 are accepted.

Consistency checks

Consistency checks compare data input into two fields before the data are accepted. This is to ensure data are consistent eg if MasterCard is selected as the credit card type on a web form, and then a number consistent with a different brand of card is entered into the account number field, the order will not be accepted.

Completeness Checks

Data will only be accepted by a system if certain mandatory fields have been completed. These checks are generally used to determine whether items of data have been missed out eg online ordering systems will not accept orders if the customer surname field is left blank.

Check digit

Certain fields may have codes to which a check digit can be attached. This digit usually becomes the last character or number of the code. When the code is entered, the check digit is recalculated and validated against the one entered by the operator. Check digits are particularly useful in supporting range checks. For example, the entered candidate number may have two digits transposed (71233452 instead of 72133452) and still pass the range check (70000000-79999999). However, if the code had used a check digit system to produce the last character then this transposition would have been picked up.

One check digit system is the modulus 11 system. Suppose there is a basic 4-digit code. Using a check digit, it will be expanded to a 5-digit code by adding a check digit. One 4-digit code might be, say, 2478. The check digit would be derived as follows.

Code digit	Weighting	Weighted total
2	5	10
4	4	16
7	3	21
8	2	<u>16</u>
		63
Check digit	1	<u>3</u>
		<u>66</u>

The check digit is a number that, when added to the weighted total as shown in the total, produces a grand total figure that divides exactly by 11. Here, a check digit of 3 takes the total to 66, which is divisible exactly by 11.

The code is therefore 24783.

If this code is keyed in incorrectly, a check digit check in the program will spot the error. For example, if the code 24783 were entered as 24873, the program would do the following check.

Code digit	Weighting	Weighted total
2	5	10
4	4	16
8	3	24
7	2	14
3	1	3
		67

This does not divide exactly by 11, so the code must be wrong.

Check digit checks are particularly useful for checking the accuracy of key codes, such as customer codes in a sales system.

Data verification

Data verification involves double entry of data values. The two sequences of data are then automatically cross-checked against each other. If they match, the data are accepted. If there are inconsistencies, the batch is rejected and an error report is generated. Verification can also be carried out manually by checking two columns of data entered into a spreadsheet on-screen.

4   Output devices

Most computer systems will use a range of output devices to communicate with users. Output devices work in a number of different ways, as described below.

Temporary display

Devices such as Visual Display Units display information on a temporary basis. Usually messages would be displayed until the user acknowledges that they have been read, but sometimes messages will scroll off the screen as more information is displayed. Many systems allow a permanent copy of on-screen information to be printed.

Printed output

The most common form of output device is a printer. Types of printer are discussed later in the chapter.

Process control

When the computer is running a production process, outputs will be direct to the equipment that is controlling the process.

4.1　Printers

A wide variety of printer types exist. Decisions regarding printer purchase should be made on:

- the volume of output required
- the speed of printing required
- the quality of printing required
- purchase costs
- running and maintenance costs
- whether a printer is to be used by a workgroup or an individual
- whether colour printing is required.

Impact printers

Accounting documents are often multipart forms such as invoices. These need to be printed out using an impact printer that physically bangs a head or needle against an ink ribbon and the document to ensure that all copies of the document are printed. Dot-matrix printers are examples of impact printers. However, they are so slow and the quality of output is so poor that they are not a viable option for most business purposes.

Ink-jet printers

Printing is achieved by guiding a high-speed stream of ink drops onto the paper. They provide faster, quieter and better quality printing than traditional dot matrix impact printers. Colour ink-jet printers are now common, and many are portable enough to be used with a laptop PC.

Laser printers

Laser printers are capable of both high speed and high quality output. The cost of purchasing and running a laser printer has fallen greatly over the last few years and they are now affordable by most businesses.

4.2　Computer output on microfilm (COM)

With computer output on microfilm, the output is recorded directly onto microfilm. The film bears a miniature image of what appears to be a printed document, although no original in fact exists.

The microfilm can be in the form of a strip or sheet. The microfilm can be made user-intelligible by special enlargers and printers.

5　Human-computer interface

The human-computer interface is the interface between the technology and human elements of an information system. Well-designed interfaces are easy to use and flexible being able to accommodate the needs of novice through to expert users.

Users tend to judge the success of an information system on the quality of its interface: Is the interface perceived as being user friendly and are system outputs in an appropriate and easy to understand form?

5.1　Interface components

The components that make up a human-computer interface are:

- the human-computer dialogue
- the terminal and keyboard design
- screen layout and appearance.

These are all explored in subsequent sections of this chapter.

5.2 Human-computer dialogue

A **human-computer dialogue** is an exchange of information between a user and the computer system via an interactive terminal.

Dialogue requirements

Dialogues should be:

1   **Natural.** The language of the dialogue, and the sequence of tasks, should be compatible with the user's view of the task being performed. Data should be presented in a logical way, and in the order that the user is accustomed to seeing it.

2   **Consistent.** The dialogue should be consistent across a system eg dates should always be entered in the same way, menus should have consistent structure and function keys should be consistent in their behaviour.

3   **Supportive.** Users should be guided on how to enter any data and provided with meaningful messages and feedback. There should be on-line help facilities to help people navigate through a dialogue, and to give context-specific assistance.

4   **Visible.** If a system is going to take many seconds to respond to a user's input, it should not leave an unchanging screen on display with no evidence for activity. Some form of icon indicating activity should be displayed informing the user to wait until the system has completed its task.

5   **Helpful.** Error messages should be clear and meaningful. 'Text only should be entered into this field' is far more helpful than 'Capture Error X2259'.

6   **Recoverable.** It is very frustrating for users to be most of the way through a long transaction, only to lose everything if the system crashes. There should be scope for saving work periodically through a data entry task, so that users can pick up from where they left off when the system is restored.

7   **Flexible.** The dialogue should be able to accommodate the needs of all users. Help messages and on-screen advice are very useful for novices. However, they become annoying for expert users and it should be easy to disable this type of feature if it is not required.

8   **Navigable.** Users should be able to see what to do at the end of any screen – whether they wish to repeat the action, perform another task, quit the system, or save the work they have completed. There should always be clear instructions for how to proceed.

Well-designed dialogues have a high degree of *usability* and tend to have a number of common features. These are:

- consistent in appearance and underlying logic

- flexible in the way that users interact with a system, catering for users of differing skills levels

- perceived as being under the control of the user in terms of the order and pace of work.

Most of these objectives are met within the modern graphical user interfaces (GUIs) such as Windows®.

The key to good dialogue is user friendliness, and this is what the analyst must seek, building in suitable help facilities and tolerance of errors.

There are five common ways for the user to communicate with the computer:

- by answering questions posed by the computer software
- by selection of an option from a menu
- by using shortcut keys
- by filling in a screen based form
- by use of a graphical user interface (GUI).

5.3 Questions

Consider the following straightforward question:

> Is the employee M (male) or F (female)?

The implication is that the user should type M or F, but this is prone to error because the user might use lowercase or might type the answer in full. In fact the question invites the answer 'Yes' from a particularly facetious or obtuse user.

This problem can be dealt with in a number of ways.

- **Radio buttons** (circles) are used if only one answer is acceptable.

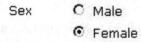

- **Drop-down lists** are used where there are a large number of options (this saves space on-screen).

- **Check boxes** (squares) are used when the user can select one or more options at the same time. Note the use of shading, here so that it is clear which box belongs to which option.

Which newspaper(s) do you read?

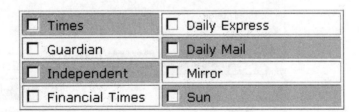

5.4 Menus

When there are a number of mutually exclusive options, a menu is a useful way to prompt input from a user. The user may highlight the option required and press the enter key (or click the mouse button).

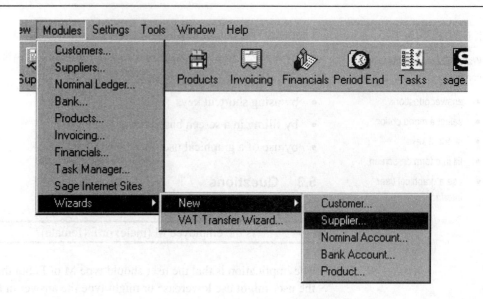

There may well be a series of menus, with one choice bringing a second menu on-screen.

5.5 Shortcut keys

Using menus and the mouse can be tedious and long-winded for experienced users. To shortcut this process, an individual key or key combination can be used to enter a specific command.

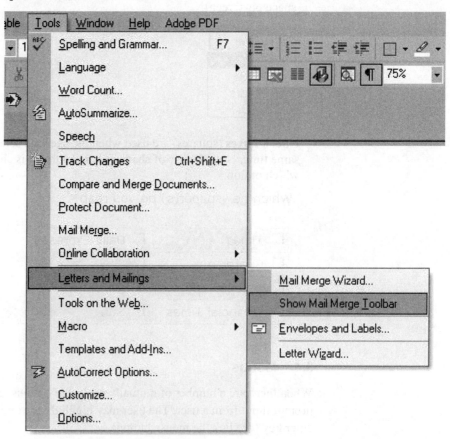

In this example (from Microsoft Word) the user could type 'Alt + T' to bring up the Tools menu and then 'e' and then 'T' (note the underlined letters in each option) to get to the 'Show Mail Merge Toolbar' option: there is no need to touch the mouse at all.

Function keys (F1, F2, etc) are also used for this purpose in some packages.

5.6 Form filling

In many systems where records containing a number of fields have to be entered, they will be typed onto a screen-based form. The form will be laid out in attractive format to make it clearer and easier to fill in. Warning messages and sound will be used to show when the user has made an error. The user typically moves from field to field using the tab or cursor movement (arrow) keys.

In the illustration below (from Sage, an accounting package) there is default form to complete with mandatory information, together with several other optional data entry forms on different tabs, such as 'Credit control'.

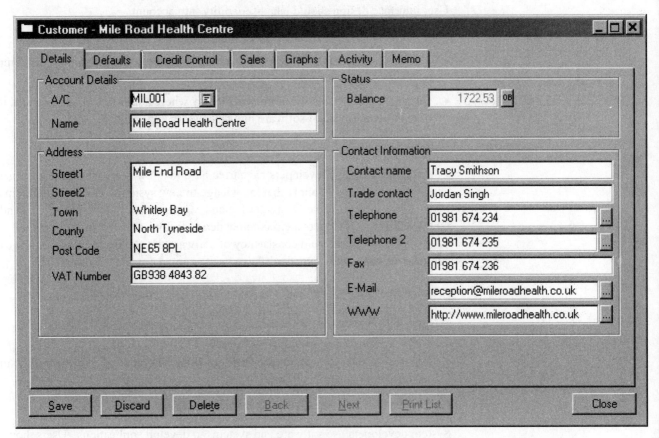

Some systems use forms that mimic hard copy originals. For entry of details from a cheque, for example, an exact duplicate of the cheque is displayed on-screen and the user fills-in the relevant fields. This helps make inputting information relatively quick and easy, as the user is already familiar with the style of the input form.

5.7 Consistency

As the cost of hardware and software has fallen in recent years, the major cost of a system has become the manpower to operate it throughout its life. This is one of the factors that has led commercial software developers to focus upon the human-computer interface. In the early 1990s, Apple Computer Inc publicised the findings of independent research that suggested the cost of operating the Apple Macintosh was significantly lower than with other kinds of personal computer because of its consistent user interface.

KEY POINT

Consistency helps users learn programs more quickly.

Consistency may also apply to the way that two different software packages function. For example, the command to save a file may be the same in a word-processing package as in a spreadsheet. If there is consistency of this kind the cost of training staff who already have some experience can be reduced. Microsoft products also provide a consistent user interface.

5.8 Flexibility and user control

Another factor driving improvement in the human-computer interface is growing appreciation amongst employers of the cost of low staff morale. Poorly designed human-computer interfaces can be a major factor contributing to poor staff morale. Inflexible interfaces that interfere rather than support the natural flow of work are particularly problematic here. Attempting to save money on interface design is now viewed as a false economy by many companies.

5.9 Classification of users

User interface design should take user ability into account.

Two categories of *computer literacy* can be identified:

- general computer literacy where a user has experience of using a range of computer packages

- software package specific computer literacy where a user is very experienced in use of a particular piece of software but lacks wider experience.

A well-designed system will meet the needs of both kinds of user.

Commercial software developers have tried hard to allow users who have good general computer knowledge to apply that knowledge to new systems. The design principle here is consistency. Apple Computer Inc and Microsoft Inc both have sets of standards which software developers are recommended to follow. Other firms have also developed guidelines to aid consistency of software developed internally. In the case of some larger firms, these standards have been adopted outside the firm.

Well-designed software will offer users support in number of ways.

Methods include:

- help screens

- tool tips - information about the functions of buttons appears on-screen if the mouse pointer lingers over the button

- wizards - the package guides users through a procedure.

System developers use software and systems to develop applications. Users, however, use applications to input and manipulate data. The difference between these two groups is important when dealing with complicated systems. Developers will need access to all of the system and its capabilities – this will affect the kind of interface they prefer. End users of the same system will rarely need access to the full system. They would normally need a simpler interface that reflects the nature of the tasks they need to do.

Distinction may be drawn between occasional and frequent users in terms of the extent of package specific knowledge each acquire of the system, the use they put the system to, the training they require and their tolerance of a poorly designed interface. Frequent users, typically:

- learn and retain a greater range of specific knowledge

- use the system to execute a fixed range of functions; the occasional user will typically use the system to make varied enquiries

- require formal training because use of the system is an important aspect of their work

- have no alternative method of carrying out their jobs, so they are more likely to persevere in learning a system that has a poor interface.

5.10 Design elements of the human-computer interface

Workstation ergonomics

Workstation ergonomics includes all aspects of the terminal and keyboard design as well as the furniture, lighting and general environment. Aspects that relate to the terminal and keyboard design are outlined below.

Terminal design

The screen should be adjustable in terms of height, angle and distance from the user. This should be independent of the keyboard adjustment described later.

Characters should not flicker or move. The use of certain kinds of fluorescent lighting with some terminals can cause these problems.

The screen should be free from glare and reflections. This should be a design feature of the terminal and not reliant upon adjustments to the ambient lighting.

The user should be able to choose either dark characters on a light background or vice versa. The contrast between the characters and background should be adjustable, as should the brightness.

The resolution of the screen should be capable of displaying sharp character images.

5.11 Keyboard design

Keyboard design is a factor that needs consideration in workstation ergonomics. Individual preferences with regard to keyboard design can be quite different. The following are some of the design features that need consideration, and where possible they should be adjustable:

1   **Key force.** The pressure required is a function of the frequency of use. Frequent users may prefer a light touch, while infrequent and inexperienced users may prefer keyboards that require greater pressure.

2   **Key shape.** The top surface of the key should be concave with a reflection free finish.

3   **Keyboard height.** The height of the keyboard should be adjustable. There should be some device that users can rest their wrists on, and this should also be adjustable.

4   **Keyboard angle.** This should be adjustable and in the range 10 to 15 degrees from horizontal.

5.12 Screen design

Layout of the display

The location of data on a screen can greatly affect the ease with which a user can locate the precise information required, and this affects the stress associated with using the system. The following suggestions are based upon what any user would expect to find on a paper-based form:

- ensure that there is sufficient space between items to ensure that they appear separate and distinct

- place important and frequently used data on the left side of the screen and arrange in descending order of importance from top to bottom

- where columns are needed give the eye something to follow when moving from one column to another to avoid accidentally changing rows

- group items together logically, and possibly put boundaries around the groups to indicate the grouping.

- input screen and input document layout must match.

KEY POINT

Good design principles:

- clearly show users what to do
- display only information essential to current task
- display all information for a task on a single screen.

What to display

Screen design should always be easy to read, presenting information in a clear and tidy manner. It should be free from any information not relevant to the task the screen or system is intended to aid. Good design principles are:

- clearly show the users what they are required to do
- display only the information essential to carrying out an action or making a decision
- display all the information needed to execute a task on a single screen; the user should not need to refer to other screens.

Input screens

The layout of input screens should be influenced by the source of the data.

1 **Data from paper forms.** Paper input forms and input screens should match. The possibility of the wrong data being entered into fields is then greatly reduced.

2 **Capturing data at source.** Where data is supplied from other sources the screen itself becomes the form that captures data the information the system needs. Here the screen should be designed using the same principles of paper form design.

5.13 Response time

There are two aspects of response time which concern the human-computer interface:

- time between the user giving a command and the command being completed
- time taken to refresh the screen when new characters are entered from the keyboard.

Screen refresh rates are critical for any application where users enter large quantities of data. Examples include word-processing and database entry. This aspect of response time is largely a function of hardware or communications capacity.

The following guidelines are pertinent to response times applying to commands.

1 **Frequently used commands** should take less than one second.

2 **System response to commands.** When a user has given a command he should be able to see that the system has acted upon it, and then see the result of the command.

3 **Consistent response.** A consistent response time for a particular command should be sought. This may mean slowing down some variants of the command.

4 **Notice of delayed response.** If the response time will be longer than the user has become accustomed to, the system should either state that the request is being worked upon or state how long the request will take to complete. More sophisticated systems will show the user details of the progress in performing a lengthy command, and also give the user the opportunity to abort the request.

5.14 Error handling

Error handling is an important part of the user interface, particularly during the learning stage. Often users are reluctant to start learning a package for fear of making irrecoverable errors.

KEY POINT

The system should prevent errors taking place by always showing the user what is required next.

The system should prevent errors taking place by always showing the user what is required next. The system should cater for the inexperienced user by clearly showing how to get detailed context-sensitive help.

Where a user carries out an incorrect action, the system should immediately identify this before any harm is done. The system should then explain to the user why what was done was incorrect. When an error is detected, only that part of the input that is incorrect should need to be re-keyed. Deficiencies in this aspect of the user interface can infuriate users with limited keyboard skills; having to re-key a screen of data because the wrong date format has been used can alienate a new user at a critical phase in their introduction to the system. Correction of the date format is an example of where systems can often correct invalid entries. Where there is a fairly limited range of codes or commands, the system can suggest a correct entry after an invalid one has been detected.

Systems should enable users to reverse commands they have given. Whilst the command may have been a valid one in terms of the system definition, users may change their minds or realise they have made an error. The ability to reverse back through the most recent commands will reduce the stress levels upon new users who are unnecessarily slow in the use of the system whilst they double check all of their entries and command choices. This facility is equally useful to the expert who carries out commands very quickly but is still likely to make mistakes.

5.15 Website design

Using a web site involves a human-computer dialogue that is similar in many ways to that involved in use of an off-line software package. Good dialogue design for a web site is similar to that for software, and involves consideration of the following:

- how should the site be structured?
- how is the site to be navigated eg buttons, text links or drop down menus?
- should a consistent page layout be used throughout the site?
- what support should be given to inexperienced web users or new visitors to the site
- what dialogue is needed when users input information into web forms?

6 Input and output document design

Input documents have two roles to play. Data is collected using them and they are then used as a basis for data entry into a computer. Careful design of documents is an essential ingredient of an effective system. Documents should provide an efficient means of transmitting information.

There are many costs associated with the use of documentation and inefficient document design will generate additional costs. Costs associated with document design include printing and handling costs.

Cost of printing

As a general rule, standard size documents are preferable (eg A4, A5) as they are less expensive than special sizes. Documentation used solely for internal purposes may use lower quality paper and printing than those used for external purposes, where the company will wish to use top-quality stationery to impress customers and others. Multi-part stationery is more expensive than single part.

Handling costs

Input forms must be easy to complete and to enter into the computer. If a form is inefficiently designed it may not be used properly.

6.1 The document description/document analysis form

Input documents used in a system will often help a systems analyst to clarify existing procedures and controls. The analyst may wish to include in his own files copies of documents used in the system, both blank documents and some with specimen data entered.

The documents themselves cannot give a complete picture and to supplement them the analyst may complete a **document description** form. An example of such a form is given below with a brief explanation of the data to be included in it:

1   **Title** – gives the form title and number with details of any alternative name commonly used for this document in the company.

2   **Purpose** – a brief description of the purpose of the document. This may help to identify unnecessary documents/copies.

3   **Originated by** – gives the place and means of origination and may identify the means of combining existing documents.

4   **Used by** – this should be related to the purpose of the document to ensure that it is only sent to those who need it. It may indicate the suitability of the layout for the user's needs.

5   **Number of copies** – minimum, average, maximum, seasonal fluctuations.

6   **Contents** – it is essential for each data item to be clearly indicated on the document. The size column indicates the maximum number of characters making up that field.

7   **Sequence** – used where the sequence of field names is different from that in the previous section.

Shown below is an example of a document description form.

Title of document				Project Name Date	
Purpose					
Originated by					
Used by					
Number of Copies			Minimum Average Maximum	} Per	
No	Field Name		Size	Comments	
Sequence of data fields					
Remarks					

6.2 Document design hints

The content and design of a document will be governed largely by its purpose and the system of which it forms part.

There follows some general advice on the design of a document for an examination answer.

Determine the purpose of the document

In an exam, read the question carefully and decide what the document is for. You may find that it is created to provide information (eg to management). You may conclude that this information (the output) should be contained along the bottom row or along the right-hand column of the document.

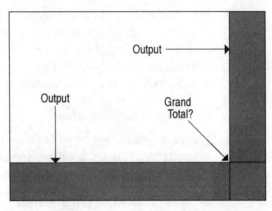

Determine the input data required

Your document will probably have to show the data items that are used to determine the output. For example, to determine the value of an invoice (output) one needs to show what has been sold, the unit price, the price net of VAT, the VAT amount and the gross price (input).

Decide the order in which to record the data

You should work from left to right across your document or work down from top to bottom (ie the process is left to right or top to bottom).

Size of the document

It was suggested earlier that documents should be a standard size. The document must be big enough to contain all the data and be easily read but not so big as to be difficult to handle and file. The solution in the examination is normally easy – use one whole sheet of A4 for each document that you have to design. This means that you have a suitably sized document and you do not have to draw the borders.

Title

The title of a form is important. It should be descriptive and preferably short. If the question in the examination gives the form a title, then use that in your answer. Write the title of the form IN BLOCK CAPITALS across the top of your answer.

Reference numbers

These are useful for re-ordering purposes. The document number should be placed in a corner of the document so that it can easily be identified when held in a file.

Headings

It is important that as much data as possible is pre-printed on the document so that only variable data needs to be entered when the document is used. Watch out in particular for the need to include:

- dates, eg DD, MM, YY. This is important in multi-national systems, since different countries have different standard ways of displaying dates.

- units, eg hours, kilos

- instructions, eg Write your name here. Please return this remittance advice with your cheque.

Multi-part sets of documents

It is often effective to print several copies of a document together on multi-part stationery, each copy usually being a different colour. Remember that it is essential to have the same data at the same position on each copy but that lower copies may have information blanked-out of them. For example, the price of goods is shown on the invoice copy but not on the despatch note copy.

Control and authorisation

Many documents will be sequentially pre-numbered and may have space for authorisation, perhaps at various levels. If you think the control and authorisation methods are appropriate, include them.

In the examination, it is important above all that your answer *looks like a document* that could conceivably *meet the objective described in the question.* You may find it useful with the examination in mind to study documents which you come across at work. Consider the contents and layout. Why has a particular design been used? Could it be improved in any way?

6.3   Output design

Output must be clear, precise and informative. A considerable amount of thought and effort is put into designing the output since, for users, it is the most important part of any system.

The first choice that will have to be made is the output medium. The two most common output media are the VDU, for temporary (or soft) copy, and printers for permanent (or hard) copy. Other output media include microfilm, CD and DVD. Output design may also be assisted by the use of prototyping. Particularly in the case of Windows applications, example screens can be produced very quickly using screen design software. These will help the user understand the look and feel of any screen before software is written to produce that design.

6.4   VDU display

The VDU is an excellent medium when decisions must be made immediately, or where the user is working interactively. If a sales order clerk is speaking on the telephone to the customer, the computer will report whether stock levels are high enough to service the order, and the clerk can accept the order.

When designing an output screen, the analyst must be sparing with the amounts of information displayed, and ensure that the screen is clear and easy to understand. The screen should identify what is being displayed, and screen layouts should be designed to fit a common style – making it easy for the user to know precisely where to look for the information displayed. Usually information will continue to be displayed until the user takes some action – such as pressing the enter key. Many systems allow users the option of producing hard copy of what appears on the screen when required.

Print-out design

After the systems analysis process has identified what output is required, it will need to be designed. Its structure will depend upon the use that will be made of it. There are basically two categories of printed out documents:

- working documents – invoices, purchase orders, statements, etc
- information presentation documents – analysis of sales, reports, etc.

6.5 Working documents

For working documents, everything is subordinated to making the document functionally efficient and effective. Many such documents are printed onto multi-part pre-printed stationery. This stationery will be designed to fit the standard house style of the organisation. The information, which varies, is printed onto the stationery at the time of document production.

The information printed at the bottom of the following statement can be read directly using an optical character reader (OCR). This cuts down the amount of clerical work required to input the details of payment received. This sort of document is known as a 'turn around' document.

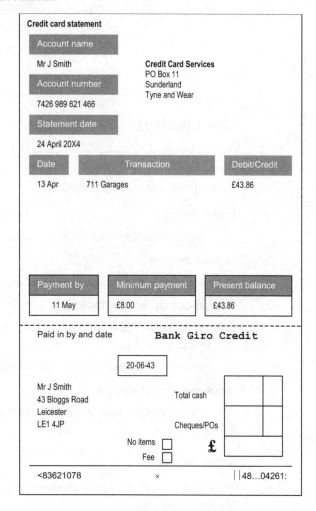

6.6 Information presentation documents

These documents are designed to be clear and understandable. As can be seen in the example below, the report specified when it was produced, what information is being presented, and what time period is covered.

J Bright

Pareto report

List of customers in diminishing size

Produced: 16.4.X4

Period covered: March 20X4

Customer	Total Sales	Cumulative sales	
A Jury plc	£66,486	£66,486	(33%)
B Kenwright	£33,204	£99,690	(50%)
C Lamb & Co	£20,310	£120,000	(60%)

Conclusion

This chapter has explored methods of data input and output together with the design of the human computer interface. Careful interface design can have significant effect on the usability and value of a system.

SELF-TEST
QUESTIONS

Input devices

1   List the main forms of input to a computer system. (2)

Output devices

2   What factors affect your choice of a printer? (4.1)

Human-computer interface

3   What are the most important characteristics of a well–designed human-computer interface? (5.2)

4   How can computer users be classified? (5.9)

Input and output design

5   What is the purpose of a document description form? (6.1)

EXAM-TYPE
QUESTION

Report layout

The extract below from a report shows information about stock levels. The report has two main purposes:

- to highlight products that are below their re-order level

- to compare the total 'value at re-order level' with the total 'stock value'. The organisation requires that total 'stock value' should not exceed total 'value at re-order level' by more than 10%.

Required:

(a) Most organisations have standards for the layout of such reports. For example, the standards may require that each report should have a title (as in stock level report).

List *five* further standard items that might apply to any system generated report. These standards may or may not have been adhered to by the stock level report extract. **(5 marks)**

(b) Briefly describe three ways in which the usability of the stock level report might be improved taking into account the main purposes of the report. (Credit will not be given for standards issues already listed in part (a) of this question). **(6 marks)**

(c) The accurate data entry of stock information is essential. In what way can errors be reduced when entering data into the system? **(4 marks)**

(Total: 15 marks)

Report extract

Stock level report

Product code	Cost per unit	Units in stock	Stock value	Re-order level	Below re-order level	Value at re-order level
98765	30	20	600	15		450
98766	60	7	420	5		300
98767	59	30	1770	40	********	2360
98768	45	21	945	23	********	1035
98769	23	53	1219	70	********	1610
98770	40	112	4480	110		4400
98771	30	67	2010	50		1500
98772	10	9	90	5		50
98773	40	7	280	5		200
98774	30	23	690	25	********	750
98775	25	45	1125	50	********	2250
98776	45	32	1440	30		1350
98777	12	10	120	10		120
98778	15	15	225	10		150
98779	45	45	2025	50	********	2250
98780	10	30	300	25		250
98781	45	67	3015	50		2250
98782	23	54	1242	50		1150
98783	80	20	1600	10		800
98784	12	78	936	15		180
98785	56	58	3248	50		2800
98786	12	12	144	10		120
98787	6	90	540	100	********	600
98788	50	2	100	5	********	250
98789	78	1	78	5	********	390
Total	881	908	28642			27565

For the answer to this question, see the 'Answers' section at the end of the book.

Chapter 12
SOFTWARE DELIVERY

This chapter investigates the different methods of obtaining software for use within an organisation. The approach to selecting software via the invitation to tender is looked at in some detail, when the successful tenderer has been chosen.

Objectives

By the time you have finished this chapter you should be able to:

- define the bespoke software approach to fulfilling the user's information system srequirements

- briefly describe the tasks of design, programming and testing required in developing a bespoke systems solution

- define the application software package approach to fulfilling the user's information systems requirements

- briefly describe the tasks of package selection, evaluation and testing required in selecting an appropriate application software package

- describe the relative merits of the bespoke systems development and application software package approaches to fulfilling an information systems requirement

- describe the structure and contents of an Invitation To Tender (ITT)

- describe how to identify software packages and their suppliers that may potentially fulfil the Information Systems requirements

- develop suitable procedures for distributing an ITT and dealing with subsequent enquiries and bids

- describe a process for evaluating the application software package, the supplier of that package and the bid received from the supplier

- describe the risks of the application software package approach to systems development and how these might be reduced or removed.

1 Software solutions

There are various ways to produce a software solution for a systems project.

- purchase a standard software package and use this without any modification

- purchase a standard software package and make suitable amendments to customise this for the organisation's specific requirements

- purchase a standard software package and add company specific modules as necessary

- pay for a bespoke system to be developed using existing hardware.

This chapter investigates the two main forms of purchase, namely the use of an **application package off-the-shelf** and the writing of a **bespoke package** (a purpose-written system). The other purchase options have similar advantages and disadvantages, particularly when compared to the bespoke solution, so they are not mentioned again in detail in this chapter.

1.1 Microsoft everything?

It is a fact that the vast majority of all computer users in the world have a version of Windows as their operating system and of Microsoft Office for day to day tasks such as word processing and spreadsheet creation.

It is also a fact that the majority of computer users in the world are familiar with these Microsoft systems. If their employer asked them to use anything else they would require extra training.

In the case of Microsoft Word and Microsoft Excel it is generally recognised – even by Apple Mac users – that these are the 'Best of Breed (BOB)' word processing and spreadsheet applications.

The fact that organisations often need to exchange files such as word-processed documents and spreadsheets is of course another compelling reason for using the software that almost everybody else uses.

We do not say all this to champion the cause of Microsoft, but simply to point out that it is likely that most organisations would only go through rigorous selection procedures for operating system and basic office software if they were considering NOT using the Microsoft products. Otherwise it can be taken as read.

The main issue with such software is how often to upgrade to the latest version.

In this chapter we are mainly concerned with the selection of other software, where there is a good deal more choice and no clear best solution, in particular accounting packages.

2 Bespoke software (purpose-written systems)

Bespoke (i.e. tailor-made or purpose-written) applications are constructed by programmers to meet the specific needs of the particular organisation in which they are found. The process of programming is extremely time-consuming and expensive, but is often the only alternative if the application is very specialised.

2.1 Preparing a bespoke system – the V model

Before a bespoke system can be implemented into an organisation, there are various design and build stages that must be completed in order to provide a relevant and robust package for that organisation. Writing bespoke software is similar to producing any other software in that the software development and testing cycle must be followed.

The V model is illustrated below.

The software development cycle

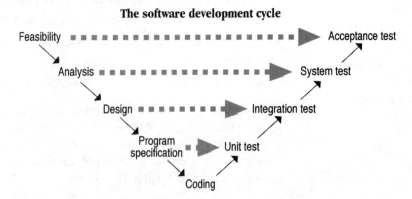

'V' refers to the two legs of the diagram. System design runs down the left leg of the V and follows testing back up the right leg. (You will be familiar with most of the stages in the design and implementation of systems from earlier studies, where the SDLC and different design methodologies were discussed.) The horizontal lines indicate the 'links' that are established between the initial design phase and the testing/implementation of the system.

The elements of the V diagram are outlined below.

(a) **Systems design**

(i) *Feasibility and analysis*

The feasibility and analysis stages will normally have been covered as part of the standard system development life cycle (Chapter 7). This means that the analysis of the requirements of the software will be available.

(i) *Design and program specification*

The design phase will involve producing a systems design specification, probably in the form of a requirements specification that can be distributed to potential writers of the software. This document will form part of the Invitation To Tender (see below) which is sent out to suppliers. Responses to the Invitation To Tender will have to be evaluated and a supplier chosen prior to the detailed program specification being produced.

Alternatively the software can be written in-house using the organisation's own software development team.

(iii) *Coding*

Once the builders of the new system have been selected, and the requirements specification for the new system completed, the team will consider the options of writing completely new software programs, or amending existing programs to meet the organisation's requirements. Part of this choice may be within the Invitation To Tender responses, especially where a software house has identified time and cost savings from amending some of the existing software. As usual, users' input will be requested at the design stage to ensure that the final system will meet their requirements in terms of functionality and usability. Prototyping may also be used to assist in trapping user requirements.

Detailed work will also be required to check the structure of existing databases and field design in the existing programmes that the bespoke system will need to communicate with. The bespoke software will need to exchange data with other programs, so it is important that the file organisation written into this system is compatible with existing software in the organisation.

(b) **Testing**

After coding of the software, the four testing stages will be undertaken.

(i) *Unit testing*

Unit testing tests individual programs operating in isolation from the other programs.

(ii) *Integration testing*

This tests two or more of the individual programs working together.

(iii) *System testing*

This tests the whole system, ensuring that all the programs work and interact correctly with each other.

(iv) *Acceptance testing*

Finally, the users of the software will perform an acceptance test, prior to sign-off of the software and its implementation into the organisation.

2.2 Advantages and disadvantages of bespoke systems

Advantages
- They are written to fit the organisation's information needs precisely.
- The organisation has complete discretion over the design of data structures.
- The system can be integrated with other applications within the organisation.
- The system can be modified to fit changing needs of the user over time.
- Bespoke systems might give a company a competitive advantage in the market place, if they can do more than competitors' computer systems.

If the programs are of interest to other organisations, they can be sold (or licensed). the information services group can thus become a profit centre.

Disadvantages
- System development takes a long time, which delays the implementation of the system.
- Bespoke systems are costly to develop and test.
- There is a greater probability of bugs (software errors) in a bespoke system.
- Support for a bespoke system will be expensive. The organisation has to bear all the cost.

2.3 Risks of bespoke application software development

The risks of using bespoke application software mainly relate to the disadvantages listed above. These risks can be overcome by:

- ensuring that users are involved at all stages in the design of the software. Any amendments to the design must be discussed with the users, and acceptable compromises found

- either taking the support and maintenance of the software in-house, or continuing the contract with the supplier. Providing maintenance in-house has the distinct disadvantage that programmers may not be fully aware of how the software was written. Trying to provide support will therefore be time consuming and potentially very costly if the software is amended incorrectly

- the data structures for the other software programs to be accessed must be stated clearly within the invitation to tender or subsequent software analysis documentation. While this may not overcome all errors in design, placing the data structures in a formal document will ensure that the supplier has notice of them, and must legally attempt to adhere to that specification.

3 Invitation To Tender

An Invitation To Tender (ITT) is a document inviting suppliers to make a bid for the supply of some specific software (or hardware) to the purchasing company. The invitation may be sent out to specific suppliers, or made as a general invitation to any supplier, perhaps via an advert in a trade journal.

The invitation to tender is likely to be for hardware, a substantial application package or for the development of a bespoke system by an outside contractor.

The ITT will define what needs to be done to achieve the system objectives and act as a basis for suppliers to put together and present their proposals.

3.1 Contents of an ITT

The invitation to tender will normally contain the following sections:

- letter of invitation
- instructions to tenderers
- conditions of contract
- form of letter and schedules
- requirements specification
- software engineering requirements.

The same format can be used for purchasing bespoke solutions or off-the-shelf packages, although in the latter case, details of software engineering may be very limited as the package is likely to require only minimal amendments.

Letter of invitation

This is the formal invitation to tender. It will specify:

- the date for submission of tenders
- contact names for technical queries
- contact names for contractual queries
- a warning that tenders received after the due date may not be considered.

Instructions to tenderers

These instructions advise the tenderer what to do and how to tender for the contract. Many of the points may seem obvious, but they have to be stated to avoid any misunderstanding. The instructions will include:

- alternatives and options where the tenderer may suggest different methods of achieving a requirement in the requirements specification, but with improved efficiency or reduced cost
- additional information that may be available from the supplier
- period of validity of the ITT
- a statement indicating whether or not prices can be varied for changes in labour rates or materials costs
- statement on the basis for prices
- statement on compliance – that is, areas of the tender that the tenderer cannot comply with, with reasons for this non-compliance.

Conditions of contract

The conditions of the contract apply to the terms of the supply of the software itself. The important areas to be included in this contract will include:

Visibility of the supplier's activities during development	The purchaser needs to be able to contact the supplier as the contract progresses to ensure that the software being designed actually meets the requirements specification and that the contract is running to schedule. As some of the work may be undertaken away from the supplier's premises, providing appropriate contact arrangements is important.
Purchaser response to queries	The contract will specify timescales for the purchaser to respond to queries raised by the supplier. The aim is to ensure that work is not unduly delayed by slow response times.

- acceptance
- warranty period
- maintenance and enhancement
- insolvency or bankruptcy
- performance and completion time
- confidentiality
- insurance copies.

Ownership rights in software	The actual ownership of software is not always clear. The contract needs to state that ownership of bespoke software passes to the purchaser, normally after the supplier has been paid, to avoid subsequent dispute in this area.
Patents, design rights and copyright	The main issue here is intellectual property rights, and whether the software written infringes on copyright of any existing software. The supplier will normally indemnify the purchaser against any breach of copyright; in effect, the supplier is confirming that the software is original work and does not infringe any other copyrights.
Indemnity and insurance	The supplier will need to arrange for appropriate insurance covering areas such as professional indemnity, product liability and legal expenses. Third party consequential damages may also be considered, although consequential loss may also be excluded by the contract.
Acceptance	How the supplier will know whether or not the purchaser has accepted the software. Some formal sign-off agreement will be stated with an acceptance certificate being produced as evidence of this.
Warranty period	This is the amount of time during which the supplier will amend the software for errors found in it. The warranty will include any errors noted in the acceptance certificate, but will exclude defects caused by the purchaser amending the software.
Maintenance and enhancement	The purchaser may ask the supplier to continue to support the software by providing ongoing maintenance and upgrades to the software. Alternatively, responsibility for these can be taken in-house.
Insolvency or bankruptcy	In case of insolvency or bankruptcy of the supplier, the purchaser will normally need access to the source code of the software so that it can be amended and upgraded in the future. One method of achieving this aim is to place the source code with a third party, to be released only if the supplier is insolvent or bankrupt. This arrangement is commonly called an 'escrow' agreement.
Performance and completion time	The contract will provide a timetable showing important milestones and estimated completion time for the software.
Confidentiality	Both the supplier and the purchaser will agree to keep confidential information that is not in the public domain. Confidentiality constraints apply to any sub-contractors as well as the main contractor.
Insurance copies	An explanation of whether additional copies of the software are available in case of loss or damage.

Form of letter and schedules

The tenderer will need to commit, in relatively high-level terms, to some additional information regarding the supply of the software and subsequent support after successful installation.

The tenderer must indicate the price and timescales for completion of the work and also for amendments and maintenance in the future need to be specified.

The tenderer will be required to state whether they comply with the requirements in the ITT. If compliance to specific sections cannot be given then these will be stated within the response to the ITT.

The tenderer will also have to supply some basic technical and project information concerning the software to be written and the method of writing the software. This information may be supplied in a form which the supplier produces.

Requirements specification

The ITT will also include the detailed requirements specification. Details of a requirements specification are covered in chapters 7, 8, 9 and 10.

Software engineering requirements

This section asks the tenderer to provide an overview of the life-cycle method that will be used to produce the software. It provides the supplier with confidence that recognised design principles will be used to write the software.

3.2 Identifying suitable suppliers

Identifying potential suppliers of software can be difficult. Although there is no absolute rule for identifying all possible suppliers of software on the market, there are a number of avenues that can be explored:

1   **Suppliers to other organisations**. An examination of the hardware or software used by comparable organisations can reveal the existence of suitable products, and how popular they are with their current users.

2   **Trade magazines**. A trawl of trade magazines will find appropriate advertisements and trade reviews and articles. Each of these must be examined critically – it should not be assumed that the articles and reviews are necessarily independent or unbiased.

3   **Consult an expert.** The company may consult with an expert. This expert may be a computer consultant with experience in the application being computerised, or may be employed by a dealer or retail establishment. It is important to consider the independence and motivation of the advice given – a dealer, for example, may receive a higher profit margin on one product than another.

When a list of suppliers has been drawn up, then the ITT can be sent and responses to this awaited!

4   Evaluating supplier proposals

Once the proposals have been received from potential suppliers, they must be compared with what was requested in the tender document, and the best one selected. The criteria used to judge the proposals can be put into three categories:

Technical

How closely do the suppliers' proposals tally with the hardware and software requirements specified in The Invitation To Tender Document?

Cost

What is the overall cost of the package offered by each supplier?

Customer support

How good is the after-sales service and warranty offered by the supplier?

Attempt to obtain the hardware and software from the same source and with a guarantee that they will be compatible. If bought from different sources and the system does not work, one supplier can blame the other's product.

4.1 Evaluating software proposals

There are many points to consider when evaluating possible purchases of application software. It is often useful to make out a checklist of the points that are most salient to the user. Some of the points that may be included on the checklist are:

How well the software fits the needs of the organisation.	This does not necessarily imply that every single requirement is satisfied – the users may be able to compromise, or to satisfy their information needs in some other way.

Can the software be tailored to fit the organisation's needs?

Sometimes packages can be modified by the supplier (at a cost) and, on other occasions, a package may have sufficient flexibility to allow the users to adapt it as required.

Other facilities.

Has the software any extra facilities that can be exploited by the organisation?

How well does the organisational structure fit in with the demands placed on it by the software?

The users should only acquire the software if no changes in structure are needed, or if any such changes will increase efficiency. A centralised system to help the sales force plan its calls efficiently would not be suitable where the sales people do not regularly visit the head office.

KEY POINT

Points to check for when evaluating proposals:

- fit to organisation's needs
- can it be tailored?
- other facilities
- fit to organisation's structure
- hardware implications
- fit with current software
- fit with future needs
- conditions of supply
- duplication restrictions
- speed
- demonstration facilities
- ease of use
- documentation
- training
- size of customer base
- security features
- maintenance offered
- updates
- cost.

Will existing hardware need to be upgraded or replaced?

Many modern PC applications are very hungry for internal memory or hard disk space, and may not be capable of running on older machinery.

Is the software compatible with existing software and file structures?

A change to a new word processing package, for example, may require all existing documents to be converted to the new format. A supplier that is eager for business may well agree to carry out the conversion process.

Is the software compatible with the organisation's future requirements?

The users may be planning to migrate to a new operating system, which would make it necessary to acquire software compatible with the new operating environment.

Under what conditions is the software being supplied?

Extra payments may be payable each year; use of the software may be restricted to single machines; a site licence may be needed for use on more than one machine; use may be restricted to machines at a single location.

What protective measures has the supplier taken against unauthorised duplication?

Although suppliers are justified in protecting their software, the measures they take can sometimes cause operational problems. The user may be unable to take a back-up copy of the original disk that the software was supplied on. If the system becomes corrupted the user may have to obtain a replacement from the supplier. There may be a delay of several days before the system can be used again.

How fast does the system run?

The user will need to be assured that the system can cope with the volumes of data that will need to be processed and stored – some software that can look satisfactory when demonstrated by a salesperson can be unusable when asked to deal with volumes of data that are greater than it was designed for.

Can the software be adequately demonstrated?

The supplier is often able to show a special demonstration version of the software running. Sometimes a restricted version (or even a full version) of the software can be lent to the user for a period of time. Many suppliers make lists of existing customers. These can be visited to see the system running in a real situation. Seeing software running can give the user a 'feel' for how it works and can provide reassurance as to its suitability.

How user friendly is the software?

It must be both easy to use and tolerant to user error. Menus, graphical interfaces and clear prompts make the software easier to use, and attractive and uncluttered screen designs make the system enjoyable to use. One strategy used by software designers to make their products user-friendly is to mimic the look and feel of more familiar software. Lotus 1-2-3, for example, is often used as a pattern for other software – both spreadsheets and other types of software.

Documentation must be both comprehensive and comprehensible.	Documentation can be at several levels, ranging from brief reference cards, through easily understood user guides to system manuals that can act as a technical reference to specialist and experienced users.
How will the user acquire the expertise to run the system?	Most suppliers offer training, and both internal and external courses may be appropriate ways for users to learn how to operate the system. Well-known packages often have many experienced users who may already be employed or who can be hired in. On-screen and written tutorials allow users to learn at their own speed.
How wide is the customer base of the software?	The existence of a large number of customers provides several benefits. Most of the bugs in the software will have been identified and corrected. There is likely to be a reservoir of expertise that can be exploited by the user, and books may have been written and training courses developed. The user can be assured that they will get what they expect from the software.
Does the software have any security features?	User numbers, passwords and encryption are useful for protecting confidential data on all types of software, and are absolutely vital in multi-user and networked systems.
What sort of maintenance and after-sales service is offered?	Maintenance and after-sales service is just as important for software as it is for hardware. A maintenance fee will usually be payable for bespoke software just as it is for hardware. The availability of a help desk is very helpful to an organisation. Many suppliers charge a subscription for access to a help desk, and some suppliers charge for each call asking for advice. The existence of this kind of charge may be a disincentive towards buying a particular software package.
Are future versions of the software likely to become available?	Many software suppliers allow users to obtain updated versions of packages at advantageous rates. If an updated version is *not* bought, the users must assure themselves that the supplier will continue to support the older versions. The user can suffer disastrous problems if support is not kept up. An example of what can happen is as follows:
	A small business acquired one of the biggest selling PC accounts packages. The version of the software that they bought was one for a different type of microcomputer. This particular version of the package did not allow for a non-integer percentage Value Added Tax. By the time the software house had found someone capable of updating the package, the small business had been forced to go back to a manual invoicing system.
What is the cost of the software?	All aspects of cost must be included in the user's calculations – purchase price, site licences, maintenance, the cost of access to help, training costs, etc.

4.2 Selecting an application package

Organisations have a great deal in common with one another – the core information processing activities are likely to be very similar from one company to the next. The basic accounting functions, for example, apply to a large majority of businesses. Many applications are served by packages that can be obtained off-the-shelf, although care must be taken in choosing the appropriate package for the specific organisation.

The selection of application package will depend on a variety of factors including those summarised in the table below:

User requirements	The package will be reviewed to check that it meets the functional requirements of users in terms of format of output, number of users etc.
Cost	Although the organisation needs primarily to purchase a package that will meet the user requirements, cost will still be important. Where there is a trade-off between these items, care must be taken to ensure that user requirements are not unduly compromised.
Interface design	The package should be easy to use and follow conventional interface design (such as Windows) to allow for ease of use and training.
Controls	The package must include appropriate controls to confirm the completeness and accuracy of processing of all data input. Access and security controls will also be required.
Updates	Appropriate and timely updates must be available. Updates are particularly relevant for software that changes frequently due to legislation or similar changes (e.g. wages software).
User manuals	Full documentation will be required in the form of detailed reference guides and probably some quick reference or similar brief guide and on-screen help.
Compatibility with existing hardware and software	The package may have to run on the organisation's existing computer systems. Software compatibility will be particularly important where data needs to be exchanged between different packages.
Support and maintenance	Support contracts to provide automatic upgrade of the software will normally be available, as will telephone support lines to help users resolve queries arising from using the software.

Information will also be required on the supplier of the package:

1 **Length of time in business.** This provides an indication of the financial stability of the supplier and is indicative that the company has a good chance of remaining in business to support the software in the future.

2 **References from other users.** These can be used to test the appropriateness of the software for the situation in the purchasing organisation, and also to check on the reliability of the supplier in providing support for the software.

3 **Availability of demonstration copies of the software.** Running the software on the organisation's own computer systems will provide one of the best methods of evaluating that software.

The normal tasks involved in choosing the application package are:

- produce a requirements listing and send this with an invitation to tender to a number of suppliers

- review the tender documents and make an initial selection of, say, three software packages

- obtain copies of those packages and test on the organisation's own computer system. Alternatively, the supplier may be asked to make a presentation to show why the purchasing company should use their particular package

- obtain user input and evaluation of each package

- obtain technical input and evaluation of each package to ensure it is compatible where applicable with existing hardware and software and provides the necessary processing capability

- test the package with test data from the organisation, paying particular reference to unusual items

- provide a final purchase recommendation, taking into account other factors such as after sales service – see below.

4.3　Advantages and disadvantages of off-the-shelf packages

Advantages

- They are generally cheaper to buy than bespoke packages are to develop.

- They are likely to be available almost immediately.

- Any system bugs should have been discovered by the vendors before sale.

- Good packages are likely to come with good training programs and excellent documentation and on-screen help facilities.

- New updated versions of the software are likely to be available on a regular basis.

- The experience of a great number of users with similar needs to those in the organisation has been incorporated into the design of the package.

- Different packages will be available for different operating systems or data structures.

Disadvantages

- They do not fit precisely the needs of the organisation – the users may need to compromise what they want with what is available.

- The organisation is dependent upon an outside supplier for the maintenance of the software; many software suppliers are larger than most of their customers, and are therefore difficult to influence.

- Different packages used by the organisation may have incompatible data structures.

- Using the same packages as rival organisations removes the opportunity of using IS for competitive advantage.

Application packages can be altered and tailored to a buyer's requirements, but amendments to an existing package have to be paid for, and so add to the purchase cost of the software. In addition, an altered package may not accept the standard updates provided by the supplier.

4.4　Comparing supplier proposals

Often, an organisation will need to weigh up a series of competitive tenders and choose the best. The tenders that they are comparing may well have different strengths and weaknesses, with no one offer providing the perfect solution. They may be tested using benchmark and simulation programs, or they may be compared using a formal procedure called weighted ranking.

4.5　Weighted ranking

KEY POINT

Weighted ranking: a number of factors that are important to the system are listed. Each factor is given a numerical weight to indicate its relative importance.

A number of factors that are important to the system under consideration are listed. Each factor is given a numerical weight to indicate its relative importance to the users. Both the factors and the weighting they are given will vary according to the system being evaluated.

Example: Weighted ranking

Factor	Weighting
User friendliness	10
Cost	7
Quality of output	8
Speed of processing	4
After-sales service	5
Security features	8

Each supplier is then ranked against each factor, thus:

		Rankings		
Factor	Weighting	Supplier A	Supplier B	Supplier C
User friendliness	10	1	2	3
Cost	7	2	3	1
Quality of output	8	3	1	2
Speed of processing	4	3	1	2
After sales service	5	1	2	3
Security features	8	1	2	3

Suppliers are then given a score that matches their ranking. In the example above, since there are three suppliers, a ranking of 1 is given a score of 3, a ranking of 2 is given a score of 2 and a ranking of 3 receives a score of 1.

		Score		
Factor	Weighting	Supplier A	Supplier B	Supplier C
User friendliness	10	3	2	1
Cost	7	2	1	3
Quality of output	8	1	3	2
Speed of processing	4	1	3	2
After-sales service	5	3	2	1
Security features	8	3	2	1

Each score is multiplied by the appropriate weighting, and the total calculated for each supplier.

Thus the total scores are:

$$
\begin{aligned}
\text{Supplier A} \quad &= (10 \times 3) + (7 \times 2) + (8 \times 1) + (4 \times 1) + (5 \times 3) + (8 \times 3) \\
&= 30 + 14 + 8 + 4 + 15 + 24 \\
&= 95
\end{aligned}
$$

$$
\begin{aligned}
\text{Supplier B} \quad &= (10 \times 2) + (7 \times 1) + (8 \times 3) + (4 \times 3) + (5 \times 2) + (8 \times 2) \\
&= 20 + 7 + 24 + 12 + 10 + 16 \\
&= 89
\end{aligned}
$$

$$
\begin{aligned}
\text{Supplier C} \quad &= (10 \times 1) + (7 \times 3) + (8 \times 2) + (4 \times 2) + (5 \times 1) + (8 \times 1) \\
&= 10 + 21 + 16 + 8 + 5 + 8 \\
&= 68
\end{aligned}
$$

The highest score is achieved by supplier A, whose proposal would be the one chosen.

This procedure may distort the result, since a slight preference for one supplier over another has the same effect as a significant preference. This problem can be overcome by allocating each supplier a score for each factor instead of a ranking. This amended procedure is more complex to carry out but is likely to lead to a more accurate result. The maximum score for each factor is given as a value of 10.

Thus the previous example might yield the following table:

			Score	
Factor	Weighting	Supplier A	Supplier B	Supplier C
User friendliness	10	10	9	5
Cost	7	7	6	10
Quality of output	8	5	10	9
Speed of processing	4	8	10	9
After-sales service	5	10	9	5
Security features	8	10	9	8

The total score is calculated in a similar way:

Supplier A $= (10 \times 10) + (7 \times 7) + (8 \times 5) + (4 \times 8) + (5 \times 10) + (8 \times 10)$

$= 100 + 49 + 40 + 32 + 50 + 80$

$= 351$

Supplier B $= (10 \times 9) + (7 \times 6) + (8 \times 10) + (4 \times 10) + (5 \times 9) + (8 \times 9)$

$= 90 + 42 + 80 + 40 + 45 + 72$

$= 369$

Supplier C $= (10 \times 5) + (7 \times 10) + (8 \times 9) + (4 \times 9) + (5 \times 5) + (8 \times 8)$

$= 50 + 70 + 72 + 36 + 25 + 64$

$= 317$

Using the amended weighting, it can now be seen that Supplier B is offering the best package.

Example: Use of weighted ranking

A small organisation wishes to computerise the production of their accounts. They run two separate companies, each with their own accounts staff but under the control of the group financial manager. They do not wish to change the way that they operate, so they need a system that can be networked over three computers, one for each company and a third for the group financial manager.

Each company's accounts staff are responsible for the day-to-day running of their business, while the group financial manager is responsible for producing consolidated accounts for the two businesses and for the management accounting function. The accounts for each of the two companies must be kept confidential.

The organisation makes out a list of factors that are important to them, allocating appropriate weights.

Factor	Weight
Ability to provide all basic accounting functions required	Essential
Networking capability	Essential
User friendliness	8
Cost	10
Management accounts capability	6
Hot line support	2
Security features	8
After sales service	4

A short-list of four accounts packages is drawn up. The packages are called Alphabet Accounts, Flying Horse, Heaven Sent and Wise. Each of these is scored against the factors described above.

Factor	Supplier Scores			
	A	F	H	W
1 All basic functions supplied	✓	✓	✓	✓
2 Networking capability	x	✓	✓	✓
3 User friendliness	7	9	10	8
4 Cost	10	2	2	4
5 Management accounts capability	3	10	8	6
6 Hot line support/training	0	5	6	10
7 Security features	6	10	7	8
8 After sales service	0	6	8	10

Solution

The first thing to note is that Alphabet Accounts does not satisfy the essential requirement of being able to be networked. Although it is by far the cheapest package, it is not a satisfactory solution to the organisation's needs, and is not considered further.

The scores for cost are corrected to 5 (Flying Horse), 5 (Heaven Sent) and 10 (Wise). Factors 1 and 2 are satisfied equally well by all three packages and do not need to be considered further. The amended table is reproduced below.

Factor	Weight	Supplier Score		
		F	H	W
3	8	9	10	8
4	10	5	5	10
5	6	10	8	6
6	2	5	6	10
7	8	10	7	8
8	4	6	8	10

The total scores for each supplier are calculated by cross-multiplying the factor weights by the appropriate scores.

Flying Horse

Total score $= (8 \times 9) + (10 \times 5) + (6 \times 10) + (2 \times 5) + (8 \times 10) + (4 \times 6)$

$\qquad = 72 + 50 + 60 + 10 + 80 + 24 = 296$

Heaven Sent

Total score $= (8 \times 10) + (10 \times 5) + (6 \times 8) + (2 \times 6) + (8 \times 7) + (4 \times 8)$

$\qquad = 80 + 50 + 48 + 12 + 56 + 32 = 278$

Wise

Total score $= (8 \times 8) + (10 \times 10) + (6 \times 6) + (2 \times 10) + (8 \times 8) + (4 \times 10)$

$\qquad = 64 + 100 + 36 + 20 + 64 + 40 = 324$

It can be seen that Wise is marginally ahead of Heaven Sent, and is the package selected. It should also be noted that the difference between Heaven Sent and Wise is very small, and further factors may be taken into account to further compare these two packages. Additional price discounts may also be available by negotiating with these two suppliers.

Conclusion

This chapter has explained the different methods of acquiring software for specific use within an organisation.

SELF-TEST
QUESTIONS

Bespoke software

1   What is a bespoke software application? (2)

Invitation to tender

2   List the main contents of an invitation to tender. (3.1)

Evaluating supplier proposals

3   What are the three main categories under which supplier proposals are evaluated? (4)

EXAM-TYPE
QUESTION

Software packages

Scenario

ZYNC plc is a large manufacturing company. It has traditionally developed many of its information systems in-house and the data processing (DP) department currently employs about 120 staff.

The following main applications are currently supported.

Application	Package / Bespoke	Year implemented	Development language
Process control	Bespoke	1989	FORTRAN
Integrated accounts	Package	1995	
Payroll	Package	1996	
Order processing	Bespoke	1991	COBOL
Quality control	Bespoke	1993	COBOL
Marketing information	Bespoke	1996	4GL

There are approximately 25 smaller applications developed in-house to respond to the needs of individual departments. However, the DP department does not have a good reputation. User departments frequently complain about missed deadlines, poor quality software and lack of functionality.

A new IT director has recently been appointed. He believes that most of the problems have been caused by the organisation's emphasis on building bespoke solutions.

His view is that 'Packages are the way forward. We can no longer afford the luxury of building our own systems.'

He is also critical of the systems development life cycle in place at ZYNC plc.

He claims that 'We have made the mistake of forcing all our system developments – whether they are bespoke systems, application packages or small one-off systems through a standard systems development life cycle (SDLC). This SDLC (listed below) has led to unnecessarily long elapsed times on projects.'

Stage 1	Feasibility study
Stage 2	Systems specification
Stage 3	Programming and unit testing
Stage 4	Systems testing
Stage 5	User-acceptance testing
Stage 6	Implementation

The new IT director proposes that all future systems will be implemented using standard application software packages. He claims that;

'*Standard packages offer cost and time savings as well as guaranteed quality.* We will be looking for packages that fit 80% or more of our business requirements. We will not be commissioning any changes to the functionality of the package. If the package does not exactly fit the business then the business must change to fit the package. We have already successfully implemented packages for accounts and payroll. We must now repeat that success in other areas of the business.'

The IT director has agreed that staffing will be kept at the current level for the foreseeable future. He states that: 'We obviously need staff to implement our package policy, although I will be looking for a significant contribution from the user areas.

Required:

(a)   Briefly explain what is meant by a:

   – software package   **(3 marks)**

   – bespoke solution.   **(3 marks)**

(b)   The IT director identifies three benefits of adopting the application software package approach.

'Standard packages offer cost and time savings as well as guaranteed quality.'

Briefly explain how the software package approach can offer each of these three benefits to ZYNC plc.

   – cost savings

   – time savings

   – guaranteed quality   **(9 marks)**

(Total: 15 marks)

For the answer to this question, see the 'Answers' section at the end of the book.

Chapter 13
COMPUTER AIDED SOFTWARE ENGINEERING

This chapter looks at methods of producing software with the aid of productivity tools. Computer Aided Software Engineering (CASE) tools are automated software tools used by systems analysts and designers to develop models for information systems specification.

In spite of the name Fourth Generation Languages (4GLs) now have less value in the development of new software, although they are still used for data extraction (SQL) and prototyping.

Objectives

By the time you have finished this chapter you should be able to:

- define a Computer Aided Software Engineering (CASE) tool and give a brief list of representative products

- describe a range of features and functions that a CASE tool may provide

- explain the advantages of using a CASE tool in the systems development process

- define a Fourth Generation Language and give a brief list of representative products

- describe a range of features and functions that a 4GL may provide

- explain how a 4GL contributes to the prototyping process.

1   CASE tools

Computer Aided Software Engineering (CASE) is one of the ways the analyst and designer can speed up the development of new systems, while improving the quality of control over the work that they do.

CASE tools mechanise some of the more routine and tedious tasks in systems and program development. They are used to speed up and make more consistent the systems development process.

There are a number of tools in existence, some of which cover the analysis phase of the lifecycle, some the design, some the build, and some the project management and control aspects. There are also some integrated CASE tools (ICASE) that cover the whole lifecycle.

DEFINITION

CASE tools are automated software tools used by systems analysts and designers to develop information systems.

The diagram below shows the facilities offered by CASE.

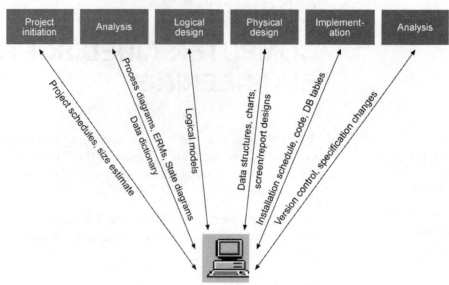

(Source: Hoffer, George and Valacich 1996 *Modern Systems Analysis and Design.* Benjamin Cummings.)

1.1   Objectives of CASE

Organisations may choose to use CASE in systems development in order to:

- speed up the development process

- standardise the development process

- ensure the quality of development models

- improve the quality of the systems

- improve and standardise the documentation produced during the development

- simplify maintenance

- improve the management of the project.

1.2   Levels of CASE

CASE tools can be categorised according to what part of the lifecycle they cover.

Upper CASE tools

Upper CASE covers tools used in the analysis phase. They include:

- **diagramming tools**, to draw process models, data models and state models according to the rules of those specific notations and methodologies

- **analysis tools** that check for completeness and consistency in diagrams, forms and reports

- **a repository** to enable integration of specification, diagrams, reports and project management information.

Lower CASE tools

These include:

- **document generators**, to help produce technical and user documentation in standard formats

- **display and report generators**, to enable prototypes of the interface to be made

- **code generators** to enable automatic generation of program and database definition code directly from the design documents.

1.3   Components of CASE

Repository

The repository is at the heart of CASE tools, especially integrated-CASE. It is a centralised database that holds all the information needed to create and maintain a software systems project, all the way from initiation through to code generation and even maintenance.

(Source: Hoffer, George and Valacich 1996 *Modern Systems Analysis and Design*. Benjamin Cummings.)

Data dictionary

This is a tool that will keep a record about all the data items in the system. Descriptions that the dictionary will hold might include: item name, textual description, synonyms, type and format, range of acceptable values, and programs, inputs, outputs etc that use that item.

Diagramming tools

The CASE tool is built to draw specific types of diagram, to specific notations. Thus a CASE tool might support all SSADM diagrams, such as SELECT. Another might support the UML notation, such as the RATIONAL suite (as well as being able to draw the shapes for that method, the tool also has the rules that support the method built into it.) Thus, a diagramming tool for SSADM would not allow a diagram that showed a data store interacting with another data store. Similarly, when a level 1 diagram is to be decomposed to level 2, the CASE tool would ensure that all the flows in and out of the level 2 boundary mapped on to the level 1 process.

Documentation generator tools

Each stage of the SDLC is responsible for further system documentation. The documents may be diagrams or reports, or data specifications. CASE will have appropriate templates, and the information from each phase is fed into the repository, so that the documents can be generated and maintained automatically.

1.4 Traditional systems development versus CASE-based development

The following table compares the main differences between traditional systems development and CASE-based development:

Traditional systems development	CASE-based systems development
Emphasis on coding and testing	Emphasis on analysis and design
Paper-based specification	Rapid interactive prototyping
Manual coding of programs	Automated code generation
Intensive software testing	Automated design checking
Maintain code and documentation	Maintain design specification

(Source: Hoffer, George and Valacich 1996 *Modern Systems Analysis and Design.* Benjamin Cummings.)

1.5 Interactive (or integrated) development environments (IDE)

An interactive or integrated development environment (IDE) is a system for supporting the process of writing software. Such a system may include a syntax-directed editor, graphical tools for program entry, and integrated support for compiling and running the program and tracing errors back to the source.

Such systems are typically both interactive and integrated. They are interactive in that the developer can view and alter the execution of parts of a program while it is being developed. They are integrated in that, partly to support this interaction, the source code editor and the execution environment are tightly coupled, e.g. allowing the developer to see which line of source code is about to be executed and the current values of any variables it refers to.

Nowadays software development is mostly done using IDE tools such as Microsoft Visual Studio.NET for general purpose applications or Macromedia XP Studio for web design and programming.

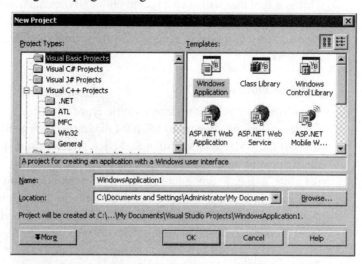

The IDE will incorporate features such as prototyping (see below), automatic generation of code and so on. As a simple illustration here is what a developer might see in Macromedia Dreamweaver when developing a database-driven web page.

```
lign="default" class="unnamed1">
nt size="1" face="Verdana, Arial, Helvetica, sans-serif"><a href="detailnew.asp?<%= MM_
etl.Fields.Item("ID").Value %>"><%=(Recordset1.Fields.Item("College").Value)%></a> </fo
lign="right" class="unnamed1">
nt size="1" face="Verdana, Arial, Helvetica, sans-serif"><%=(Recordset1.Fields.Item("Po
lign="default" class="unnamed1">
nt size="1" face="Verdana, Arial, Helvetica, sans-serif"><%=(Recordset1.Fields.Item("El
lign="default" class="unnamed1">
nt size="1" face="Verdana, Arial, Helvetica, sans-serif"><%=(Recordset1.Fields.Item("Us
lign="default" class="unnamed1">
nt size="1" face="Verdana, Arial, Helvetica, sans-serif"><%=(Recordset1.Fields.Item("Pa
```

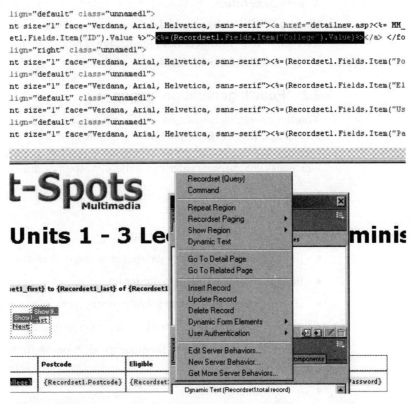

The screen is split into two so that the programmer can see both the programming code and the results as they will appear to the user. Changes in the code are immediately reflected in the display. The code for complex tasks such as inserting or updating a record in a database can be generated automatically simply by choosing an option from a menu and filling in a form: there is no need to write the code from scratch, although it can still be modified by hand if necessary.

2 Fourth generation languages

2.1 Generations of computer languages

Computer languages are sometimes said to have passed through four different generations:

First generation

This was machine code with programs being written in binary code only. The programs were very complex to write and extremely difficult to read and debug. Maintenance was equally difficult. The programs were written for a particular machine, and could not be installed on another machine afterwards.

Second generation

Assembler languages. These used symbolic code to provide instructions to the computer. While they were slightly easier to understand, they were still very similar to machine code, which limited their usability. These too were written for just one machine, and were not portable.

Third generation

High-level languages such as FORTRAN, COBOL, C, C++, Java and Basic. The languages were much easier to use as many of the commands were close to English. Most of the mainstream software that we use today is written in C and C++. They are also called General Purpose Languages (GPLs).

Fourth generation

In spite of the implications of the term 'fourth generation' a 4GL is not a superior alternative to a third generation language. They were developed to serve specific purposes and their main factors are outlined below.

2.2 Fourth generation language

'Fourth generation languages' or 4GLs were special-purpose application builders customised to specific applications, such as generating business reports. They may be contrasted with general purpose languages (GPLs) or '3GLs' such as Cobol or C, with which a skilled programmer can build almost anything.

Martin (1982) provides a list of the desirable features of this type of language. The main points from this list are:

- centred on a relational database

- links to other proprietary databases to assist overall system development

- integrated and active data dictionary

- simply query language to allow programmers and users to access the data

- integrated screen design tool, or screen-painter

- a dialogue design tool to facilitate production of dialogue boxes including the use of graphics

- a report generator

- procedural coding facility to document procedures in written or software terms.

4GLs first sprang up in the 1970s. Their selling point was simplicity. 4GL functions were expressed in ordinary English and linked together with everyday syntax. The best-known example is SQL, which we will look at in a moment.

In the early 1990s networks were migrating to the client/server basis and databases from flat-file to relational systems, and operating systems from proprietary languages to Unix and Windows. This meant that all the applications and files that had grown up in the mainframe/minicomputer world needed to be ported into this new environment. 4GLs turned out to be ideal for the purpose. The essence of the technology changed from application development to legacy management, and that is largely where it remains.

In the mid-90s, the Internet gave rise to another wave of complexity that 4GLs were able to help with, as every computing context started to demand specialised application development tools.

In practice, however, this space has been occupied by languages such as Perl/CGI, ASP and PHP. Nevertheless, as mentioned, one of the original 4GLs was SQL, and this is more important than ever in the modern environment.

2.3 Example of a 4GL: SQL

Microsoft Access (and most other major database packages) uses a language called SQL or Structured Query Language to perform highly sophisticated data extraction.

SQL is deceptively simple: statements are in this form

SELECT such and such data

FROM such and such table of data

WHERE such and such criteria apply

In Microsoft Access you don't actually need to know any SQL to create a simple query. For instance here is an example of a query created 'visually' within a central heating firm's database.

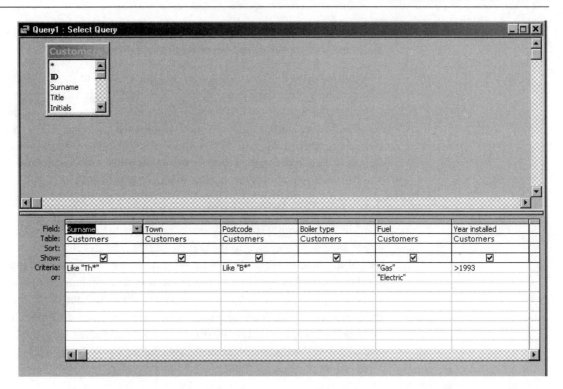

When it is run this query will return only the fields Surname, Town, Postcode, Boiler type, Fuel and Year installed, not any of the other fields there might be in the database such as street names or other information about the customers. And it will only return records where the surname begins with 'Th', the Postcode begins with 'B', the Fuel is Gas or Electric, and the Year installed is after 1993. We could add as many more selection criteria as we wanted. This example might be used to plan the driving route of a service engineer.

3 Prototyping

KEY POINT

Prototyping is the production of a working model of a system.

Prototyping is the production of a working model of a system. Working models are used in many areas of business, from the production of new cars to the setting up of a call centre in a service industry. The use of prototypes minimises the risk that the item being designed will not fit the needs of the organisation and allows experimentation without the high cost of failure.

Under the traditional methods of system development, users specified their requirements to the analyst and project team, who then developed the system based on those requirements with little or no further user involvement. Prototyping lets the user view the system during development and make amendments or corrections as required.

3.1 Throwaway and working prototypes

The throwaway model acts as a communications device between user and developer and aids in the learning process. The user is better able to explain his requirements from the model developed by the prototyper and the prototyper is better able to demonstrate how the proposed system is intended to operate. This kind of prototype is usually built very quickly and would not include aspects of the system such as security, performance, error handling procedures, etc.

An example of a throwaway prototype is one developed for screen-based dialogues. There would not be any underlying database, nor would there be facilities and codes for storage or data manipulation. Screen-based dialogue simulation enables the analyst to lead the user through a series of screens and explain how each screen is used. The user is able to relate to the system and is in a better position to say whether the system meets his requirements and expectations. This kind of system may be a simple shell and contain no working capacity.

The working prototype is an extension of the throwaway model and will incorporate and implement some of the system's important features.

The prototype will be constructed using similar tools to those used in the construction of an actual system. The user interface style will be similar to that of the final implementation, thus enabling better evaluation of the system. As the data dictionary screen and data definitions will have been preserved, these can be used for the final construction. A sub-system is taken and developed into a working prototype, which is in turn used to form the basis of the new system.

3.2   Working prototyping

Working prototyping (or evolutionary prototyping) is an alternative approach to developing systems, akin to RAD (Chapter 7). The developer constructs a prototype of part of the functionality of the new system. S/he tests and refines it with the user until it reaches the desired quality. At that point, it is actually handed over to the user as a working system, with all of the data converted and the non-functional requirements implemented. Another set of required functions are then developed in the same way, and that prototype added to the original handover. In this way, the system is developed with the users' help in a piecemeal fashion, but in a way that means they can use the most urgent parts of it sooner.

3.3   Advantages of prototyping

The final design is highly likely to fit user needs

It is often difficult for inexperienced users to visualise what the computer can do for them and to define what they need. By having concrete examples it is easier to visualise what the computer can do for them and to define their needs fully and precisely.

Employees are involved in the systems development process

Because of the dynamic way that prototyping develops systems, employees working in the user department are fully involved in the development process. They are more likely to identify the system as being *their* system. This will help to ensure that the system is properly defined, and will reduce the likelihood of dysfunctional behaviour.

Identification of problems

Once a full system has been developed, it is very expensive to eradicate any bugs in the programs or difficulties in the way the users relate to the system. With prototyping, the systems analyst or users can identify any problems or omissions and eliminate them. The user-friendliness of the system can be guaranteed.

Code generation

Prototyping tools may be capable of automatically producing a series of programs written in a third generation language. This makes prototyping a very cost effective way of developing systems.

3.4   Disadvantages of prototyping

The principles of prototyping are so fundamental to good software development that modern development tools have prototyping facilities built in. The disadvantages for the most part relate to older, stand-alone prototyping tools.

- Many prototyping tools are hungry for computer processing resources and expensive to buy.

- The development process may become sloppy and unstructured, wasting money and resources and making planning difficult. The greatest danger here is 'requirements shift' whereby users, seeing how much the computer can do, think of more and more extra requirements to add on to the specification.

- Prototyping tools often require data to be in a specific format. Existing data files may require conversion before they can be input into the prototype

- Some prototyping tools are restrictive in the way that systems can be developed, and may not allow hand written codes to be linked in

- Code produced by code generators may well be less efficient than that produced by an experienced programmer

Conclusion

This chapter has explained CASE tools and the way that they can assist in the development of systems. Fourth Generation Languages are also important, particularly in the field of prototyping.

SELF-TEST
QUESTIONS

CASE tools

1   What is a CASE tool? (1)

2   Explain the advantages of CASE tools in systems development. (1.4)

4GLs

3   List the main features of a Fourth Generation Language. (2.2)

Prototyping

4   What are the advantages of prototyping? (3.3)

EXAM-TYPE
QUESTION

Prototyping

In the context of systems development:

(a)   Explain what is meant by a prototype.   **(3 marks)**

(b)   Describe two advantages and two disadvantages of using a prototyping approach to systems development.   **(8 marks)**

(c)   Select two facilities usually found in a fourth generation language (4GL) and explain their application in developing a prototype system.   **(4 marks)**

(Total: 15 marks)

For the answer to this question, see the 'Answers' section at the end of the book.

Chapter 14

TECHNICAL INFORMATION SYSTEMS REQUIREMENTS

KEY POINTS

Performance of a system covers:

- Response and turnaround times
- Ability to deal with volumes of transactions
- Availability of system

These are known as non-functional requirements.

DEFINITION

Response time is the interval between data entry by the terminal user and receipt of the result of any processing activity that has taken place.

This chapter discusses some of the technical requirements of a system, such as performance and volume requirements, various 'housekeeping' activities and the purpose of an audit trail. Many systems need to interface with other working systems in the organisation and, in some circumstances, outside the organisation, too.

Objectives

By the time you have finished this chapter you should be able to:

- define and record performance and volume requirements of information systems
- discuss the need for archiving, backup and restore, and other 'housekeeping' functions
- explain the need for a software audit trail and define the content of such a trail
- examine the need to provide interfaces with other systems, and discuss the implications of developing these interfaces
- established requirements for data conversion and data creation.

1 Performance and volume requirements

When the requirements document is completed, there will be entries for what is known as **non-functional** requirements. Non-functional requirements are descriptions of the expected performance of the system. They will typically refer to issues such as response and turnaround times and requirements relating to volumes of both data and transactions, availability, usability, security and privacy. Usability requirements were described in Chapter 11; security and privacy requirements will be covered in Chapter 15.

1.1 Performance

Turnaround and response times

A justification for many systems is that they will turn transactions round faster than the system being replaced, so saving time and cutting costs. The analyst may have discovered, for example, that to respond to a customer order by taking the order, despatching the goods and sending the invoice currently takes 1 hour of effort, and 8 elapsed hours. The integrated ordering-stock management and invoicing system built to replace this was justified by the calculation that the computer time is reduced to half a minute and the elapsed time reduced to 2 hours, most of which is the manual work in the warehouse and despatch bay. A further justification was that this improvement in turnaround time means that the system can cope with a massive increase in throughput, resulting in greater profits for the company.

Testing may have shown, on a small test database and a single terminal, that this target performance was met comfortably. On implementation, however, the performance may significantly degrade because in fact there are a hundred sales staff accessing the system simultaneously, reading and updating a database several hundred times larger than the test one, and so the whole cycle is slowed significantly. We would hope that it is still faster than the current system, but the expected turnover of the business will be lower than predicted.

There have been cases where the turnaround times have been disastrously slow. In the 1980s, the UK Passport Office, for example, installed a new system that took two months to turn passport applications around, as opposed to the fifteen days that the old system took.

A manager may have requested the facility to make enquiries on stock levels, or customer details, or on line sales summaries, and expect to be able to call them up on screen within 3 seconds. If, because of weight of traffic and quantity of data, the system cannot give him/her the information for 10 seconds, they will be disillusioned and sceptical about the system. The requirements document must capture the expected response time, and the system must be designed to ensure that it is met. This may be captured as a part of each individual requirement, or it may be specified as a 'global' non-functional requirement, meant to apply to every enquiry in the system.

Volumes of transactions

In October 1989, the Brussels Stock Exchange was out of action for two days after the computer systems crashed, unable to handle the unexpectedly high volumes of transactions. An air cargo system was unable to deal with the volume of transactions passing through it, and the ensuing backlog caused the company's warehouse to overflow. After two weeks, the whole system was shut down. Sadly, there are many other horror stories of systems that failed to deliver what they promised, and led instead to very costly embarrassment and, in some cases, business failure. As with the two cases cited here, it was not *what* the systems was specified and programmed to do that led to failure, but *how* they achieved it, i.e. the non-functional, performance measures.

When collecting and specifying requirements for the new system, the analyst must identify what the volumes of traffic are expected to be:

- how many users will use that function
- what is the expected maximum number of transactions per day, or hour
- what growth is expected in the number of transactions over the next 6 or 12 months.

Without a clear picture of these figures, the designer cannot build an optimum system.

Availability

Another important non-functional requirement is the availability of the system. Some systems, especially those supporting e-commerce, and safety critical systems, need to be available for 24 hours a day, 7 days a week; others only need to be working for standard office hours.

Whichever, the desired availability of a system, and of the functions within the system, must be specified in the requirements document, and will be part of the assessment of its performance. There should be a realistic expectation: to say that a system must be fully available 100% of the time does not allow opportunity to take back-ups and perform other necessary housekeeping. To say that it must be available 99.99% of the time suggests that it can be down by no more than 1 hour in a year. This is not a realistic expectation, and should be challenged. More likely is that part of the system can be taken down, and the rest of the system work on a degraded performance for an agreed period. For example, if a system is built to capture orders, validate them, allocate stock, prepare despatch notes and invoices, while generating purchase notices where necessary, it may be allowable for most of the system to go off-line, as long as orders can be captured, to be processed later when that part of the system comes back on line. MG Hotels have stipulated that they require their booking systems to be available from 6am until midnight for seven days a week. They have found that these hours allow prospective visitors from most of the time zones to call to make reservations. However, should the central database crash during those hours, they will accept a level of service that will let them take the visitor's details, and details of their requirements, so that as soon as the system is restored they can make the reservation and call them back with either confirmation, or alternative provision.

They originally wanted the system to be available for 24 hours a day, 365 days a year, but the designers pointed out that while this could be achieved, it could only be done at a greater cost than MG thought worth paying. This level of service could have been achieved by running a duplex system, i.e. two precise copies of the system running simultaneously for the whole time, so that if one system failed, the other could cut in at once and preserve the service. This is acceptable in a safety-critical system, such as air traffic control, or nuclear power station control, but not for a system such as required by MG.

The lesson from this is that any level of availability is obtainable, but the more rigorous the requirement, the greater the cost to achieve it. The users, designer and project manager must address the results of losing service for a certain period, and its cost to the operations; if it results in substantial loss of business the company may decide that it is preferable to pay a great deal extra for the service; if it might result in loss of life, there is no question, but the company must pay what is needed to ensure continuous availability.

Accuracy

A functional test of a system's performance will be accuracy of its output. This is a feature that will be checked during each phase of testing. Accuracy covers both the stored data and the output. Thus, the invoice produced by the system must tally with the value of the goods despatched, which in turn must tally with the original customer order. In the process, the quantity of stock held must be decreased by the appropriate figure once it has been allocated to the order. A combination of initial testing, and continuing audit, should ensure that this aspect of performance is satisfactory.

Level of accuracy is significant in management reporting. A list of orders taken and their value must be accurate to the exact penny, so that it can be reconciled with the monies received and due. However, a senior manager who is looking at summary information regarding sales figures for such and such a region for the last six months will only expect the figures to be accurate to, say, the nearest £100,000. Any finer level of accuracy than that will become meaningless. Each level, therefore, of a reporting system or MIS has its own requirements for levels of accuracy. These too will be identified and recorded in the requirements document.

The Directors of MG Hotels will be concerned to see how many bookings take place across the whole chain over a year, to the nearest £100,000. Directors of a particular country's division will be concerned to see how many bookings there were over the year to the nearest 1,000, and a regional manager within the country will look to the nearest 500. Managers and supervisors in each individual hotel need to know the precise number of guests due to arrive day by day, and the precise number who have stayed and paid.

2 Housekeeping requirements

2.1 Archiving

Archiving

When data pertaining to a transaction is completed, it can be either deleted from the system completely, or put into storage elsewhere, perhaps for later reference. For some form of transactions, there are legal requirements (see below), while for others, such as personnel systems that store details of employees, there may be a need to keep details of ex employees for the purpose, say, of providing references for future employers. This storing of old data is called *archiving*. Archiving will be on either magnetic media such as tapes or disk packs, or optical media such as CD or DVD. If the company is only seeking to save space (see below), it may hold the archive in a human readable form such as microfilm or microfiche. The operational system will never be able to access such data again, but human eyes can find and refer to it if desired.

There are two reasons for archiving old data:

1   to save space on the operational system

2   to have the data available to answer enquiries, and be able to conduct trend and pattern analyses.

Saving space

The longer the system is in operation, the larger the database grows. An order processing system will, by definition, add new orders and new customers every day of its operation. There will come a time when, if old data is not purged, there will not be space to add new records. Before that time, allocated file space will become so clogged with new data that the speed of processing degrades to an unacceptable level as the programs try to work through two or three levels of overflow in order to find the required data for the transaction. After a certain time following a transaction, it is unlikely that the record will be needed for further action, so it should be removed from the operational database. For legislative reasons, financial data should be kept for seven years following the transaction; this does not mean that it should be kept with 'live' data for the full seven years. More probable is that perhaps a year after the transaction is completed, it will be archived on secure storage elsewhere. Optical disks are frequently used for archive purposes. The archived data can be retrieved and read, but will not be updated.

Available for enquiries

After data is archived, the organisation may still want to interrogate it using various techniques to try to identify trends in customers' buying patterns, or to determine a product's long-term viability. If the data was completely deleted when the transaction time was completed, the company could not make use of it for these purposes. This would severely handicap its operations and decision-making ability in a competitive environment; keeping the information available in an archive allows it to be interrogated, while not interfering with the performance of the live system.

MG Hotels could use the reservation information gathered over the last five years to assess not just simple trends such as which times of year are most popular for bookings, but could identify demographic trends, such as demand for single rooms among certain age groups, or reasons for group bookings over a particular period, in order to target their advertising campaigns, and perhaps to put together packages that will appeal to identified sectors of the market.

2.2   Back-up and restore procedures

Every system should be prepared for accidents, disasters and failure. The simplest way
to prepare for these is to take regular backups of all data, transaction and program files.
This involves copying all files on the database, particularly the most volatile and
commonly accessed files, onto a safe medium away from the live system. The
principle is the same for a stand-alone PC or for a mainframe system. Typical backup
media would be CD, or a Tape Streamer. These allow large volumes to be saved at
high speed.

For the duration of the downtime, losses can be expected to escalate. It is, therefore,
essential that the time when the computer system is unavailable be kept to a minimum.

Requirements for backup

Strategies for recovery can be based on a number of strategies; whichever strategy is
employed will affect how the technical requirements are specified. Three common
strategies are:

* file generation
* checkpoints
* logs/journals.

These are described below.

1   File generation

These refer to master files on the database. In MG Hotels case these would
include Guest files, Reservations files, Bills files, Corporate files.

Each of these files is backed up onto a storage medium at the end of a business
cycle (perhaps a day); the transactions that updated them during that period are
also backed up. The backups are usually kept for two periods, so that three
versions of back-up are kept in total: the current one and the two previous ones.
These are known as Grandfather - Father - Son generation. This allows re-
constitution from the three earlier versions of the files, if there should have been a
major disaster. Usually, re-constitution is required from the Son generation only.
This form of backup – restore is commonest on mainframe applications.
Technical requirements would include the filespace needed to store the
generations, and time needed to take the backups.

2   Checkpoints

A checkpoint is a mechanism used on large batch applications, not on on-line
applications. A checkpoint is a point in time during the run when the progress
and status of the work is recorded. Should there be a crash subsequently, the run
can be restarted from the checkpoint rather than going back to the beginning of
the run.

A requirement would be to stipulate which transaction runs are to be
checkpointed, and at what frequency.

3   Logs/journals

The journal (or log) electronically records the processing history of the whole
system. It records the transactions, updates, errors, faults. As part of its function,
it will record the state of the data record before it is updated, and after (Before-
image and After-image). This allows an audit trail (see below) for the system, as
well as an immediate diagnostic source in case of trouble or suspected corruption.

Requirements would be to stipulate the details recorded in the log, and how it is to
be reported.

The purpose of the housekeeping functions is to ensure both accuracy and performance, congruent with the users' stipulation. This entails recognising that mishaps and breakdowns do occur, for many reasons, and the system must be able to recover from them.

System recovery

The response to a potential disaster, such as the loss of all or part of the computer system, should be managed. The best way of doing this is by means of a **contingency plan**. The plan itself will be specified as a response to the technical requirements.

As the importance of computing within an organisation continues to grow, so the effects of a breakdown of the computer system are potentially even more damaging. In addition, the computer system is increasingly exposed to the potential threat of hackers and the introduction of computer viruses.

For the duration of the downtime, losses can be expected to escalate. It is, therefore, essential that the time when the computer system is unavailable be kept to a minimum.

A number of common standby plans are discussed below. The final selection would be dependent upon the estimated time that the organisation would function adequately without computing facilities.

1   Creation of multiple data processing facilities on separate sites, with the smallest site being capable of supporting the crucial work of at least one other site during the calculated recovery time. This strategy requires hardware and software compatibility and spare capacity. It is calculated that approximately only 20 per cent of computer usage is critical, so the volume selected for temporary transfer can be kept to a minimum.

2   Reciprocal agreement with another company. Although a popular option, few companies can guarantee free capacity, or continuing capability, which attaches a high risk to this option.

3   A more expensive, but lower risk, version of the above is the commercial computer bureau. This solution entails entering into a formal agreement that entitles the customer to a selection of services.

4   Empty rooms or equipped rooms. The former allows the organisation access to install a back-up system, which increases the recovery time but reduces the cost. The latter can be costly, so sharing this facility is a consideration.

5   Re-locatable computer centres. This solution involves a delay while the facility is erected and assembled and larger computers cannot usually be accommodated.

    The effectiveness of the contingency plan is dependent on comprehensive back-up procedures for both data and software. The contingency plan must identify initial responses and clearly delineate responsibility at each stage of the exercise – from damage limitation through to full recovery.

    The greater the effort invested in the preparation of a contingency plan, the more effectively the organisation will be able to mitigate the effects of a disaster.

3 Software audit trails

It is often useful to be able to trace the path of transactions through a computer system. Part of the value of a software audit trail is to enable the system to be thoroughly tested during project development, but it also allows management to investigate any cases of fraud, or false transactions.

A **software audit trail** for a computerised accounting system can be defined as 'a register of the details for all accounting transactions' (Sage plc).

The specific trail for a system will be designed with the aid of the Internal Auditor. The trail must give certain information about each transaction: who made the transaction, at which terminal; on what date and at what time the transaction was carried out, and which files/records were accessed.

Some operating systems have logging/journal facilities as an integral part of them. Essentially, however, a software audit trail is a list of transactions entered into a system and of transaction activities. It can be printed out in detail or in summary form, when required. External auditors often ask for a printout of the software audit trail when they carry out their audit work.

Sensitive data, e.g. payee codes, should be subject to a separate audit report showing when the data was read, written to or updated. It should show also the before and after state and the data causing the change.

As well as it being a convenient tool to monitor the progress of a system, it is a legal requirement in many countries, including the UK, to provide *audit trails* of all financial transactions in public and other companies.

An audit is an inspection, verification and, in some cases, correction of business accounts. The auditor must be an independent person, with no vested interest in what is being inspected. External auditors are appointed to look after the interests of shareholders or owners; internal auditors ensure to corporate management that resources are being used wisely and well, and that its assets are safe.

Auditors may sample outputs rather than inspect every single transaction. They will also ensure that controls and procedures are faithfully observed.

3.1 Work of the internal auditor

The work of the internal auditor regarding information systems management will include the following:

- Liaising with the project team and providing recommendations on the controls that can be implemented in systems. These controls are likely to focus on establishing an audit trail within the information system so that transactions can be followed through the system.

- Reviewing controls within existing systems and recommending improvements to those controls.

- Reviewing the work of the project team; specifically ensuring that the project quality plan is being followed and that documentation being produced meets the quality standards.

- Monitoring any systems change and reviewing the completeness and accuracy of data being transferred from one system to another.

- Liaising with the external auditor to provide information on the controls within information systems, and where necessary performing tests of those controls for the external auditor.

The important distinction in all of this work is that the Internal auditor is reviewing and checking systems and the work of the project team; production of original documentation is normally avoided. If the internal auditor produced documentation, then an independent check on the accuracy of that work could not be carried out.

An accountant will also be involved more in the budgeting, monitoring and reporting on the financial aspects of a project. The extent of involvement will normally depend on the size of the project, and the need for specialist assistance in determining the financial success of a project.

4 Interfaces with other systems

Very few computer systems work in isolation; they will almost certainly have some links to other systems whether this is via the Internet or to other network servers. As computer systems are developed, or as they are used over time within an organisation, there will be a need to ensure that appropriate links between computers are established and maintained.

In the case of a new system, part of the analysis and design phases of the SDLC will be to review what links are actually required for the new system, and then plan to provide those links. For example, if a user requires up-to-date information from a specific source, then links to that source will be included within the system.

Needs for links to other systems may also develop over time as users' jobs change or new systems and sources of information become available. Upgrading an existing system to provide the required links may be difficult, especially where the existing system was implemented without any thought to the future requirements of users. Specific problems that may be faced include:

- lack of appropriate cabling for network or other access
- lack of hardware capabilities, for example to fix additional network cards into the computer
- insufficient memory to run upgraded software
- incompatible software
- lack of IT staff to check and test any changes.

The analyst will need to test any amendments to the system carefully to ensure that there are no clashes with existing software and to check that existing systems do work correctly following any amendment. In many cases, minor amendments will simply not be made; instead, many minor amendments will be grouped together and one 'major' change will take place.

Links to other computer systems may be required for various reasons including:

- access to third party information (including Internet access)
- provision of services to third parties (such as extranets)
- communication between departments in an organisation, where each department maintains its own servers
- access to value added networks and electronic data interchange services
- sharing of information worldwide within an organisation (using Lotus Notes or similar system)
- communication via e-mail.

5 Data conversion and data creation

Data conversion means the transfer of data from one system onto another system, which normally involves some reorganisation of the data itself, such as creating new fields. **Data creation** involves setting up or creating new data from scratch. Data creation is likely to be needed in most data conversion situations, especially where new master files or databases are to be established.

Data conversion will be required in situations such as:

- a new software system is introduced which replaces but is not immediately compatible with an existing system

- two information systems, which provide similar data are amalgamated into one system

- two organisations, with different information systems, merge and one common information system is required

- details of how to approach the data conversion process are to be found in Chapter 17 of this text.

During the analysis and design phases, the format of all data fields will have been specified; if the system is being mapped onto an existing computerised system, there may be a mismatch between the data fields across the two systems. In this case the specification must stipulate how the mapping is to be achieved.

Another problem that can occur during the conversion relates to the volatility of the data, i.e. how rapidly and how much of it changes. All standing reference data can be transferred early in the process; when the new system is to go live, all the data must be accurate and up to date. This means that the changeable data can only be converted at the last minute; as an alternative, all the most recent transactions can be saved, to be run against the data just prior to implementation. The technical requirements for conversion must identify the changeable data, and what strategy is to be used to ensure accurate and timely conversion.

Example – payroll system

You are responsible for implementing a payroll system for weekly paid employees, using a bought-in package on a stand-alone microcomputer system. There are 3,000 records (one for each employee) in the current manual system. Each record is held on a card. The information about each employee comprises personal details (personnel number, name, date of birth, grade, section, rate of pay, allowances, deductions from pay etc), held in the top section of the card. In the body of the card are held a series of line entries, one for each week of the year. As each week is worked the details are entered in the appropriate line: gross pay; tax and national insurance, by reference to the relevant tables; and net pay.

Required:

(a) Fully describe a procedure for transferring data from the manual to the computer to create the master file prior to going live on the new system.

(b) Specify the checks and controls to be incorporated into the process to ensure that the computerised master file is accurate, complete, up to date and suitable for running the live system.

Solution

(a) File conversion takes place during the last stages of systems development. Once the new system is in place then all data has to be transferred onto it. This process can take a considerable time when converting from a manual to a computerised system.

The way in which files are converted depends, to some extent, upon their size and complexity. In this case, there are 3,000 records for input onto a stand-alone microcomputer.

Assuming that there is only one input device, presumably a keyboard, the following sequence of events is likely to occur.

- The changeover will be thoroughly planned and a suitable time identified. In the scenario given, it would not be feasible to run any sort of parallel system and as the package being used is a bought-in package, then it will have been tried and tested and will be free from 'bugs'.

- Once a time has been chosen it is necessary to ensure that all the data held within the present system is accurate and up to date. Dead records should be removed from the system.

- The records will be in continuous use, therefore they will have to be entered in batches. Alternatively, all the cards could be photocopied and then entered onto the system.

- Initially, only the static data will be entered on the computer. This includes such data as name, address, personnel record number etc. A record will be created for each employee containing all their personal static data.

- Once the static data has been entered then it will be a relatively easier task to enter the up-to-date variable information. This method avoids data becoming out of date before the system is in operation.

- Once all the data has been transferred to the computer, tests will be carried out using test data to ensure that the system is working correctly.

- Hard copies of all records would be printed out in order for employees to verify their record and also in order to comply with the terms of the Data Protection Act.

Amendments will be necessary from time to time, as in the case of changes in tax tables and national insurance rates. However, there should be standard programs within the package to facilitate amendment.

(b) Controls that would be incorporated into the process to ensure that the computerised master file is accurate, complete, up to date and suitable for running the live system would include the following.

- The controls exercised to check the completeness and accuracy of the existing manual system.

- The controls over the total number of records and the values imposed on certain key fields. Data entry should be controlled by use of a batch register to ensure that all records have been entered.

- Data should be validated by input programs to check correctness of input.

- Strict control should be exercised over any rejected records.

- Notes and records should be kept of any changes to the manual system prior to conversion.

- A check should be made by record once the data has been entered and this should be compared with the manual records.

- A full test run should be initiated in order to check the system's and operator's accuracy.

Conclusion

This chapter has described the technical requirements for a new system and the importance of specifying these in tandem with the functional requirements and technical design of a system.

SELF-TEST
QUESTIONS

Performance and volume requirements

1   Why is performance information on computer systems recorded? (1.1)

Housekeeping requirements

2   What is the difference between archiving data files and backing up data files? (2.1)

Audit trails

3   How can the internal auditor assist in the systems development process? (3.1)

Interfaces with other systems

4   What are the implications of a system having to interact with other computer systems? (4)

Data conversion and data creation

5   Explain the problems involved in converting data before implementation. (5)

EXAM-TYPE
QUESTION

Disaster Recovery

'Disaster Recovery' is a charity that flies aid to the sites of natural disasters such as floods, earthquakes, volcanic destruction etc. It keeps stockpiles of provisions such as blankets, tents, water purification units and tablets, preserved foods and some clothing. When there is news of a disaster, the provisions are loaded onto trucks and landrovers, and flown to the site as soon as possible. The charity raises money by public donation, fundraising campaigns and a large network of retail outlets in UK towns.

Disaster Recovery has commissioned a new integrated information system to manage the stock levels, and also to track the whereabouts of volunteer drivers, trucks and aid that is in transit.

Because most of its money is earmarked for disaster relief, the Directors have stipulated a low budget to cover basic functionality, not wanting to divert too much money from the core activity.

You are a consultant working on the specification. Write a report for the Directors explaining the technical requirements that the system may need to meet, and explaining why this may demand a higher investment than they wish to make.

(15 marks)

For the answer to this question, see the 'Answers' section at the end of the book.

Chapter 15

SECURITY AND LEGAL REQUIREMENTS

Information systems have to be monitored to ensure that they continue to work efficiently, to ensure that they comply with relevant legislation and to check that they are safeguarded from threats such as viruses and hackers. All of these issues are discussed in this chapter with specific reference being made to UK legislation.

Objectives

By the time you have finished this chapter you should be able to:

- describe the principles, terms and coverage typified by the UK *Data Protection Act*

- describe the principles, terms and coverage typified by the UK *Computer Misuse Act*

- discuss how the requirements of the UK Data Protection and UK Computer Misuse legislation may be implemented

- explain the implications of software licences and copyright law in computer systems development

- discuss the legal implications of software supply with particular reference to ownership, liability and damages

- describe methods to ensure the physical security of IT systems

- discuss the role, implementation and maintenance of a password system

- explain representative clerical and software controls that should assist in maintaining the integrity of a system

- describe the principles and application of encryption techniques

- discuss the implications of software viruses and malpractice.

1 The Data Protection Act 1998

The Data Protection Act was initially introduced into UK law in 1984 for two major reasons:

- to counteract the threat to privacy caused by the increased ability of computers to hold, transfer and process personal data. Personal data is information about an individual

- to enable the UK to meet its obligations to ratify the Council of Europe Data Protection Convention. When fully operational, this convention will enable the countries that have signed it to refuse to allow data to be transferred to other countries that do not have equivalent data protection laws.

The Act was amended in 1998, the new Act becoming law on 1 March 2000. This was required to comply with the European Union's *Data Protection Directive*, which extended the scope of the legislation from just computer records of personal data to manual records as well.

> ### KEY POINT
>
> The Data Protection Act:
>
> - counteracts the threat to privacy
>
> - meets requirements of *Data Protection Convention*.

One feature of the Act is that the transfer of personal data outside the European Economic Area (basically the EU) is restricted. Personal data may only be transferred outside the EU if the other country has a similar level of data protection law.

Another feature of the 1998 Act is that it gives more powers to individuals whose details are being held; for example, the individual's explicit consent is required when processing sensitive data such as racial origin, criminal convictions or political opinions.

1.1 The scope of the Act

The Act applies to **personal data** of data subjects that is processed by, or on behalf of, data controllers.

The Act gives rights to individuals:

- to access personal data held about them by a data controller

- to seek compensation for any loss or damage suffered from the misuse of such personal data.

For the purposes of the Act, data is information recorded in any form. This can include data processed by equipment operating automatically, or data kept in manual records. There are various exclusions from the need to notify under the Act, including data held for standard business purposes. Note that manual records that have some logical filing system (structured data in terms of the Act) are included under the Data Protection legislation. However, if those records are simply used to maintain an organisation's accounting records, then there is normally no need to notify (that is register under the Data Protection Act).

Personal data is data relating to a living person who can be identified from the data itself, and which is in the possession (or likely to come into the possession) of a data controller. However, data concerning deceased persons or companies is not within the scope of the Act. A person who is the subject of personal data held by a data controller is known as a **data subject**.

A data controller is a person who determines the purpose for which, and the manner in which, personal data will be processed and used. The 1998 Act refers to 'data controllers' whereas the 1984 Act referred to 'data users' in this context. Data is held or controlled when all the following conditions apply:

- the data forms part of the data processed or intended to be processed by, or on behalf of, that person

- the person controls the contents and use of the data

- the data is in the form in which it has been, or is intended to be, processed.

The implication is that a data controller does not have to own the computer on which personal data is held. For example, a computer bureau could process the data on behalf of the data controller, but it is the data controller who decides how the data should be processed. On the other hand, physical custody of a floppy disk containing personal data does not make that person a controller if he has not, and does not intend to, process it.

1.2 The Data Protection Register

This is a register of data controllers and bureaux compiled by the Data Protection Commissioner.

The register lists names and addresses of all users and bureaux together with general details of the nature of the personal data held and the purposes for which it is held. One or more addresses will be provided to which data subjects may write to request access to the data that relates to them.

1.3 Provisions of the Act

The 1998 Act gives a data subject, with some exceptions, the right to examine the personal data that a data controller is holding about him or her. Individuals may write to a data controller to ask whether they are the subject of personal data, and they are entitled to a reply.

The data controller may charge a nominal fee for providing the information, but is required to reply within a certain time.

Where personal data is being held, the data subject has the right to receive details of:

- the personal data that is being held

- the purposes for which the information is being processed

- the recipients to whom the information might be disclosed.

The data subject is also entitled to receive this information in a form that can be understood. In practice, this usually means providing the data subject with a printout of the data, and an explanation of any items of data (such as codes) whose meaning is not clear.

Any individual who suffers damage as a result of improper use of the data by the data controller is entitled to compensation for any loss suffered.

1.4 The Data Protection principles

The Data Protection Act establishes eight general principles or standards to be observed by data users and bureaux. Failure to comply with these principles can result in seizure of data and unlimited fines. The Secretary of State has the power to amend the principles. The principles are as follows:

Personal data held by users

1   The information in personal data should be obtained and processed fairly and lawfully.

(Obtaining the data fairly means that it should be collected from the data subject, and the data subject should know why it is being collected. Personal data must not be collected by deception or coercion.

Processing the data fairly means that the data subject should have given his or her consent, or that the processing is necessary to perform a contract to which the data subject is a party, or that the processing is necessary to comply with a legal requirement, and so on.)

2   Personal data held shall be held only for one or more specified and lawful purposes, and shall not be further processed in any manner incompatible with that purpose or those purposes.

(This means, for example, that a data controller cannot collect personal data for one purpose, such as to provide an Internet service to a private customer, and then use the data for another purpose, such as marketing other services – unless the data controller has specified those purposes.)

3   Personal data shall be adequate, relevant and not excessive in relation to that purpose or purposes for which they are processed.

(A data controller should not collect more personal data than is actually needed. In this respect, a **data dictionary** can play a useful role in system development. A data dictionary sets out the role and purpose of every item of data held in a system, so that all the personal data held on the system can be justified.)

4   Personal data shall be accurate and, where necessary, kept up to date.

(The data controller should take reasonable steps to make sure that the data is accurate and up-to-date. One way of doing this is to write to data subjects periodically, and ask them to verify their personal data, or to notify the data controller if any details should be changed.)

5   Personal data held for any purpose or purposes shall not be kept for longer than is necessary for that purpose or those purposes.

(When the original purpose for collecting and holding the personal data no longer exists, the data should be destroyed. For example, when an employee leaves an organisation, the organisation should destroy all records relating to past appraisals of the employee.)

6   Personal data shall be processed in accordance with the rights of data subjects under this Act.

7   Appropriate technical and organisational measures shall be taken against unauthorised or unlawful processing of personal data and against accidental loss or destruction of or damage to personal data.

8   Personal data shall not be transferred to a country or territory outside the European Economic Area (EEA) unless that country or territory ensures an adequate level of protection for the rights and freedoms of data subjects in relation to the processing of personal data.

One of the main duties of the Commissioner is to encourage data controllers to comply with these principles. The registrar will investigate complaints that these principles have been contravened and may issue the following:

- an enforcement notice requiring the recipient to comply with the principles within a set time

- a deregistration notice threatening to remove the recipient from the register

- a transfer prohibition notice forbidding the transfer of specified data out of the EEA.

If a data controller is deregistered and may no longer process personal data, that could effectively put them out of business. The controller may appeal to a Data Protection Tribunal against these notices.

Reasons for processing

Personal data cannot be processed unless one of the following exclusions for processing is met:

- The data subject consents to the processing. Consent must be explicitly obtained; it cannot be implied. In other words the data controller must ask the data subject whether personal data can be processed prior to that processing taking place.

- Processing is the result of a contractual agreement.

- Processing is a legal obligation.

- To protect the vital interests of the data subject.

- Processing is in the public interest.

- Processing is required to exercise official authority.

There are exemptions to the legislation. These might be exemptions from the Act altogether or from certain parts of the Act. Typical exemptions relate to information held for national security purposes, information about crime, information about taxation, data held for health, education and social work, payroll and accounting applications, the domestic use of computers and personal data held by unincorporated clubs and societies.

Sensitive data

Also, data which is deemed to be sensitive cannot be processed without the express consent of the data subject. Sensitive data is data relating to racial origin, political opinions, religious beliefs, physical or mental health, sexual preferences or trade union membership.

2 The Computer Misuse Act 1990

Until the introduction of the *Computer Misuse Act* in 1990, two highly damaging activities were not against the law. These were hacking into computers, and the deliberate infection of computer systems with viruses. Although an offended organisation could use the civil courts to seek damages for losses suffered, there was no effective legal protection against these two misdemeanours.

2.1 Hacking

Hacking is the gaining of unauthorised access to a computer system, and perhaps altering its contents. Hacking might be done in pursuit of a criminal activity or it may be a hobby, with hackers acting alone or passing information to one another.

Although computer hacking is commonly associated with outsiders breaking into a computer system, the law also applies to unauthorised access to an organisation's computer systems by its own employees.

2.2 Viruses

A virus is a piece of software that seeks to infest a computer system, hiding and automatically spreading to other systems if given the opportunity. Most computer viruses have three functions – avoiding detection, reproducing themselves and causing damage. The damage caused may be relatively harmless and amusing ('Cascade' causes letters to 'fall' off a screen), but are more often severely damaging. In recent years viruses have been spread by email address books around the world within a very short time, and inflicted considerable damage to systems, and the businesses that depended on them.

Hacking and viruses are examined in greater depth later in this chapter.

2.3 The criminal offences created by the Act

This act was designed to outlaw hacking, the introduction of viruses and the unauthorised copying of data. Three new offences were created by the Act:

Unauthorised access to a computer (hacking)

It has become illegal to gain access or to attempt to gain access to a computer system without authorisation. It is not necessary to succeed in gaining access to be guilty of this crime.

The maximum penalty is up to six months in prison and/or a fine.

For example, an employee of a company might gain unauthorised access to the payroll records, perhaps by using the password of an authorised user, and look at the salaries paid to the company directors.

KEY POINT

Offences created by the Act:

- unauthorised access (hacking)

- unauthorised access with intent to commit another offence

- unauthorised modification of data or programs.

Unauthorised access with intent to commit another offence

The maximum penalties for this crime are significantly greater than for unauthorised access alone:

- On summary conviction an offender is liable for up to six months in prison and/or an equivalent fine.

- On conviction or indictment an offender may be imprisoned for up to five years and/or an unlimited fine.

For example, an employee of a company might gain unauthorised access to the employee records, and find information about an employee that he or she can then use for blackmail.

Unauthorised modification of data or programs (introduction of viruses and computer sabotage)

A person is guilty under this offence if the intention is to prevent or hinder access to any program or data or to compromise the reliability of data or programs.

The penalties for this crime are the same as for the crime of unauthorised access with intent to commit another offence.

2.4 What you need to know about data legislation

You need to be aware of the scope and terms of the Data Protection Act and the Computer Misuse Act, and the data protection principles.

You should also give some thought to how the requirements of the Act can be enforced. For example:

- How can an organisation enforce the requirement of the data protection principle 5 that personal data should not be held for longer than its purpose? A comment has already been made about the possible use of a data dictionary in this context.

- How can offences under the Computer Misuse Act be prevented or detected if they occur? Control over access to computers (both physical access and access through passwords and user names) and the use of firewalls and anti-virus software are all possibilities.

3 Copyright law and software contracts

Copyright in general terms is the right to publish, reproduce and sell the matter and form of a literary, musical, dramatic or artistic work. The owner of the copyright can therefore sell the item that the copyright relates to, and can stop other people from selling the same work because they are breaching the copyright obtained by the original author.

KEY POINT

The Copyright, Designs and Patents Act of 1988 provides the same protection to the authors of computer software as it does to literary, dramatic and musical works.

Within the UK, the *Copyright, Designs and Patents Act* of 1988 provides the same protection to the authors of computer software as it does to literary, dramatic and musical works. However, selling software is slightly different from selling a book or painting, for example. When computer software is sold, it is not sold outright to the purchaser. Instead, the purchaser is granted a right to use that software as explained in the user licence. This normally means that only one person at a time can use the software, and that making of copies of the software is limited to back up purposes only. The purchaser cannot therefore simply copy the software onto another CD or floppy disk, as this would breach the copyright.

Most software suppliers allow more than one person to use one copy of the software, where, for example, the software is loaded onto a network server, and a licence to use multiple copies of the software has been purchased.

Some software can be copied legally; this is **shareware**. The software can be loaded onto a computer and tested; however, if the user decides to keep the software, then a royalty payment is due to the author. **Freeware** is software that can be copied and used without charge, although the software author retains the copyright to that software. Finally, **public domain software** is freely available and sharable software that is not copyrighted.

Anyone convicted of an offence under this Act can expect a fine of unlimited amount plus a prison sentence of up to two years.

3.1 Software contracts – off-the-shelf software

Software contracts can be in respect of either packages or bespoke software. The contracts governing most packages are standard. As explained above, users are normally licensed to use a copy or copies of the software; they do not own the software as such and the licence can be withdrawn if the contract is breached.

The important terms found in package software contracts govern the user's rights of use and limit the software vendor's liability.

A typical licence agreement is reproduced below:

Software Licence Agreement

1   **WHAT THIS IS.** This sheet contains the Software Agreement (the 'Agreement'), which will govern your use of the ABC Company software package 'XXXXX'.

   YOU AGREE TO THE TERMS OF THIS AGREEMENT BY THE ACT OF ORDERING OR RUNNING OR INSTALLING THE SOFTWARE.

2   **GRANT OF LICENCE.** On acceptance of your order, ABC Company will grant you, and you will accept, a limited licence to use the ordered software, user instructions, and any related materials (collectively called the 'Software' in this Agreement). You may use one copy of the software. If installed on a network, only one user may use the software at any time.

   You may not transfer or sublicense, either temporarily or permanently, your rights to use the Software under this Agreement without the prior written consent of ABC Company.

3   **TERM.** This Agreement is effective from the day you receive the Software and continues until you return the software to ABC Company. You must also certify in writing that you have destroyed any copies you may have recorded on any system.

4   **ABC COMPANY'S RIGHTS.** You acknowledge that the Software is the sole and exclusive property of ABC Company. By accepting this Agreement, you do not become the owner of the Software, but you do have the right to use the Software in accordance with this Agreement. You agree to use your best efforts and all reasonable steps to protect the Software from unauthorised use, illegal reproduction, or illicit distribution.

5   **YOUR ORIGINAL DISKETTE/HARD DISK COPY.** You may use the original software to make a hard disk copy for the purpose of running the Software program. After making a hard disk copy place the original software in a safe place. Other than the authorised hard disk copy, you agree that no other copies of the Software will be made.

---

6 **LIMITED WARRANTY.** ABC Company warrants for a period of ninety (90) days from the effective date of this Agreement that, under normal use, and in accordance with the installation instructions, the software will not prove defective, that the program is properly recorded and that the accompanying instructions are substantially complete and contain all the information which ABC Company deems necessary for the use of the program. If, during the ninety day period, a defect in the Software should appear, you may return the software to ABC Company for replacement without charge. Your sole right with respect to a defect in the Software is replacement of the Software.

EXCEPT FOR THE LIMITED WARRANTY DESCRIBED IN THIS PARAGRAPH, THERE ARE NO WARRANTIES, EITHER EXPRESSED OR IMPLIED, BY THIS AGREEMENT. THESE INCLUDE, BUT ARE NOT LIMITED TO, IMPLIED WARRANTIES OF MERCHANTABILITY OR FITNESS FOR A PARTICULAR PURPOSE, AND ALL SUCH WARRANTIES ARE EXPRESSLY DISCLAIMED.

7 **LIABILITY.** You agree that regardless of the form of any claim you may have, ABC Company's liability for any damages to you or to any other party shall not exceed the license fee paid for the Software.

ABC COMPANY WILL NOT BE RESPONSIBLE FOR ANY DIRECT, INCIDENTAL, OR CONSEQUENTIAL DAMAGES, SUCH AS, BUT NOT LIMITED TO, LOSS OF PROFITS RESULTING FROM THE USE OF THE SOFTWARE OR ARISING OUT OF ANY BREACH OF THE WARRANTY, EVEN IF ABC COMPANY HAS BEEN ADVISED OF THE POSSIBILITY OF SUCH DAMAGE.

8 **TERMINATION OF AGREEMENT.** If any of the terms and conditions of this Agreement are broken ABC Company has the right to terminate the Agreement and demand that you return the Software to ABC Company. At that time you must also certify in writing that you have not retained any copies of the Software.

9 **GOVERNING LAW.** This Agreement is to be governed by, and interpreted in accordance with the law of England.

3.2   Software contracts – bespoke software

The user should have more say when negotiating for bespoke programs to be written. Of particular importance will be who owns the copyright to the program and the source code. Unless otherwise stated, the law will assume that the software writer will own these. The full list of matters that should be addressed is as follows:

- precise description and specification of the software
- performance warranties (that it will operate with certain response times)
- price
- terms of payment
- dates for completion
- acceptance tests and period for acceptance
- penalties for late delivery and poor performance
- conditions of use
- ownership of copyright
- ownership of source code
- documentation
- training
- warranties
- after-sales service and levels of support

- protection against copyright infringement
- confidentiality.

All these items will be included in an agreement to write the software, prior to that writing being commenced.

4   Security, privacy and threats to the organisation

Security and privacy are both important considerations in the design and operation of information systems in an organisation. Their importance is evidenced by the fact that both have been the subjects of legislation within the last few years. The protection of the organisation's security and the individual's privacy must be key aspects of the organisation's information technology strategy.

4.1   Security

DEFINITION

Security is:

- the protection of data and programs against unauthorised access, change or modification
- the assurance that the system can operate as designed and the users can receive the services they need
- the protection of hardware against damage
- the protection of humans against injury and harm.

Security can be defined as:

- the protection of data from unauthorised access, change or modification
- the protection of programs from unauthorised change or modification
- the assurance that systems operate as designed, and that users continue to receive the services that they need
- the protection of hardware against damage
- the protection of humans against injury and harm.

The damage to data, software and hardware can be caused deliberately or accidentally, and may be caused by 'act of God' or by human malice or error. The assurance that systems operate as defined implies that system faults are also within the broad definition of security problems.

Security, therefore, is a wide and important part of the management of IT, and must be taken very seriously. A security policy should consider the avoidance or minimisation of threats, the prediction and detection of problems and the recovery from problems.

4.2   Privacy

DEFINITION

Privacy is the right of an individual to control the dissemination or use of data that relates to him or herself.

Privacy is the right of an individual to control the dissemination or use of data that relates to him or herself.

The volume of data that can be held on a computer, the speed with which it can be transmitted, and the ability of the computer to link several sets of data pose especial problems. Personal information can be misused much more effectively on computer than with manual systems. The dangers of this misuse led to the *Data Protection Act* (above).

The Privacy and Electronic Communications (EC Directive) Regulations 2003

This legislation, deriving from an EU Directive, is designed to protect consumers and businesses from unsolicited electronic communication, usually known as 'spam'. Marketing via e-mail and SMS (text message) is now permitted only if recipients have given prior consent or **'opted-in'** to receive information via these channels. This puts the onus on the sender of the mail.

The regulations state that explicit permission must be obtained from a consumer before contacting them via email or SMS for the first time.

The legislation does allow businesses to contact existing customers who have already given their email address or mobile number and also those consumers who have enquired about a product or service via email or SMS. By showing an interest they are deemed to have given permission to be contacted again in the future.

Any form of electronic communication sent to an individual must always contain a clearly stated unsubscribe option which is free for the recipient of the email / SMS. Businesses will be evading the law if they continue to communicate with a consumer once they have opted-out from communications. Breaking the law can result in fines of up to £5,000.

A cookie is a text file or piece of software placed on the user's hard drive by a website that the user has visited. It records details about the user (such as the user's contact details or preferences) so that the user can be recognised on future visits. It is often used by e-commerce sites as a means of memorising items placed on a shopping cart.

The regulations introduce certain limitations on the use of cookies on websites requiring basic information about them e.g. what they store and the consequences of not accepting them, as well as the opportunity to reject them.

Finally, the regulations forbid the use of electronic mail for direct marketing purposes where the identity or address of the sender is concealed or disguised or where a valid reply address has not been provided.

The impact of the regulations is limited because most spam originates from outside the EU, where there are either no laws or the laws are less stringent. In the US, for example, the CAN-SPAM Act 2003 allows businesses to send unsolicited messages until the recipient **opts out**. In other words the onus is on the receiver rather than the sender of the mail.

4.3 Threats

There are always threats to an organisation during the operation of any system, whether the system is manual or computer-based. Computer systems are much more vulnerable to risk because of the power and speed of the computer, and because problems are more difficult to identify.

The extra problems of computer systems are:

- Data stored on magnetic media is much more liable to undetected corruption or loss.

- The computer can be accessed remotely via the public communications network – unauthorised people can access and change data.

- No automatic trace of computer transactions is created. If a problem occurs, it may be impossible to correct or even detect inaccuracies in the data.

- The computer can carry out processes so fast that a great deal of damage can be done by the time that an error has been detected.

- The computer does not have an automatic 'feel' for what is reasonable.

Types of threat

DEFINITION

Five basic threats:

- physical damage to hardware or computer media
- damage to data
- damage to humans
- operational problems
- industrial espionage/fraud.

Five basic types of threat to an organisation relate to information technology.

Physical damage to hardware or computer media

Malicious damage, poor operating conditions, natural disasters and simple wear and tear can physically damage machinery and storage media such as disks, tapes and diskettes. These carry a triple threat – the cost of repair or replacement of hardware; the danger of damaged data or program files; and the cost of computer down time. This is discussed in greater detail below.

Damage to data

Hackers, viruses, program bugs, hardware and media faults can all damage data files. The havoc caused by damaged data is made worse if it is not detected and rectified quickly.

Damage to humans

Computers and peripherals can cause hazardous conditions for operators and users, who can receive electric shocks, trip over wires, gash themselves on sharp corners, or be injured in fires. Sometimes physical precautions against computer damage can themselves create danger. Some units, for example, are protected against fire by being flooded by CO_2 gas. If someone were trapped when this happens, serious injury or death may result.

RSI – repetitive strain injury is an injury caused by constant repetition of specific activities such as the use of keyboards. It can cause long-term problems and has forced many individuals into premature retirement and their employers have had to pay large damages claims.

To avoid physical trauma to users of computer equipment, attention should be paid to their needs when designing workstations and setting up the computer installations. Measures that can be taken to protect staff include:

Good ergonomic design

Workstations should be designed for comfortable use by the people who are going to use them. The lighting must be such that there is no glare or reflection from screens. The screens themselves should be designed to reduce the amount of flicker, which is extremely tiring to the eyes. Furniture must be of a comfortable height for the average user, and should be adjustable to fit the needs of the non-average user. The designers of workstations should also avoid sharp corners and projections that users could accidentally hurt themselves on. Wires should not be in a position where people can trip over them.

Ducting and false floors

To avoid the damage to both users and equipment that can be caused by tripping over cables, these should be fed through ducting or passed through false floors and false ceilings.

Safety awareness and training

Most accidents are caused by human error, so it is important to stress awareness of safety in the workplace. A high priority must be placed on the well-being of staff, which will cut down on absenteeism and sickness, reduce costs and increase the effectiveness of staff.

Operational problems

Program bugs and operational mistakes can cause significant problems, ranging from the need to resuscitate files and repeat computer runs, to the possibility of losing customers.

Industrial espionage/fraud

Industrial espionage and sabotage can yield significant advantages to competitors, and fraud and blackmail are also significant threats.

DEFINITION

The basic causes of problems:

- human error

- technical error

- natural disasters

- fraud, espionage, sabotage

- poor personnel relations.

4.4   The underlying causes of problems

The basic causes of problems are:

1   **Human error.** The most prolific cause of problems is human error.

2   **Technical error.** Hardware or software malfunction is another significant risk, with communications equipment giving especial problems.

3   **Natural disasters.** Natural disasters (bad weather, earthquakes, fire, flood, etc.) cannot be avoided completely, but their possibility must be catered for.

4   **Fraud, espionage, sabotage.** The deliberate actions of individuals can result in significant loss, whether these actions are for personal gain, for competitive advantage or for revenge or malice.

5   **Poor personnel relations.**

5   General protective measures

Although many of the measures discussed below will be described in more detail later on, it is relevant at this point to list a number of measures that organisations should take to protect themselves whenever they build information systems.

1   **Physical security.** Access to hardware should be controlled and restricted to authorised personnel. This will reduce the chances of physical sabotage, accidental damage and hacking.

2   **Protection against remote access.** Passwords and user numbers can be used to limit the chances of unauthorised people accessing the system via the public communications network.

3   **Back-up procedures**. Data should be backed up on a regular and systematic basis. This will enable problems to be overcome with the minimum of trouble.

4   **Strict operating procedures.** Imposing strict operating procedures and controls reduces the chances of human error.

5   **Attention to health and safety.** All dangers should be eliminated from the working environment by passing cables through ducts and being alert to safety hazards. The danger of RSI and eyestrain will be reduced by the careful ergonomic design of workstations and the use of flicker-free visual display units.

6   **Encryption of data.** If data is encrypted, the only people who can read the data are those who have the key to the encryption technique. This means that even if an industrial spy were to gain access to a computer system or intercept a communications link, the damage they could do would be limited.

7   **Vigilance.** The most dangerous situation is where people become overconfident and blasé. All people in the organisation should be alert to danger at all times.

6   Physical threats to computer installations

Poor security may result in physical damage to a computer installation – either accidental or deliberate. It may also allow unauthorised access by ill-intentioned or ham-fisted people. In either case, protective measures must be taken.

For an organisation to plan its defence against any kind of threat, it must make a catalogue of the dangers that it faces before counter-measures can be developed.

6.1   Physical threats

Physical threats can result in many kinds of damage to an installation. All parts of the system are vulnerable, including the machinery, the environment, computer media, software and the people using the system. The resulting damage can be so crucial that companies can be completely bankrupted by physical disasters that they have not properly protected themselves against. Physical threats include:

Fire

Fire is a very serious hazard to a computer system. It can damage or destroy every part of a computer installation – hardware, software, data files and the original transaction documents. Even the people involved and the fabric of the computer installation are at risk from fire.

It is not just the flames that cause the damage; heat, smoke, dust and the substances used to fight the fire are all very destructive.

Flood

Water can be extremely damaging to any kind of electrical equipment. Rivers and seas overflowing may cause flooding, or it may be caused by the results of fighting fires within the building. Computers sited in the basement or ground floor of buildings are more susceptible to flooding than those sited on upper floors, although the floor immediately underneath a water tank may also be at risk.

Weather

Bad weather can harm an installation by physically damaging the fabric of the building, by damaging hardware or computer media, or by interrupting the power supply. The worst damage is caused by extreme weather such as high winds, torrential rain or thunderstorms, but long term erosion or weathering can also degrade the fabric of the building and harm the computer installation.

Although the threats posed by wind, rain and extreme temperatures are significant, the most common weather-based threat is lightning. This can act in a number of ways:

- A lightning strike on a building may damage its fabric or burn out electrical cabling and other equipment.

- The cabling connecting different machines in a network may be struck. This can damage several machines at the same time, and disable the network.

- Overhead pylons carrying high voltages are very commonly struck by lightning. This can cause power surges and spikes in the electricity supply to the computer installation and damage equipment several miles from the lightning strike. Data files corrupted by this occurrence must be reconstructed and can cause a great deal of down time in an unprotected organisation.

Natural disasters and terrorist attack

Earthquakes and explosions are potentially disastrous to people, machinery and buildings. They are also likely to disrupt communication lines. Damage caused by terrorists may be an accidental side-effect of an attack on another target, or it may be specifically aimed at a commercial or military organisation.

Uncontrolled physical environment

A great deal of equipment and computer media needs to be operated in a controlled physical environment. Although it is less important for PCs, they are still susceptible to many hazards. Dangers include:

- dust
- heat
- cold
- humidity
- spillages (e.g. coffee, tea, soft drinks and food)
- static electricity
- magnetic fields
- power failure, irregular current, surges and spikes.

Deliberate physical attack and fraud

In addition to the sort of terrorist attack described above, computers are also liable to attack from disgruntled employees, ill-disposed members of the public, thieves, industrial spies, blackmailers and extortionists, and other criminals. There are a number of such hazards that installations need protecting against:

- hardware sabotage
- hardware theft
- software piracy
- blackmail and extortion
- copied or stolen data
- unauthorised alteration of programs
- false transactions being applied to data files
- loss of confidentiality
- physical interception of data communication
- the use of detection equipment to show what is being displayed on computer monitors. Equipment similar to television detector vans can intercept the radiation from a monitor and display a facsimile of what is displayed on the screen. This equipment can operate over a distance of many metres.

7 Countering physical threats

Once the physical threats to an installation have been catalogued, measures can be developed to counter them. Many of these measures will cost money, but others may just entail the introduction of good working practices.

Those counter-measures that do cost money need to be cost-justified. The cost-justification will not always be formally carried out, but management will need to know how much their counter-measures are costing.

The actions that can be taken to protect against physical threats can be categorised as follows:

1 **Preventative measures.** All possible measures must be taken to stop problems from occurring.

2 **Detective measures.** If a problem has occurred, the organisation must find out what has happened so that the effects are minimised.

3 **Corrective measures.** After a problem has been discovered, its effects must be minimised and the organisation must take action to return the situation to normality.

The problems that do escape the net of the preventative measures adopted by the organisation may reveal weaknesses that need to be countered in the future. Planning against threats must be regarded as an ongoing process.

7.1   Protection against fire

There is a range of measures that can be adopted to protect against the risk of fire or alleviate its consequences:

- training of staff to be alert against fire
- control of combustible materials
- regular fire drills
- smoke and heat detectors
- fire alarms
- fire doors and automatically closing doors
- automatic extinguishers: carbon dioxide and water sprinklers (where appropriate)
- manual foam-based extinguishers
- regular backing up of files and transaction data
- fire-proof, water-proof safe for back-up media
- holding back-up materials off-site
- regular servicing of machinery and maintenance of electrical equipment
- the use of computer bureaux if machinery is damaged
- planned redundancy – the availability of more than one machine, so that work can be transferred onto another machine if one is affected
- insurance cover.

Not all of the above measures are adopted in every organisation – some measures are alternatives to others – but there is often a synergy between some of the above measures, with several measures being more effective if they are used in combination. Insurance premiums are likely to be reduced if insurance companies are satisfied with the other measures adopted. Regular backing up of data is of little use unless the back ups are stored in a fireproof safe or at another location.

7.2   Protection against floods and the weather

Several of the measures to protect against fire have a more general value. The regular taking and safe storage of back ups, the use of external bureaux or planned redundancy, and the use of insurance policies to mitigate the results of disasters are examples of general-purpose protective measures.

Some of the more specific measures are:

Careful siting of hardware

Computer machinery should be installed away from dangers. Organisations will usually avoid the basement and other areas that are vulnerable to flooding. Most computers of any kind, including PCs, microcomputers, will not be put into temporary office buildings unless operational reasons dictate that they should be.

Regular building maintenance

If the building is well maintained, there is less chance that leaks will cause major problems.

Shielded cabling

Cables and wires are vulnerable to water as well as to lightning strike. If there is a weakness in the cable insulation, electricity will track across a damp surface causing further degrading.

7.3   Power failure

Back-up generators

In the event of a power failure, a back-up generator can be switched on to enable processing to continue. These generators may be tripped automatically to minimise disruption.

Current isolators

Specialised equipment can be connected to the power supply to flatten out spikes and other uneven patterns in the amount of electricity coming through. Spikes can cause computers to make errors and damage disk contents.

Current isolators minimise the danger of damage to computer media or hardware.

7.4   Physical attack

Shatter-proof glass

Shatter-proof glass will minimise the problems caused by explosions and similar terrorist activities.

7.5   Environmental control

One of the most powerful protections against physical threats is to isolate the computer installation as far as possible from the rest of the world. The degree to which this can be done will depend upon the size and value of the computers and the importance of the systems that run on them. Mainframe computers are likely to be enveloped in a protective cocoon, whereas personal computers have fewer external protections and must be more inherently robust – more tolerant to imperfections in their environment. Some machines are built to withstand extreme conditions, especially those that are designed to be used outside.

More generally, however, business computers have protective measures built into their environment. These measures include:

Separate area

A separate or segregated area will enable the section of a building containing the computer facilities to be totally controlled. Air conditioning and dust controls will ensure that the computer equipment operates under optimum conditions.

Static control mats

Static control mats dissipate static electricity before it can build up into a damaging charge.

Separate electrical supply

Spikes, surges and dips in the electricity supply are not only caused by problems in the public network. There may also be problems caused locally within the building itself. A particular danger is when more than one piece of electrical equipment shares the same circuit. Switching on a power-hungry piece of equipment is likely to cause a significant dip in the power available to machines that are already switched on. Even machinery such as electric kettles and vacuum cleaners can cause problems to computers. It is unwise, therefore, to connect sensitive equipment such as computers to circuits shared by other machinery.

Restricted access

Many of the physical threats to a computer installation that we have discussed earlier are caused by unauthorised individuals gaining access to the computers. Restricting access to the computers by the installation of security mechanisms will minimise these risks. A discussion of some of these security measures can be found later in this chapter.

7.6 Protection against fraud and data theft

Once people have gained access to computer facilities, they may try to enter false transactions or to copy data. There are a number of measures that can be taken to detect when this is happening and to avoid likely problems. The measures that can be taken include the use of physical devices, operational procedures and security software.

The sort of security procedures that may be adopted include:

Strict controls over input/processing/programs and division of duties

There should be no confusion over which person should be doing each job. In this way, the chance of problems occurring is very much reduced; if problems do occur then it is much easier to establish what has happened and to rectify the situation.

Internal audit review systems

It should be possible to trace back all the events that affect data files. An audit trail will enable management to identify when any problems have occurred and find out what the causes of those problems were.

Encryption of data

Data may be coded so that it is not understandable to any casual observer who does not have access to suitable decryption software. Encryption provides a double benefit. It protects against people managing to gain access to the system, and it protects against the tapping of data whilst being transmitted from one machine to another.

Shielding of VDUs

To protect against people with detection equipment being able to view remotely what is being displayed on VDUs, the units may be shielded to prevent the transmission of radiation that can be detected. Computers containing sensitive material can also be sited so that they are out of the range over which detector vans can operate. Some defence establishments have been known to install PCs accessing sensitive information in metal-lined rooms with no outside windows, to eliminate the chance of unauthorised individuals viewing what is being shown on the screen.

8 Physical access control

Reducing access to sensitive areas can cut down considerably on the risks posed by intruders. It will minimise the probability of hardware theft, espionage, sabotage and all other kinds of computer crime. It also reduces the chance of non-criminals causing inadvertent damage.

There are various basic categories of controlling access to sensitive areas. These include:

- security guards

- physically lockable working areas

- safes and lockable cabinets.

An organisation may have a mixture of different devices to restrict access.

There is likely to be a security guard controlling access to the whole building. Especially sensitive areas are likely to be very tightly controlled – this would include the main computer facilities. Security in other parts of the building is likely to be much lighter, sometimes depending on the operating procedures of an individual department.

Physical security within the computer department

Security in the computer department itself is likely to be very tightly controlled. Some of the controls that may be operated are:

- the computer department being sited in a secure part of the building, often on an upper floor

- access past a separate reception or security desk

- access being via locked doors which may be opened in one of a number of different ways:

  - typing in a personal identification number (PIN)

  - an electronic key card

  - conventional keys may be issued to authorised personnel

  - combination locks requiring a person to type in a set sequence of digits, which can be periodically changed

- closed circuit TV used to monitor what is happening in a particular part of a building – this may be backed up by security video cameras.

- doors automatically locked in the event of a security alarm

- computer equipment electronically or physically tagged to activate an alarm if an attempt is made to carry it out of the building or computer area.

Other devices, such as machines which can identify fingerprints or scan the pattern of a retina, are often seen in TV programmes.

8.1 Data security

The first line of defence against interlopers is to control physically who is allowed near to the computer. The second line of defence is to reduce the damage that can be caused when the first line of defence is breached.

This can happen when an interloper succeeds in getting past the security measures or when a hacker manages to access the computer remotely.

In either case, it is vital to prevent unauthorised users from changing or viewing data, and to limit the damage that they can do. There are a number of points to consider.

Theft of disks

Diskettes, data sticks and CDs (both referred to hereafter as disks) are vulnerable to theft and to damage. Although the disks themselves are not valuable, the data they hold can be. They can be easily smuggled out of a building in a briefcase or a pocket, and disk security is often a weak link in an organisation.

Disks should not be left lying around on desks and working surfaces. They may be lost, stolen, inadvertently reused or damaged by spillages of hot drinks. Disks should be locked away when not being used, and should be filed for easy reference. All disks containing important information must be backed up on a regular basis.

Theft of printout

Computer printout may well contain confidential data. Many industrial spies make a habit of investigating the rubbish for useful titbits of information. Disks are also sometimes discarded and, even if files have been deleted, the data on them can be

---

KEY POINT

It is vital to prevent unauthorised users from changing or viewing data, and to limit the damage that they can do.

recovered. Both printout and disks should be shredded or otherwise destroyed before being thrown away.

Unauthorised access

Passwords and user numbers are used as a way of identifying who is authorised to access the system. There may be several levels of password, with particularly sensitive applications protected by multiple passwords. There may also be a system of electronic handshakes; these enable the computer to recognise which terminal is accessing it. This allows some applications to be restricted only to certain terminals. These protections can also be used to help track down the culprits when a security breach has occurred.

It is important to maintain strict security over the passwords used. Unauthorised users may discover passwords in several ways. For example, a written reference to the password may be secreted somewhere near the computer (often taped to the underside of a desk drawer). The hacker may be able to guess the password from knowledge of the private life of an authorised user; the password or user number might be worked out through trial and error (sometimes carried out systematically by a computer program); the password may have been 'lent' or otherwise discovered because of carelessness.

PIN numbers are used in certain circumstances. These personal identification numbers can be used in combination with magnetic strip cards to reinforce security. Cash dispensers are a typical example of this kind of protective measure.

9   Passwords

The British Computer Society's definition of a password is: 'a sequence of characters that must be presented to a computer system before it will allow access to the system or parts of that system.'

The sequence of characters referred to above can be any combination of letters, numbers or symbols. The system in use will determine such factors as the maximum/minimum length of password permitted; characters which may not be allowed (*, ?, -, for example), whether the password is case-sensitive, etc. The administrators of the system can usually set the properties of the individual's account: when/if the password expires (obviously the security of the system is improved if a user has to change the password regularly); if the user is able to change their own password, etc.

When a password is entered, the characters entered should not appear on the screen (but may appear as, for example, asterisks; this confirms to the user the number of characters entered). This will prevent disclosure of the password to any onlooker.

The use of passwords is to increase data security and restrict access. These objectives, however, need to be balanced against the resultant inconvenience and, if taken to extremes, a reduction in value of the system to users.

A password may be required at boot-up, i.e. when the machine is first switched on. If this level of security is used, care must be taken to ensure that this password is not forgotten; great inconvenience ensues if no one can easily gain access to the machine at this level!

In the case of a LAN, a password will usually be entered in conjunction with the user identity. The user identity will be displayed as it is typed in – whereas the password should not appear as it is typed.

9.1 Problems with passwords

Password systems can only be effective if users use them conscientiously. There are several inherent problems with such a system:

- Authorised users may divulge their password to a colleague: this may arise because allowing temporary access in this way may be perceived as being more convenient than going through the process of setting up the colleague with their accounts.

- Many passwords may have associations with the user (e.g. son's name and age: brian14; house name and number: 19bellfield); these can be discovered by experimentation.

- Passwords are often written down close to the computer (e.g. pinned to the notice board inside the office), left on a yellow 'post-it' in a desk drawer or even attached to the terminal!

To protect passwords and user numbers against discovery, a number of precautions should be adopted:

- Users should be required to change their passwords regularly.

- Passwords should be memorable but not obviously related to a user's private life (common password choices such as children's or pets' names or birthdays).

- Users should be encouraged never to write down their passwords. Mnemonic methods should be suggested as an *aide-mémoire* (e.g. making up a phrase or nonsense sentence using the numbers and initial letters).

- Passwords should be case-sensitive and passwords should be a combination of numbers as well as letters.

- There should be strict controls over passwords – they should never be 'lent' or written down where they can be easily seen.

- There should be automatic sentinel or watchdog programs to identify when a password has been keyed incorrectly.

An alternative to passwords is for the user to have a card or badge; this can be used to establish the identity of the user, but passwords may then be required in conjunction with the use of the card.

10 Logical access system

10.1 The role of a logical access system

Physical access controls involves restricting unauthorised access to the hardware of a system. In comparison, logical access controls involves those who do have access to a computer or terminal; this may take the form of restricting access to specific data application software.

A **logical access system** involves a system of facilities developed and maintained to protect data or software from the potential dangers of unauthorised access.

The potential dangers to data that may exist resulting from unauthorised access are as follows:

- It may be **inaccurate**. This situation may be difficult to detect as the system itself will ostensibly be functioning normally, but will in fact be producing inaccurate figures. The danger here is that management decisions may be reached using incorrect information.

- It may be **falsified**. This may be done to gain some advantage, to the detriment of the organisation.

DEFINITION

A **logical access system** involves a system of facilities developed and maintained to protect data or software from the potential dangers of unauthorised access.

- It may be **disclosed**. Information may be made available to individuals who have not been granted access to it, or to the public in general.

- It may be **lost**. This may occur at any stage (i.e. before, during or after processing).

10.2 The operation of a logical access system

Initially, the security risks with regard to computer-based should be assessed considering the potentialities identified above.

The next stage entails classification of data in terms of sensitivity. Suggested classifications may be:

- **public data**: giving wide access to read/copy

- **limited access data**: specific users in personnel or finance

- **private data**: access to identified individuals only.

A logical access system should, therefore, be capable of the following:

- establishing the user's identity by means of an ID code

- verifying the user, usually by means of a password

- confirming that the user has authorised access to the requested data.

To accomplish this the system should be capable of:

- identifying each user by means of a logical identifier

- matching the identifier with the terminal being used, to ascertain that access is from an authorised location

- controlling access to specified data and resources by users, terminals/computers

- logging accesses and usage of resources to facilitate auditing.

10.3 Password maintenance

Passwords require a simple system to ensure that they remain effective. The system would normally include the following features:

- a system for issuing instructions to users regarding the setting up of passwords

- a record of the scope of each user name and password

- a system for enabling forgetful users to obtain a new password

- periodic reminders to users to change their password

- automatic expiry of passwords after a certain time.

11 Hacking

Hacking is the deliberate accessing of on-line systems by unauthorised persons.

Management often requires that the contents of certain files (e.g. payroll) remain confidential and are only available to authorised staff. This may be achieved by keeping tapes or removable disks containing the files in a locked cabinet and issuing them only for authorised use.

The introduction and growth in the use of on-line systems has meant that alternative precautions need to be taken. Security at the terminal should be adequate; the terminal can be locked and/or kept in a locked room. Access and use should be properly recorded and controlled.

As organisations have grown to depend more and more on systems and the data stored on them, individuals and other organisations have become increasingly interested in gaining access to those systems and the data.

KEY POINT

Typical data classification:

- public data

- limited access data

- private data.

KEY POINT

A logical system should:

- establish user's identity

- verify user

- confirm that user has authorised access to requested data.

DEFINITION

Hacking is the deliberate accessing of on-line systems by unauthorised persons.

Since the 1980s, a class of highly intelligent individuals has emerged. These people use their knowledge of systems to gain unauthorised access to systems for their own purposes. The perpetrators, hackers, often consider hacking to be fun, and it is not necessarily done with malicious intent.

As modems and PCs have become more widespread, the threat of hacking has increased. Due to changing working practices, many systems now have dial-up facilities; this facilitates entry into the system by the hacker after the telephone number has been obtained or by means of an auto dialler. To exacerbate the situation, hackers, having obtained numbers, make these available over the Internet.

11.1 The dangers stemming from hackers

A knowledgeable hacker can conceal any evidence of their deeds by disabling the journal or console logs of the main CPU.

Once hackers have gained access to the system, there are several damaging options available to them. For example, they may:

- gain access to the file that holds all the ID codes, passwords and authorisations
- discover the method used for generating/authorising passwords
- develop a program to discover users IDs/passwords
- discover maintenance codes, which would render the system easily accessible
- interfere with the access control system, to provide the hacker with open access to the system
- generate information which is of potential use to a competitor organisation
- provide the basis for fraudulent activity
- cause data corruption by the introduction of unauthorised computer programs and processing onto the system (computer viruses)
- alter or delete files.

11.2 Firewalls

A firewall is the most important security component to prevent hacking if the network in the organisation is also connected to the Internet. Firewalls may either be physical boxes, or the server may have a program on it (software) that performs the same function.

- A hardware firewall is generally a small box which sits between the computer and your modem. A business network is most likely to have a hardware firewall since these can protect more than one computer at once.

- A software firewall (for example Zone Alarm, Norton Internet Security) runs on the user's computer in the background. The most recent operating systems, such as Windows XP have a built-in firewall.

- It is, of course, possible to use both types.

Firewalls have always been important but they have become much more so as more and more people have broadband connections to the Internet that are "always on" (to a hacker, "always on" means "always vulnerable").

11.3 Other controls to help prevent hacking

By specifically identifying the risks that the hacker represents, controls can be designed to help prevent such activity occurring. Examples include:

Physical security

Check that terminals and PCs are kept under lock and key, and ensure that, where dial-in communication links are in place, that a call-back facility is used. (In call-back, the person dialling in must request that the system calls them back to make the connection. The system will only make a call to a pre-defined telephone number that is assigned to that specific user. This stops unauthorised users using a modem attached to the system to log in from an unidentified location.)

User authentication systems

There should be software controls over access. User authentication systems have two elements: user names and passwords.

User names

Each employee with authority to access some of the computer system files and programs is given a user name. Typically, each computer terminal will display the username of a particular individual, although this can be altered by keying in a different name. An individual user might be allowed access to some parts of the computer system but not others.

Passwords

In addition to user names, access is also protected by passwords. Each user of the system has an individual password, and has to key in the password correctly in order to gain access. To prevent an unauthorised person from 'stealing a password' by looking over the shoulder of an authorised person as he or she keys in a password, the screen displays asterisks as the password is keyed in, rather than the actual letters and numbers of the password.

The controls over passwords must be stringently enforced and password misuse should represent a serious disciplinary offence within an organisation. Associated with the password is a list of files, and data within files, which the user is allowed to inspect. Attempts to access unauthorised files or data will be prohibited by the operating system and reported at the central computer. For example, an order clerk using a VDU would be allowed access to the stock file, but not to the employee file. Similarly, the clerk would be allowed access to the customer file for purposes of recording an order, but would not be able to inspect details of the account.

Data encryption

Files can be scrambled to render them unintelligible unless a decoding password is supplied. Encryption can also be applied to data before transmission, so that it is unintelligible to eavesdroppers. (See below for more on Encryption.)

System logs

Every activity on a system should be logged and be subject to some form of exception reporting, e.g. unusual times of access could be reported.

Audit trails

Sensitive data, e.g. payee codes, should be subject to a separate audit report showing when the data was read, written to or updated. It should show also the before and after state and the data causing the change.

Sensitive users

Every facility must be accessible by at least one person. This should not mean that the same person has access to every facility. The system should allow a different user to be assigned to specific facilities as a form of segregation of duties, so that at least some form of collusion would be required, e.g. to generate an automatic payment on a non-existent supplier account.

Random checks

This approach checks who is doing what at random intervals on the system, and ensures that they are authorised for those activities.

12 Encryption

Encryption provides a defence to enhance physical security measures.

Encryption is the technique of disguising information to preserve its confidentiality; this should occur during transmission and when stored. Encryption derives enciphered text from plain text, thus transforming the latter into an unintelligible form; in simpler terms, it is a method of scrambling the data in a message or file so that it is unintelligible unless it is unscrambled (or **decrypted**).

The process of encryption and decryption comprises an algorithm and a key; the algorithm is the operation itself, which transforms the data into cipher, and the key controls the algorithm; changing the value of the key can alter the effect of the algorithm so that the conversion for each key value is completely different.

Computers, because of their computational power, facilitate sophisticated encryption techniques that would otherwise be unrealistic. The cryptanalyst must devise a system with a cost of decoding which is sufficiently high to deter a potential unauthorised decoder but which has, at the same time, a level of sophistication no higher than necessary, as this slows down the processing time – which costs money.

Cipher keys may be different for each file or message, but they will usually be applied to groups. Often the same key is used for encryption and decryption, so both the sender and the receiver must know it, which increases the possibility of it becoming known to an unauthorised user.

If the encryption and decryption keys are different, they can be constructed so that a potential eavesdropper may gain complete knowledge of the encryption process and key and yet still be unable to unscramble the data, even with the aid of sophisticated computer equipment. The encryption key may be made generally available, and then it is know as a **public key.** The person receiving messages encoded with the public key retains a different (**private key**) that is needed to decrypt the message. Because the private key is kept secret, the person sending a message with the public key will know that only the intended recipient of the message can decrypt and read it.

So, if you make a purchase on the Internet, almost all vendors will confirm that you are on a secure link so your credit card details are safe. All this means is that your credit card details are encrypted using the vendor's public key; only the vendor has access to its own private key, making the transfer of data very secure.

Of course, you may argue that computers are so fast they can break encryption systems quickly. However, as noted above, the power of computers to search for decryption keys has lead in recent years to producing keys that would take a significant amount of computer time to break. Two encryption systems, PGP (Pretty Good Privacy) and RSA (named after the inventors Rivest, Shamir and Adleman and marketed by RSA Data Security Inc.) are examples of this type of encryption system.

13 Computer viruses

13.1 Types of computer viruses

A further security and control issue, which has been highlighted in recent years, is the growth of computer viruses. A **computer virus** is a small program that, having been introduced into the system, proliferates; its purpose is to spread extensively, impairing both data and software. As the name suggests, they have the ability to infect a whole computer system. The infected programs may then act as carriers for the computer virus, with the end result that the infection process can have a spiralling effect. The potential for the damage a virus can cause is restricted only by the creativity of the originator. Given the mobility between computerised systems and the sharing of resources and data, the threat posed by a viral attack is considerable.

Viruses can be categorised as:

- **trojans** – whilst carrying on one program, secretly carry on another
- **worms** – these replicate themselves within the systems
- **trap doors** – undocumented entry points to systems allowing normal controls to be bypassed
- **logic bombs** – triggered on the occurrence of a certain event
- **time bombs** – which are triggered on a certain date.

Once a virus has been introduced into the system, the only course of action may be to regenerate it from back up. However, some viruses are written so that they lie dormant for a period, which means that the back ups become infected before the existence of the virus has been detected; in these instances restoration of the system becomes impossible.

13.2 Preventative steps against computer viruses

It is extremely difficult to guard against the introduction of computer viruses. Steps may be taken to control the introduction and spread of viruses, but these will usually only be effective in controlling the spread of accidental viruses by well-meaning individuals. The actions of hackers or malicious employees are less easy to control. Preventative steps may include:

- control on the use of external software (e.g. checked for viruses before use)
- use of only tested, marked disks within the organisation
- restricted access to diskettes and CDs on all PCs/workstations.

Anti-virus software is available to protect against viruses, although the focus of these programs is to detect and cure known viruses; they will not always restore data or software that has been corrupted by the virus. As new viruses are being detected almost daily, it is virtually impossible for the virus detection software to be effective against all known viruses. More recent anti-virus software includes has an ability to look for particular signatures or patterns of computer code, which imply a virus may be present. These programs have decreased the success of virus attacks, although one of the effects of these types of programs is to provide a new challenge for authors of computer viruses.

It is now usual for users connected to the Internet to receive regular updates of their anti-virus software by downloading a new version of the software from the software supplier's web site, in response to an on-screen prompt. All anti-virus software will supply these updates for the period covered by the licence (usually one year). After that time, the anti-virus software may continue to function for existing viruses but will not be updated for new viruses. It is essential to update the licence when it runs out to retain the protection against new viruses.

14   Disaster recovery plans

An unexpected disaster can put an entire computer system out of action. For large organisations, a disaster might involve damage from a terrorist attack. There could also be threats from fire and flood damage. A disaster might simply be a software or hardware breakdown within a system.

Disaster recovery planning involves assessing what disasters might occur that would pose a serious threat to the organisation, and trying to ensure that alternative arrangements are available in the event that a disaster occurs.

In the case of a computer system for a clearing bank, this would mean having an entire back-up computer system in place that could be brought into operation if a disaster puts the main system out of action.

Not all organisations have extensive disaster recovery plans. Certainly, however, back-up copies of major data files should be kept, so that in the event that the main files are destroyed, the data can be re-created with the back-up files.

Conclusion

This relatively lengthy chapter has provided the background to maintaining the security and integrity of computer systems. The need to comply with legislation and implement appropriate controls to guard against specific risks facing an organisation's computer systems has also been discussed.

The following table provides a summary of measures for dealing with risks to systems.

Potential threat	*Counter measure*
Physical damage, due to fire or flooding. Also damage caused by physical conditions such as dust, heat, cold, humidity, power failures, magnetic fields	Make sure that the procedures in event of a fire are well documented and that staff are trained in what to do. Provide fire extinguishers and smoke/heat detectors, fire-doors. Obtain insurance cover. Computer equipment might be located in a segregated area in which air conditioning and dust controls operate effectively. Static control mats and uninterrupted power supplies can be used. Off-site facilities can be pre-arranged to cater for the possibility of total destruction of the in-house computer equipment. Off-site back-up copies of data files should be maintained.
Damage caused by human interference, such as unauthorised access resulting in theft, piracy, vandalism	Access to the computer room should be restricted to authorised personnel only. Doors to the secure area should be locked and require either PIN code, conventional key, combination locks, or electronic keys to open them.

Potential threat	Counter measure
	Closed circuit TV and security guards are also possible solutions.
	The hardware itself can be physically or electronically tagged to sound an alarm if it is removed from the building. Where possible hardware can be locked down, or locked in cabinets.
Operational problems, such as program bugs and user operational errors	Thorough testing of new programs should help to minimise the risk of software errors (bugs) although it is unlikely that testing will eliminate the risk of software errors entirely. The procedure to follow in the event of finding a bug should be clearly documented and made known to all the staff .
	Strict operating procedures should be followed to control and reduce the number of user errors. Adequate training of all staff members will help.
Data corruption, e.g. viruses, hackers	Sentinel software, such as virus checkers should be run and updated regularly to prevent corruption of the system by viruses. Firewall software should provide protection against unauthorised access to a system from the Internet.
	Passwords and user numbers can be used to limit the chances of unauthorised people accessing the system via the public communications network.
Data theft, e.g. fraud, industrial espionage, loss of confidentiality	Data encryption techniques allow only those individuals with the encryption key to view the data in an understandable form.
	Passwords and user numbers can be used to limit the chances of unauthorised people accessing the system via the public communications network.
	Physical access controls should also apply here.
Human resource risks, e.g. repetitive strain injury, headaches and eye strain from VDUs, risk of accidents caused by tripping over loose wires	The Health and Safety Officer should ensure that the work area is free from all avoidable hazards, for example all cables should be in ducts and should not run across an office floor.
	Careful ergonomic design of workstations should help to reduce the risk of repetitive strain injury. Anti-glare screens will reduce eye strain.

The Data Protection Act 1998

1   What is personal data? (1.1)

2   What prohibitions are imposed on the transfer of data? (1.4)

The Computer Misuse Act 1990

3   What were the new crimes created by this Act? (2.3)

Copyright law and software contracts

4   In what way is the Copyright, Designs and Patents Act of 1988
relevant to computer software? (3)

Physical threats

5   What are the main physical threats to computer systems? (6.1)

Countering physical threats

6   How can an organisation protect its computer systems and data against
fraud? (7.6)

Passwords

7   What are the inherent problems associated with the use of passwords? (9.1)

A logical access system

8   What is a logical access system? (10.1)

Hacking

9   What controls may be implemented to prevent hacking? (11.2, 11.3)

Encryption

10   What is encryption? (12)

Computer viruses

11   What is a computer virus? (13.1)

EXAM-TYPE
QUESTION 1

Data security

(a)   An organisation may hold sensitive data on computer. A logical access system
is essential to protect such data. What is a logical access system, and how does
it work?   **(8 marks)**

(b)   Explain the meaning of the following terms relating to data security:

    (i)   encryption   **(4 marks)**

    (ii)   hacking   **(4 marks)**

    (iii)   computer viruses   **(4 marks)**

(Total: 20 marks)

Security factors and the Computer Misuse Act

(a)   You are an outside consultant specialising in computer security brought in by an organisation to advise on the security aspects relating to a new computer centre.

   (i)   What potential physical threats would you make your client aware of; what precautionary measures would you suggest; and what techniques would you propose should be implemented to control access to the computer centre?   **(6 marks)**

   (ii)   You also feel that a contingency plan is an essential aspect of the new computing facility.

            Explain to the client the purpose of such a plan, how it might be developed, and the standby options that are available.   **(8 marks)**

(b)   The *Computer Misuse Act* came into force in August 1990. What are the three offences that the Act defines?   **(6 marks)**

(Total: 20 marks)

Chapter 16
QUALITY ASSURANCE AND TESTING

The specification and production of software, like all human endeavours, can be affected by errors or incompetence. The costs that can result from errors in software systems can be large in both financial and human terms. Software errors can potentially threaten the financial health of enterprises or the physical health of human beings.

The disciplines of quality assurance and testing are employed to ensure the delivery of software systems of known and reproducible quality.

Objectives

By the time you have finished this chapter you should be able to:

- define the characteristics of a quality software product
- define the terms: quality management, quality assurance and quality control
- describe the V model and its application to quality assurance and testing
- explain the limitations of software testing
- participate in the quality assurance of deliverables in requirement specification using formal static testing methods
- explain the role of standards and, in particular, their application in quality assurance
- briefly describe the task of unit testing in bespoke systems development
- define the scope of systems testing
- distinguish between dynamic and static testing
- use a cause-effect chart (decision table) to develop an appropriate test script for a representative systems test
- explain the scope and importance of performance testing and usability testing
- define the scope and procedures of user acceptance testing
- describe the potential use of automated tools to support systems and user acceptance testing.

1 Quality software

1.1 What is quality software?

The aim of all software developers is to produce high quality software. However, what is meant by quality software may vary from developer to developer or between what the user expects from the software and what the developer is prepared to provide.

Whatever view is taken regarding software quality, the following characteristics will normally apply to it:

Reasonably bug-free. It is difficult, if not impossible, to ensure that complex software written today is 100% bug free. However, there is an expectation that software will perform its main activities accurately without any errors occurring.

Delivered on time. Organisations will rely on delivery dates for software, either because their systems need changing (due to changes in tax laws, for example) or because revised systems are needed to implement specific client services or other objectives. Delivering that software on time will therefore help organisations to meet

KEY POINT

Quality software is:

- reasonably bug-free
- delivered on time
- written within budget
- meets initial specification
- meets quality control standards.

their obligations and objectives. If software is delivered ahead of schedule, the service will be perceived to be significantly better.

Meets initial specification. Software is written to meet a requirements specification. The purchaser of the software will expect that the specification is adhered to when the final product is delivered. Meeting the specification provides good evidence that the software production has been correctly planned with appropriate focus onto user requirements.

Meets quality control standards. In other words, the software has been written to meet appropriate quality control standards, set by the ISO (International Organisation for Standards) and the IEEE (Institute of Electrical and Electronics Engineers). Meeting these standards provides good evidence that the software will be robust and adhere to the initial specification.

The actual mix of objectives to be met may vary depending on the software being written and the user groups interested in maintaining quality. For example, accountants may require that quality software is written within budget, while users require that quality software is user-friendly, providing an easy-to-understand user interface. Whatever the mix of objectives, the software must do the job expected of it, meeting the software specification originally developed.

2 Quality, quality and more quality

Quality is maintained at three different capacities within an organisation, namely:

- quality management

- quality assurance

- quality control.

2.1 Quality management

Quality management suggests a concern that the organisation's products or services meet their planned level of quality and perform to specifications.

2.2 Management role

Management has a duty to ensure that all tasks are completed consistently to a standard that meets the needs of the business. To achieve this they need to:

- set clear standards

- plan how to meet those standards

- track the quality achieved

- take action to improve quality where necessary.

Setting standards

To manage quality, everyone in the organisation needs to have a clear and shared understanding of the standards required. These standards will be set after taking account of:

- the quality expected by the customers

- the costs and benefits of delivering different degrees of quality

- the impact of different degrees of quality on:

  - the customers and their needs

  - contribution to departmental objectives

  - employee attitude and motivation.

Having decided on the standards these must be communicated to everyone concerned to ensure that the right standards are achieved. Documentation of the standards must be clear, specific, measurable and comprehensive.

Meeting the standards

Having decided on appropriate quality standards management should then:

- agree and document procedures and methods to meet the standards
- agree and document controls to ensure that the standards will be met
- agree and document responsibilities via job descriptions and terms of reference
- prepare and implement training plans for employees to ensure they are familiar with the standards, procedures, controls and their responsibilities.

Tracking the quality

After the process to achieve quality has been set up, an information system to monitor the quality should be set up. This is called quality control.

When a good system to track the quality has been achieved, it can be used constructively to improve quality and work on problem areas.

Employees within the organisation have a huge influence on the quality of their work and to gain their commitment and support the management should:

- publish the quality being achieved
- meet regularly with the staff involved to discuss the quality being achieved as well as the vulnerabilities and priorities as they see them. They should also agree specific issues and action points for them to work on to improve quality
- encourage ideas from the staff about improvements and consider introducing short-term suggestion schemes.

Structured walkthroughs

A review technique that is commonly used at various stages throughout the project is a *structured walkthrough.*

It is a means by which the project team may undertake a review and determination of the current state of the project in respect of the time schedules being met and the expenditure of project budget.

The review is designed to detect and remove any errors within the project to date without casting blame in any direction within the project team. It enables errors in design, logic and coding to be detected early. The review is a good communication vehicle for project team members.

In essence it is a review of the work done by the developer and by other project members (excluding the organisation's management). The developer sets up the walkthrough and determines the members that should be present. Each member receives the review material at least 4–6 days in advance of the meeting.

Walkthroughs are sometimes used to complete a phase in the development cycle and act as a condition of entry into the next phase of the cycle.

The timing at which the walkthrough is completed is critical. If it is completed too early within the project's life, there is not enough material available to make sense of the project status. If completed too late, too many unalterable decisions may already have been made.

There are four types of walkthrough:

- *Specification walkthrough*. The functional requirements of a computer system as expressed in the specification are reviewed.

- *Design walkthrough*. If the functional requirements have been incorrectly stated, it is important to find a solution to the problem.

- *Code walkthrough*. This reviews the program listing and could uncover program analysis or design problems.

- *Test walkthrough*. This is to ensure the adequacy of the test data for the system.

2.3 Quality assurance

KEY POINT

Quality assurance:

- establishing standards

- establishing procedures to those standards

- monitoring quality, work-in-progress and finished products

- act when quality falls below standard.

Quality assurance is the title given to the more traditional view of quality. It may be defined as the process of:

- establishing standards of quality for a product or service

- establishing procedures or production methods that ought to ensure that these required standards of quality are met in a suitably high proportion of cases

- monitoring actual quality

- taking control action when actual quality falls below standard.

Quality assurance is the term used where a supplier guarantees the quality of goods supplied and allows the customer access while the goods are being manufactured. This is usually done through supplier quality assurance (SQA) officers, who control the specification of the goods supplied.

KEY POINT

Supplier quality assurance officers control the specification of the goods supplied.

Some companies follow Japanese practice and use supervisors, workpeople or quality circles to control suppliers' quality. These representatives or the SQA officer may enter suppliers' plant, to verify that production is to the correct specification, working tolerances, material and labour standards. For example, the Ministry of Defence would reserve the right to ensure that defence contractors produce to specification, since defective work could mean the failure of a multi-million pound aircraft, loss of trained pilots and possibly ground crew as well as damage to civilian life and property. Likewise, a weapons system failure could have disastrous consequences.

One great advantage of SQA is that it may render possible reduction of the in-house quality control headcount, since there will be no need to check incoming materials or sub-assemblies or components.

2.4 Quality control

KEY POINT

Quality control is concerned with maintaining quality standards, usually through procedures to check quality of bought-in materials, work-in-progress and finished goods

Quality control is concerned with maintaining quality standards. There are usually procedures to check quality of bought-in materials, work-in-progress and finished goods. Sometimes one or all of these functions is the responsibility of the research and development department on the premise that production should not self-regulate its own quality.

Statistical quality control through sampling techniques is commonly used to reduce costs and production interruptions. On some occasions, where quality assurance has been given, customers have the contractual right to visit a manufacturer unannounced and carry out quality checks.

In the past, failure to screen quality successfully has resulted in rejections, re-work and scrap, all of which add to manufacturing costs. Modern trends in industry of competition, mass production and increasing standards of quality requirements have resulted in a thorough reappraisal of the problem and two important points have emerged:

1   It is necessary to single out and remove the causes for poor quality goods before production instead of waiting for the end result. Many companies have instigated 'zero defects' programmes following the Japanese practice of eradicating poor quality as early in the chain as possible and insisting on strict quality adherence at every stage. As Crosby points out in his book Quality is Free, this is cost effective since customer complaints reduce dramatically.

2   The co-ordination of all activities from the preparation of the specification, through to the purchasing and inspection functions and right up to the function of delivery of the finished product, is essential.

It is accepted that it is not possible to achieve perfection in products because of the variations in raw material quality, operating skills, different types of machines used, wear and tear, etc. Quality control attempts to ascertain the amount of variation from perfect that can be expected in any operation. If this variation is acceptable according to engineering requirements, then production must be established within controlled limits and if the variation is too great then corrective action must be taken to bring it within acceptable limits.

2.5   The V model and its place in quality assurance and testing

The V model was studied in Chapter 12 and is now considered again in the context of quality. It is illustrated in the figure below. 'V' refers to the two legs of the diagram. System design runs down the left leg of the V and follows testing back up the right leg. You will be familiar with most of the stages in the design and implementation of systems from studies in Chapter 7, where the SDLC and different design methodologies were discussed.

The software development cycle

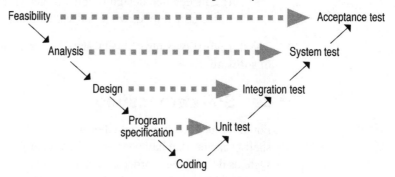

2.6   Three quality links

The V model illustrates three quality links that are established between the design and testing/implementation phases.

(a)   The first quality link is between the feasibility and analysis sections of the model (the specification) and the system testing and acceptance testing section of the model. The specification provides the detailed requirements of the system, while the verified system includes the final user acceptance testing and final handover of the system. The purpose of acceptance testing at this stage is to ensure that the original requirements have been met. Checking that this is the case provides some assurance regarding the quality of the final product, although the quality of the underlying software may still be in doubt.

(b)   The second quality link is between the *design* and the *integrated software testing* sections of the model. During the design stage for software, the specific objectives for that software will be stated along with the different software modules that will have to be written. The software is then written and the different modules tested individually and together to ensure that they work correctly. The quality check then occurs when the integrated software is compared to the specification for that software. The tested software should meet the initial design; if this is not the case then amendments to the software will be required.

(c) The third quality link is between the *individual program specification* and the *unit testing* sections of the model. This check tries to ensure that the individual software modules have been written and tested correctly. The overall design for the software is broken down into the different software modules. Each module is written, tested and debugged and then compared to the actual module design. As with the other quality checks, the module design, and the actual software produced should match with each other. If there are any differences, then the software module will need to be amended.

Following the V model therefore provides three quality checks in the writing of software, which hopefully ensures that the final software package is as error free as possible. One of the main strengths of this model is that it follows the normal hierarchy of software specifications, namely:

(i) The functional specification is a precise description of the required behaviour of the software. That is, it describes what the software should do rather than how the software achieves its goals and may also specify constraints on how this may be achieved. This separation is often described by saying that a functional specification defines the functionality of the software.

(ii) The design specification, which describes the architecture of a design that implements the functional specification. Components within the software and the relationship between them will be described in this document.

(iii) The detailed design specifications, which describe how each component in the software, down to individual units, is to be implemented.

The three quality control checks above correspond to these three levels of specification of software.

3   Software testing

For all bespoke systems, whether written in-house or externally, and for any off-the-shelf packages that have been modified in any way, testing is an integral part of the systems development process. The main standard for software testing is contained in the ANSI/IEEE standard 829-1983 – *Standard for Software Testing Documentation*. Some software testing may also be performed by computer, in which case the abbreviation CAST (computer aided software testing) may be encountered.

Testing broadly follows the structure of the V model, although some testing systems (which we follow in this text) do recognise four distinct stages of testing, as outlined below.

3.1   Stages of testing

Testing can be broken down into four basic stages:

KEY POINT

Four stages of software testing:

- test the logic

- test each program with data

- test system as a whole

- acceptance testing.

1   Unit testing

The technique of dry running can be used to make sure that the logic that has been set down by the analyst is correct. The programmer or analyst will trace by hand the progress of a number of sets of data through the structure diagrams or program flow charts. If all data produces the results that are expected, the individual programs can be written. The individual program will also be tested 'live' with test data in isolation from other programs.

2   Integration testing

Each program is thoroughly tested with test data as above and also tested with several other related programs. As explained earlier the test data is carefully selected to make sure that all sections of the programs are working correctly. The testing process is carefully documented – with the data being tested, expected results, actual results and any action taken as a result of the test being recorded. The test documentation produced is an important part of the overall system documentation, being especially vital for system maintenance.

Integration testing should cover:

- checking the interface with other programs and systems work
- correct functioning of feasibility and validity checks on input data
- correct functioning of branching and looping
- impossible values (e.g. negative stock) which causes confusion
- adequate storage and buffer areas
- proper batch control totals
- the correct form of the output
- any operational problems in running the programs.

3   System testing

Once it has been established that individual and groups of programs are working correctly, the system must be tested as a whole. This is an equally important task, and the results should be documented in the same way as those for the testing of programs. It is not only the software that is evaluated during the system testing process, it is also important to test operating procedures, staffing levels, etc.

System testing must be carried out prior to installation (off-line testing) and immediately after implementation (on-line testing). The more off-line testing that is carried out, the lower the risk of failure during implementation. However, off-line testing cannot possibly find all of the problems with a system, as some will only appear during live operation.

The system testing extends beyond program testing to include:

- interfaces between programs
- suitability of input documents
- any practical input problems
- availability of information when required
- ability to modify data
- procedures to deal with special situations
- audit requirements
- ability to handle seasonal peaks
- viability of hardware
- practicability of operating procedures.

Testing is normally carried out by feeding test data into the system, and then comparing the actual results with the desired results as the following figure illustrates:

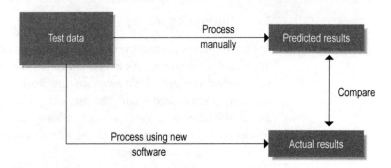

Test data can be artificial or taken from actual transactions.

It is important that at some time during testing:

- data is processed through all stages

- the data is of sufficient volume to represent actual transactions

- all the processing is carried out by the users, rather then the project team

- all extremes of data are used to test the program suite.

4 Acceptance testing

The earlier stages of testing can be carried out by the systems development team. The users of the system must be involved at the last stage to ensure that the system is usable for them. It is just as important to ensure that the users will accept a system as it is to make sure that it performs to its specification. The users operate the system with test data, with their use of the system being monitored closely, and the users reporting on their experiences.

The involvement of users in the development process and the use of prototyping can cut down the problems that may be revealed during acceptance testing.

The producers of software packages also need to assure themselves that their software will be well received by their customers. Pre-production copies are sent to selected companies for their appraisal. Not only does this enable the software house to assess how popular the package is likely to be, it also allows any remaining bugs to be identified and eliminated. This process is often called beta testing.

3.2 Dynamic and static testing

Software testing can be carried out in a dynamic or static environment.

Dynamic testing is the process of evaluating a system or component of that system based upon its behaviour during execution.

Static testing is the process of evaluating a system or component of that system without executing the program or system.

The difference between the two testing methods is that dynamic testing means the program is actually running, while static testing is carried out by reviewing the program code, i.e. the program is not running.

There is a place for both types of testing within software development. A static test has the benefit that the program can be viewed in isolation. Other programs cannot affect it and it is not reacting with other programs. Many logical and code errors can be found by simply reviewing the code prior to running.

However, dynamic testing is essential before any software is implemented. It is only in live testing that the actual results of running the program can be seen and any potential conflicts within the program or between the program and other programs on the same computer be identified. Dynamic testing can last for days, and may involve users running the software to try to isolate as many bugs and errors as possible before the final software release date.

3.3 Overview of testing methods

As noted above, static testing methods mean testing the software, but not actually executing that software. The aim of testing is to ensure that the software is as bug-free as possible, while also meeting the initial design specification.

The design specification to be tested may have up to three different layers of documentation:

- the functional specification, which provides a precise description of what the software should do
- the design specification which explains how the functional specification will actually work
- the detailed design specification, which describes how each part of the software will be implemented.

Each element of the design specification has its own testing level:

- **unit testing** where each part of the software is tested to ensure that the detailed design for that unit has been correctly implemented
- **software integration testing** where groups of units of the software are tested together until all the units are working with their related units.
- **system testing** where the software is integrated into the final product and a check made to ensure that the functionality defined in the functional specification is actually available.

3.4 Static testing plan

The design of tests for software follows the same basic principles as actually writing the software. Testing will be carried out on the overall strategic objectives of the software, followed by lower-level tests on the detailed design specifications being carried out later.

The steps that will normally be carried out in testing software for appropriate quality using static testing methods will normally include:

1. **Formulate a testing strategy.** This provides a statement of the overall approach to testing, identifying what tests are to be applied and which techniques or tools are to be used. The test strategy itself is normally part of the overall quality plan in producing the software.

2. **Developing a test plan.** The plan states what items are to be tested and at what level they will be tested. The sequence of testing and the test environment will also be explained. In this situation, the test environment is a review of the documentation, rather than a live test.

3. **Design the tests to be used.** Using a static testing system, the tests that can be used are relatively limited. One of the main tests will be reviewing the program code for functional and/or logic errors.

4. **Carry out the tests**. Each test will be stated as a test procedure, specifying the exact processes to be followed in carrying out the tests. This type of detail is required to ensure that the test is valid and repeatable.

5. **Document results of tests.** Any errors found in reviewing the software will be formally documented. This provides a record of errors as well as a review sheet for programmers to check the completeness of clearing the errors found.

6. **Re-test.** Finally, the software may need to be re-tested to ensure that the errors found have been remedied.

3.5 Rules for software testing

As software is being tested, it is useful to remember the following rules:

- always test against a specification – testing without a specification implies that there is no need for the test as nothing of value is being tested
- document the testing process
- use different forms of testing techniques such as static and dynamic testing to provide a complete testing plan
- test positively, checking that the software does what it should do, and negatively, that it doesn't do what it shouldn't.
- have the right attitude to testing – it should be a challenge and not a chore.

3.6 Limitations of software testing

Although software is normally tested quite extensively, there are still some limitations in the testing methods and amount of testing that can be performed.

Limitations in software testing therefore include:

Not possible to test most software fully

It is not usually possible to test most software fully. For example, a standard of testing all paths through a program is achievable, but testing all combinations of paths through the program would probably not be achievable.

Not testing all possible values

Test data not testing all the possible types or values of data input that may occur within the system. For example, the range of data being tested may include values up to and including £999,999.99; because this appears to be the highest value that will be required in the system. However, in a few years, this value may be exceeded as values of transactions increase and inflation increases the overall price level. A broader range of values should be tested to ensure that the software can process them effectively and allow for future expansion of the system.

Inadequate error messages

Ensuring that all error messages contain adequate explanations of the error occurring. Many error messages are quite understandable to the program writers, but not necessarily to the users of the software. Users must be involved in the software testing to ensure that they can understand error messages and are aware of the appropriate action to take if an error does occur.

Not testing all the functionality of the software

The test plan may not cover all the functionality of the software. This may happen where software has been amended away from the initial specification, but inadequate documentation of those changes has been maintained. If the test plan is based on the initial specification then these changes will be omitted from the testing.

Inadequately documented testing process

The testing process is inadequately documented. This may occur, for example, due to human error or lack of complete documentation to record the tests actually taking place. The main risk is that errors in the software are not correctly recorded, and so those errors are not resolved prior to the software going forward to full system testing.

Inappropriate focus to the testing

Inappropriate focus to the testing. The software can be tested to check that it does what it should do rather than checking to ensure that it doesn't do what it shouldn't. Negative checking is as important as positive checking to ensure that the software responds appropriately to error situations or unusual data. For example, the need to allow for high value items was discussed above; although this is positive testing in that values above zero are expected. The software should also be tested to ensure that values below zero (values that are not expected) or alphabetical characters being entered into that particular field are actually rejected as being incorrect.

The basic rules of software testing noted earlier must be adhered to. Any attempt to rush testing is likely to result in failure, as errors in the software may not be detected.

4   Decision tables and test scripts

Decision tables are used as a method of recording in tabular form a decision-making process and the consequent actions. As we shall see they can be used to develop test scripts.

The decision table has four quadrants together with headings for the title and rule number and takes the following form:

Title	Rule number
Condition stub	Condition entry
Action stub	Action entry

Draw thick or double lines between the four quadrants.

1   The **condition stub** lists all the possible conditions that may exist within the system.

2   The **action stub** is a list of all the actions that may be taken depending upon the circumstances that may exist.

3   The **condition entry** section gives the various combinations of conditions that can exist in the system. Each combination (or rule) is equivalent to a particular route through a program flowchart.

4   The **action entry** indicates what action to take for each particular rule. It indicates what operation symbols appear on a particular route through a program flowchart.

4.1   Types of decision tables

There are three main types of decision tables:

1   **Limited entry** – in which a condition in the condition stub is phrased to provide a yes or no answer. The condition entry section has 'Y' or 'N' to indicate the condition. Only 'X' is entered into the action entry section to indicate the actions required.

2   **Extended entry** – in which various conditions are included in the condition entry section and the description of an action is given in the actions required.

3   **Mixed entry** – is a mixture of (1) and (2).

We will only consider the limited entry decision table in this text.

Example: Limited entry decision tables

William is a student studying for an accountancy examination. If it is Saturday he does not study, but goes out. On other nights when it is not raining, he goes jogging. On any other night he studies.

Produce a decision table for this situation.

Solution

(a) The conditions that affect his action are:

1   is it Saturday?

2   is it raining?

(b) These can be entered into the condition stub.

The actions that he might take are:

1   go out

2   go jogging

3   study for examination.

(c) Calculate the number of condition combinations. The maximum number is 2^n where n = the number of conditions calculated in (a). Here there will be 4 condition combinations, which is 2 squared. Draw one vertical column for each condition combination in the entry section of the table.

(d) Complete the condition entry section of the table by using the **halve-rule**. This means that you halve the number of columns in the entry section $(4 \div 2 = 2)$ and write Y twice and N twice in the condition entry. Then halve the number to write alternative Y and N in the condition entry.

(e) Complete the action entry writing an X if an action is appropriate to the condition combination.

Condition	1	2	3	4
Is it Saturday?	Y	Y	N	N
Is it raining?	Y	N	Y	N
Go out	X	X		
Go jogging				X
Study			X	

(f) Now remove redundant rules. These are identified by looking for columns where the action entries are the same, and the condition entries differ in one condition only.

This applies for rules 1 and 2, so that columns 1 and 2 above become column 1, column 3 above becomes column 2, etc:

Condition	1	2	3
Is it Saturday?	Y	N	N
Is it raining?	-	Y	N
Go out	X		
Go jogging			X
Study		X	

4.2 Advantages and disadvantages of decision tables

Advantages:

- **analysis** – the construction of a table is a valuable aid to analysing a decision-making process, to ensure that all possible conditions have been explored, and unnecessary conditions eliminated

- **communication** – a decision table is a convenient way of explaining a decision-making process to someone else

- **conciseness** – the decision-making process is represented clearly in the minimum of space. It is sometimes easier to see what decision is taken in particular conditions than by tracing the lines of a flowchart

- **convenience** – a decision table is easier to reproduce (e.g. using a spreadsheet) than a flowchart

- **standardisation** – standard forms can be used for the completion of decision tables far more readily than with flowcharts

- **programming** – some high-level languages allow a decision table to be converted into a program. This is possible only with limited entry tables

- **intelligibility** – the layman understands decision tables more easily than program flowcharts.

Disadvantages:

- they become cumbersome when the number of conditions and the number of rules is high

- they are not always suitable for planning programs. (Generally, program flowcharts are better.)

4.3 Using test scripts

A test script is a list of tests that new software must be attempted on new software prior to that software being accepted as finished. The script will provide information to the user or programmer, showing precisely the tests to undertake, and how to identify and record error conditions that may arise during the testing.

The actions to take from identifying errors during testing can be explained in the form of a decision table, as shown overleaf:

Example

An analyst investigating an order processing system has found the following rules are applied by order clerks:

All orders received by the company are checked by order clerks. The order clerk first calculates the value of the order and adds that value to the customer's current credit balance. If the credit balance exceeds the customer's credit limit then the current payment record is investigated. All such customers who have no invoices older than 30 days are notified that their order is 'on-hold' and that the order has been passed to the accounts manager who will contact them in the next three days. However, if the credit limit is exceeded and any invoice is older than 30 days, then the order is rejected. If the customer has not exceeded the credit limit then the current payment record is still investigated to find whether there are invoices older than 30 days. If there are, then the order is processed but a reminder letter is sent reminding the customer of the payment terms. In all other circumstances the order is processed without query.

(a) Construct a Decision Table for the process described above.

(b) Explain how such a table would assist in testing the software that will support this process.

Solution

(a)

	1	2	3	4
Exceed credit limit?	Y	Y	N	N
Any invoice > 30 days	Y	N	Y	N
Reject order	X			
On-hold order		X		
Pass to Accounts Manager		X		
Process order			X	X
Send reminder letter			X	

(b) Defining test cases (or test scripts) is an important element of testing. When testing a process (such as part (a) of this question) it is important to define all the possible permutations of the conditions and predict the outcomes in advance of testing. This is what the decision table has achieved. Four different test cases have been defined and the required outcomes have been marked in each column with the letter X. Each of these cases will be executed in testing and the actual outcomes compared with the predicted ones.

5 The role of standards

5.1 Standards used in software testing

There are various standards that are used concerning the writing and testing of software. Within the UK, the British Standards Institution initially set many standards, although worldwide, other standards are also available developed by the International Standards Organisation (ISO) and the Institute of Electrical and Electronics Engineers (IEEE).

The ISO 9000 family of standards concern quality systems and are assessed by external auditors. They actually apply to many kinds of production and manufacturing organisations, not simply software development.

ISO 9000 is more properly referred to as BS EN ISO 9000, the BS indicating that it is endorsed by the British Standard Institution (BSI), and the EN indicating that it is endorsed by the European Committee for Standardization (CEN).

Quality management standards began in the UK with BS 5750 in 1979. This was reissued in 1994, in slightly modified form, as BS EN ISO 9000 which had three parts: ISO 9001, 9002 and 9003.

The 1994 version has been entirely superseded by the 2000 version. The numbers 9002 and 9003 are no longer used.

The family includes four principal standards.

- ISO 9000:2000. *Quality management systems. Fundamentals and vocabulary.* This describes basic concepts and specifies the terminology for quality management systems.

- ISO 9001:2000. *Quality management systems. Requirements.* This specifies the requirements for a quality management system where an organisation needs to demonstrate its ability to provide products that fulfil customer and applicable regulatory requirements and aim to enhance customer satisfaction.

If an organisation wishes to obtain independent certification of its quality system it will be audited and assessed according to the requirements set out here.

- ISO 9004:2000. *Quality management systems. Guidelines for performance improvements.* This is a more detailed version of ISO 9001:2000: it includes (word for word) all the key sections of ISO 9001:2000 but it adds further notes explaining

KEY POINT

ISO 9000:2000 standards:

- ISO 9000: 2000: *Quality management systems. Fundamentals and vocabulary*

- ISO 9001: 2000: *Quality management systems. Requirements.*

- ISO 9004: 2000 *Quality management systems. Guidelines for performance improvements.*

- ISO 19011: *Guidelines on Quality and/or Environmental Management Systems Auditing*

the requirements in more detail and giving examples. It is meant to be used for guidance purposes, not for certification.

- ISO 19011. *Guidelines on Quality and/or Environmental Management Systems Auditing.*

The IEEE standards tend to focus on the actual testing of software, not the initial development. There are many standards covering a wide variety of situations, but some of the main ones are:

- IEEE 829 – 1998 *Standard for Software Test Documentation*
- IEEE 1008 – 1987 *Standard for Software Unit Testing*
- IEEE 1012 – 1998 *Standard for Software Verification and Validation.*

5.2 Performance testing and usability testing

Performance and stress testing

Performance testing evaluates the compliance of a system or component with specified performance requirements.(IEEE).

Performance testing can be extended into **Stress Testing**, which tests the software under increasing workload demands. The initial specification for the software will provide some guidance concerning the numbers of transactions to be placed through that software. However, demands on software tend to increase over time, so it is useful to know exactly how many transactions the software will actually cope with before it 'falls over' or breaks.

In stress testing, the number of transactions is increased until the software effectively breaks. Checking the total number provides a good guide to the limits of the software. This type of testing is frequently used on web sites to try and determine the number of 'hits' that a site can cope with before it breaks. Popular sites must be able to cope with thousands of hits an hour. Stress testing is extremely important in commercial web sites; if the website becomes unavailable due to volume of hits, then the company cannot make any sales!

Usability testing

Usability testing checks the ease with which users can learn and use a product. Clearly this is subjective, and will depend on the targeted end-user or customer. User interviews, surveys, video recordings of user sessions, and other techniques can be used. Programmers and testers are usually not appropriate as usability testers.

User acceptance testing

User Acceptance Testing is an end-to-end test of a system or application, involving the end user, which verifies that the system provides the required business functionality and correctly produces the expected business information. It also allows the user to test the non-functional, or performance, requirements before accepting the system.

User acceptance testing is normally carried out towards the end of the development of the software. Within the V model (see above) user acceptance testing comes after module and systems testing. The main objective of the testing is to ensure that the system specification has been met in the software. Users will have a test script and test data to run against the new software, and note errors or deviations where the output does not meet the original specification.

Where differences from the specification are found, then difficult decisions may need to be made concerning amending the software, or accepting it 'as is' with an incomplete specification. Amendments at this stage may be difficult, hence the decision to accept the differences. However, if the V or similar model of systems development has been followed, then situations where the software does not meet the specification should be rare.

6   Use of automation in systems testing

If all testing had to be performed manually, then this would be very time consuming and quite boring (imagine pressing the same key on a keyboard every few seconds for an entire day to run the same program!). Fortunately, a lot of testing can be automated, saving considerable amounts of time, and providing a more reliable testing environment. The results of automated testing can also be stored and evaluated statistically to identify trends which could otherwise be missed.

Automated testing means writing a test script which will then automatically run tests such as regression tests on the software that is being developed. Specific activities that the automated testing tool will be able to perform include:

- Record and replay test scripts as required.

- Track, report, and chart all the information about a quality assurance testing process.

- Detect and repair some of the problems associated with the software being tested.

- View and edit your test scripts while you are recording.

- Use the same script, without modifications, to test an application on multiple software platforms.

Testing can be carried out by the same organisation that is writing the software; however there are also some specialist software testing organisations.

Conclusion

This chapter has explained the importance of testing software to ensure it is as error free as possible, and outlined some of the main techniques that are used to carry out that testing. It is unlikely that you will have practical experience of testing, so ensure that you understand the principles of testing, and can spot weaknesses in any testing system you may find in an examination question.

Quality software

1   What characteristics normally apply to quality software? (1.1)

Quality, quality and more quality

2   What is quality control? (2.4)

3   Draw a picture of the lifecycle, linking the testing stages with the development stages. (2.5)

The role of standards

4   Why are standards needed in software testing? (3)

Software testing

(a)   Two stages of computer software testing are:
- systems testing

- user acceptance testing.

Briefly describe each of these two stages.   **(10 marks)**

(b)   Certain deliverables in the development life cycle cannot be easily tested because they are in the form of written documentation. This is particularly true of deliverables in the analysis stage, such as dataflow diagrams and entity-relationship models (logical data structures).

Explain how the correctness and quality of these deliverables can be checked.

(5 marks)
(Total: 15 marks)

For the answer to this question, see the 'Answers' section at the end of the book.

Chapter 17

IMPLEMENTATION METHODS AND ISSUES

This chapter discusses the implementation of a new system and the testing that can take place to determine the success (or otherwise) of implementing that system. The different implementation strategies are discussed, along with the main differences between parallel running and direct changeover. The various reports that can be produced following implementation are also mentioned.

Objectives

By the time you have finished this chapter you should be able to:

- plan for data conversion and creation

- discuss the need for training and suggest different methods of delivering such training

- describe the type of documentation needed to support implementation and comment on ways of effectively organising and presenting this documentation

- distinguish between parallel running and direct changeover and comment on the advantages and disadvantages of each.

1 System implementation strategy

1.1 Introduction

The implementation stage of a computer system can be considered to be a project in its own right. In some very large organisations, some analysts actually specialise in implementation activities. It is the stage when the theoretical design becomes a working, practical system.

It is the user department that carries the major workload here. Without careful planning, the result is always chaotic. This is the most crucial stage in the attainment of a new, successful system and in providing user confidence in it.

It is normal to encounter a variety of problems at the implementation stage of a computer system; the more complex the system, the greater the likely number of problems.

To some extent the problems will be unavoidable. Many, however, can be avoided or lessened by proper planning and control.

The implementation procedures should be designed so that:

- most problems are anticipated and avoided

- the unavoidable problems can be managed.

The prerequisites of implementation are:

- the systems specification must be complete

- programs must be fully tested

- planning must be complete

- the required resources must be available or provided for
- operation techniques must be fully planned
- a fallback system must be fully planned.

1.2   Implementation tasks

The tasks involved in any normal implementation process are given in the diagram below:

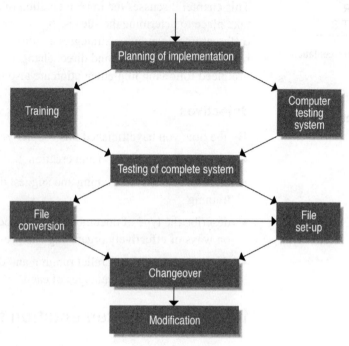

In greater detail, the activities below are linked to the major tasks in the diagram:
- allocating premises
- hardware commissioning
- design/coding/testing of programs
- designing new forms
- staff training
- writing instruction manuals
- production of complete set of systems documentation
- testing for user acceptance
- changeover planning
- file conversion
- system testing.

1.3   Staff training and education

People are a vital part of any system. The introduction of a new system must mean changes in roles and relationships and, by their nature, most people resist change.

If the system being introduced is opposed by some or most staff, it is less likely to be successful. A new system may involve the recruitment of new staff, redundancy, or the need for new skills for existing staff.

It is part of the task of the project team to ensure that user staff are involved in the new system from the earliest design stages. Where their jobs change, then the nature of the changes and details of the necessary training should be explained. If redundancies are anticipated, then these should be made clear to staff at an early stage.

The project team should therefore:

- arrange presentations to staff on the use of the new system and the effect this will have on the work. A positive approach is necessary to help alleviate any fears concerning their own employment. Questions should be encouraged

- a training schedule should be prepared and circulated in order that everyone is aware of what is taking place and when.

Management's role is to handle the other staff ramifications of the implementation. They should:

- encourage staff to apply for any new jobs created rather then pressurise them into re-training

- provide counselling services to discuss individual fears regarding their future. Re-training in other areas should also be discussed

- ensure staff are re-trained without loss of pay or pressure of work put upon them.

It is useful to send senior staff not directly involved in the operation on computer appreciation courses if they are unfamiliar with such systems. It may also be necessary to recruit specialist staff.

Education complements training: it explains the background to the changes and the reasons for them, providing the foundation for confidence in, and commitment to, the new system. A good deal of educational effort goes into the presentation of seminars to management under such titles as 'What every manager should know about the computer'.

Training is dealt with in more detail later in this chapter.

1.4 Testing

Testing includes both the testing of the individual programs, and the testing of the whole system as an operating entity. Faults not found during testing will reveal themselves more expensively later in the operation. Therefore the testing must be comprehensive. Systems testing was explained in detail in Chapter 16 of this text.

1.5 Data conversion

Most commercial systems are file-based, depending on the processing of one or more files. These files must be created before the system is operational. File conversion is the process of moving data from files in the existing system into files in the new system. These files could contain different information, and will be in a different format. File conversion might be from a manual system to a computer system, or from an existing computer system to a new computer system.

Creating the basic data files is an important but often time-consuming task. There are five different scenarios:

1   **The data is available in hard copy.** This data must be collated onto input forms and then entered into the system. This process is likely to be time-consuming and labour intensive and may require the hiring of temporary staff to ensure that data entry is done in a timely manner. If the data entry is on-line, it is often better to use the temporary staff to carry out the ongoing work while the existing staff enter the data. This helps with training and helps test the system.

2   **The data is in hard copy form but some data is missing or incomplete.** If this data is crucial it must be researched or estimated.

- data is partially available on magnetic media

- part or all of the data is contained in a central database.

3   **The data is fully available on magnetic media from existing applications.** This is the easiest situation to deal with, although it is still important to validate or verify the data after it has been converted.

4   **The data is partially available on magnetic media.** The additional fields should be researched or estimated as in the scenario above.

5   **Part or all of the data is contained in a central database.** The data dictionary must be updated as appropriate.

The main stages are shown in the following figure:

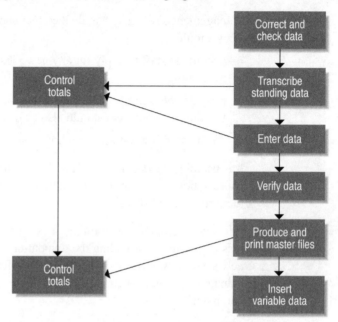

The diagram shows standing (or reference) data being set up first. This produces a skeleton file and can often be done well in advance of the changeover date, as the reference data is static. Only the variable data remains to be dealt with at the changeover date. Skeleton files therefore help to reduce the time pressure of file conversion.

Dead records will be identified and eliminated before conversion. The data must be as 'clean' and as accurate as possible before being printed into the new system.

It is essential that adequate reconciliation details are maintained to agree the old system's control total with that produced by the new system. Control over conversion can be by:

1   **One-for-one checking.** This involves checking each record on the old system to a record on the new system.

2   **Sample checking**. Where numbers are too large for one-for-one checking, statistically monitored samples can be checked.

3   **Control total checking.** This involves checking the total number of records from the old to the new system.

4   **Programmed checking.** This involves using a computer program to assist in the conversion, e.g. when converting from a bureau system to an in-house system, a computer program might be used to handle the conversion and reformatting of master files.

When the file conversion is from an existing computer system to a new computer system, program routines will be available (in the case of application software packages) or can be written (in the case of bespoke systems) that will do some of the file conversion automatically.

1.6   Going live

The key moment is when the new system is introduced and goes live.

This moment must be carefully fixed and agreed by all parties involved. It is essential that at this stage:

- all staff training is complete
- all systems are fully tested
- all documents are available for use
- the cut-off procedures on the old system have been properly established.

Accountants will readily appreciate how, unless there is a proper cut-off, transactions could be processed twice, or missed entirely.

It is essential that during the early stages after going live, the new system be carefully monitored to ensure that the data is being properly processed.

There are four approaches to achieving these objectives. Note that only parallel running and direct changeover are in the syllabus.

1   **Parallel running.** This involves running the new system in parallel with the old system and making a comparison of the results of both. If the new system performs exactly the same as the old system as far as control details are concerned, then the go-ahead can be given for live running. Despite the theoretical advantages, this is difficult to manage and nowadays is rarely used.

2   **Direct changeover**. This involves the direct changeover from the old to the new system without any parallel running. Direct changeover is often the only practicable approach to changeover although there is clearly the danger that the new system will not work correctly and that the organisation will be in serious trouble. It is essential that the method of control be clearly established.

3   **Phased changeover** is where a complete section of the existing system is run on the new system. This entails a greater degree of safety than a direct changeover with less disruption at any time. The section chosen needs to be a complete section. If that part is successfully run, then other parts of the existing system will be transferred over to be run on the new system, until eventually the whole of the system has been changed over.

For example, if the accounting system were being computerised, first convert the sales ledger. If successful, then convert the stock system and so on.

4   **Pilot operation.** Here, the changeover is carried out department-by-department or branch-by-branch. Thus, if a manual sales ledger is being converted, it might be carried out geographically area-by-area.

The actual approach used will depend on the specific application and the existing systems. Direct changeover is simple but can be risky. Other methods are more complex and can sometimes create the problems they are designed to avoid.

1.7   Advantages and disadvantages of some changeover methods

Parallel running

Advantages

Parallel running provides a safer systems changeover environment because a backup system (that is, the old system) is available should the new system fail. Provision of the backup will help to minimise any disruption.

The changeover method is also safer because the output from the new system can be verified as being correct by comparing it to the output from the old system. Direct changeover does not provide this facility as only one system is ever running.

Disadvantages

The disadvantages of parallel running revolve around the additional cost and work involved with this changeover method. Additional costs result from having to run two systems in parallel with additional staffing and other resources that this may entail.

There will also be an extra workload imposed on staff. In addition to this costing the organisation more in terms of wages, employees may also become overworked, resulting in errors being made in using the computer system. It may be difficult to identify whether errors actually relate to system weaknesses or human error caused by tiredness.

Because parallel running provides a back-up, initial testing of the system may be less rigorous, as there is the assumption that processing errors will be identified during the parallel run.

Staff may not commit fully to the new system because they have the old one to fall back on.

Direct changeover

Advantages

Direct changeover is one of the quickest methods of systems changeover; basically processing stops on the old system and then immediately starts on the new system. There may be a brief delay while data is transferred between the two systems.

Direct changeover minimises the cost of systems changeover. As there is only one system running at a time, there will be a reduced requirement to pay staff overtime or to hire in temporary staff to help with running two systems at once.

Disadvantages

The main disadvantage with direct changeover is what to do should the system fail. As there will be no backup system in place, the cost of rectification in financial terms as well as loss of business can be extremely high.

However, direct changeover may be the only possible method of changing systems. For example, if running two separate systems would be confusing, then direct changeover will be used.

2   Training

2.1   The need for training

Training is needed for two reasons:

- if staff are not adequately trained, they will not operate the system correctly or efficiently

- if staff feel that they are being asked to perform tasks that are outside their capabilities, they may become demoralised and alienated.

Investment in systems will only be worthwhile if the expected benefits that were identified in the feasibility study develop. That is unlikely to happen if training is inadequate and the organisation risks wasting its investment.

Training will be needed when:

- a new system is introduced
- there is a material change to a system
- a new staff member is recruited
- someone's job changes within the organisation
- someone's job changes as part of a general development programme
- reminder or booster courses are needed to keep skills fresh.

2.2 Types and levels of training

You will be familiar with the three levels within organisations: strategic, tactical and operational. The information needs of staff depends on the level at which they are working and their training needs are similarly affected.

Operational level

Operational level staff are mainly responsible for recording transactions. Typically they will be entering amounts into the accounting system, taking telephone orders for sales, etc. Their tasks are routine, repetitive and limited.

Their training will be targeted at the specific skills they need, eg how to enter a sale, or how to answer a customer query about a product.

Tactical level

Staff at this level have some management tasks. Their jobs are more open-ended and their use of computers will have to be more flexible. Typically they will need to know how to operate the management information system. They will probably also need to know how to set up a spreadsheet and simple database.

Their training will be targeted at some specific skills (for the MIS) but also at equipping them with more general skills.

Staff at this level may be in a career structure and some training will equip them for their next jobs in the organisation.

Strategic level

At this level, managers will be using MIS systems, decision support systems and executive information systems. They will need training in how to operate these. It is also likely that they would want some spreadsheet skills.

The types of training outlined above have all been about skills in using computers. However, as managers become more senior they may also need training in how to manage information systems. For example, senior managers should know that it is wise to have a feasibility study before contracting for a new system and that security is an important aspect of any IT system. Therefore, training about managing information systems should form part of a manager's development.

2.3 The training plan

The development of a training plan can be represented by the following diagram:

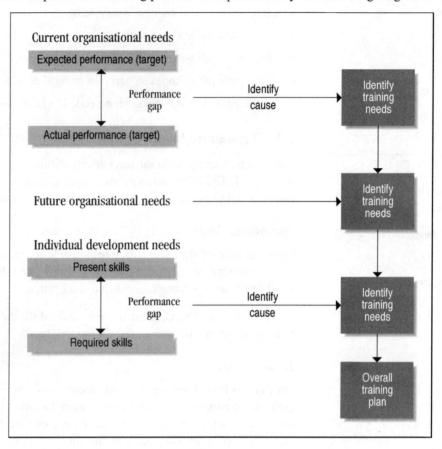

Let's see some examples of training needs:

1   A mail order organisation finds that its level of bad debts is running above budget. It identifies that the principal cause of this is that operators are over-riding the computerised credit limit system.

     The training need is that operators should be told when manual over-ride is permissible. This training could be achieved by a simple memorandum or could be told to the operators during regular staff meetings.

2   An organisation is shortly to introduce a new system. This will require extensive training of all staff who are going to use it. An extensive training program is planned at the offices of the software house who will use case studies to mimic real life scenarios.

3   A young staff member who is on a management trainee scheme will soon be moved to the treasury department. A specific training course is arranged on the operation of the company's cash and foreign exchange management system.

2.4   Methods of delivering training

There are many different methods of delivering training to employees in an organisation. The precise method or methods chosen will depend on various factors including budget, availability of training rooms and simply time available for training at the time of implementation of a new system.

The training methods that can be considered will include the following.

Classroom-based training

Classroom training normally provides use of the real software, but in a training environment. Trainees will be using the real software, but only processing data against dummy or training files specially set up for the course. While the training method tends to be relatively labour-intensive (possibly one trainer to six trainees), it does provide an excellent training environment as trainees can ask the trainer questions and receive an immediate response.

Computer-based training (CBT)

Alternatively, the training course can be produced on a CD or a website; the trainee can then run the course where and when it is convenient for them to do so. While the training method does provide flexibility in terms of location and time, it is expensive and time consuming to produce. The CBT may not use the real software, but rather use prototype screens built into the CBT itself. The functionality of the software will be limited, limiting the usefulness of the system.

Case studies and exercises

Both classroom tuition and CBT can be supplemented with case studies and exercises based on the processing of the real software. Case studies are essential to the understanding of the software, because they duplicate the processing of actual items in the software. They are usually quite easy to produce and they do help the user understand exactly how the new software will work.

Reference material

Following on from training, some form of reference material will be required so that users can remind themselves of the content of any training course or find more detailed technical information as required. The reference material provided will normally be a mixture of course manual containing the exercises, reference manual explaining how the system works, quick reference card demonstrating shortcuts and commonly used procedures and finally some form of electronic help system. Generally, the more types of material that can be provided the better, because users can then choose their own method of obtaining information about the software.

At desk training

Training can also be provided at the employees' desks as they are using the software. Trainers are employed to 'floor walk', that is, monitor the work of a number of employees for a day and then provide advice and assistance when problems in using the software become apparent.

Alternatively, training can be provided literally at the employee's desk. This gives the benefit of working on the real software, but can be frustrating for the employee and trainer due to distractions from telephones, e-mails and other members of staff wanting to communicate with the employee being trained.

3 Documentation

The word 'documentation' refers to a very wide range of reference materials used in the running and maintenance of computer systems. It takes various forms, ranging from the very technical to the completely non-technical.

The level of documentation will vary according to the situation. Bespoke or internally produced software will require very comprehensive documentation enabling it to be maintained, whereas a package will require only enough documentation to enable the organisation to exploit the package's full capabilities. The ISO 9000 standards require that implementation, as with any other quality activity in the analysis and design of a new system, is correctly documented. Similarly, the standards require project managers to use those tools and techniques, which they consider appropriate for the situation. So, the scale of implementation may change, and this will result in different standards of documentation being produced; however, that documentation must always be adequate for the specific situation.

3.1 Types of documentation

The first category of documentation that must be kept is that which was used in the initial system development process – the feasibility study, system specification, program specification, test data, security precautions, etc.

Details of all changes to the system must be recorded and documented to the same standard as the original system. *All* copies of all documentation must be updated when changes are made. Costly errors too often occur when someone referring to an outdated manual operates the system. Most organisations require changes to be authorised and justified formally.

The second category of documentation is that aimed at helping the users. It includes user manuals, help screens, handy reference cards, CDs and various other references designed to make life easier for the users.

3.2 User manual

During the development of a system it will be necessary to produce documentation to support the system in use, and to aid further development or modification. The user manual is designed to support the training of users, and to provide them with a reference guide in case they experience problems during the operation of the system.

The user manual will be written in non-technical language, and will normally include the following sections.

• system objectives

• system overview

• input stage activities

• processing and storage activities

• output: on screen

• reports

• appendices: a glossary of technical terminology

• input screens, with a completion guide

• sample reports

• error messages, and what to do about them

• fault reporting procedures

• support details and helpdesk contact numbers.

3.3 Technical manual

The technical manual is designed to be used by future project teams who may need to fix, modify or upgrade the system. Its language will be far more technical than that of the user manual and its contents will differ.

A typical technical manual might contain the following:

• system objectives

• system overview

- performance specification
- technical specification
- appendices
- data dictionary
- dataflow diagrams, entity models and life histories
- program specifications
- likely upgrades and fixes required in the future
- contact details for the original designers and developers

3.4 Support services

No matter how well trained the users are (see above), the unexpected can still happen, and provision must be made to give the users specialist help as and when they need it.

This specialist help can take various forms. Purchasing staff may be needed to obtain special stationery and supplies. Computer and telecommunications staff may have to deal with hardware problems. Various software specialists may be asked to help users work with the computer operating system, networks and applications software.

Providing users with access to the relevant expertise is an important part of system implementation that is sometimes forgotten. The implementation plan should make sure that whatever support services will be needed are available as soon as the system goes live.

Conclusion

This chapter has explained some of the activities that take place towards the end of a project such as the implementation of a new system. The need for appropriate training was also mentioned with the importance of maintaining appropriate documentation.

SELF-TEST QUESTIONS

Systems implementation strategy

1   What are the main tasks involved in system implementation? (1.2)

2   How can control of system conversion be maintained? (1.5)

3   What are the four main methods of system changeover? (1.6)

Training

4   How is an overall training plan developed? (2.3)

Documentation

5   What are the normal contents of a user manual? (3.2)

Chapter 18
POST-IMPLEMENTATION ISSUES

This section of the manual discusses the post-implementation of a new system and the reviews that can take place to determine the success (or otherwise) of that system. The various reports that can be produced following implementation are also mentioned in this section.

Objectives

By the time you have finished this chapter you should be able to:

- describe the metrics required to measure the success of the system

- discuss the procedures that have to be implemented to effectively collect the agreed metrics

- explain the possible role of software monitors in measuring the success of the system

- describe the purpose and conduct of an end-project review and a post-implementation review

- describe the structure and content of a report from an end-project review and a post-implementation review.

1 System monitoring (system audit or post-implementation review)

After the changeover is complete and the new system is running, it should continue to be monitored for a period, to establish whether:

- the advantages claimed for the new system are being obtained in practice

- target dates are being met

- costs are as estimated

- any unforeseen problems have arisen

- redundant work has, in fact, been discontinued

- the outputs of the system (e.g. management reports) are being properly used

- the procedures for detection and correction of errors are working properly

- too many errors are occurring

A company would expect to hold a post implementation audit six or twelve months after the system has gone live, during which these issues will be examined.

1.1 System evaluation

The main reason for software evaluation is to check that the system requirements agreed at the beginning of any systems project have been met.

Evaluation, or determining the success of the system can be less than straightforward as various aspects of its impact are not quantifiable or easily identifiable. There are, however, some elements, which can provide a useful gauge:

1   **Significant task relevance** considers the effect of using the system. For example, minutes of meetings may be distributed more quickly as a result of introducing electronic mail into the organisation.

2   **Perceived value.** The willingness of user departments to contribute to a specific upgrade may provide a useful indicator as to the value they ascribe to the system.

3   **Systems logs.** In the case of a system which is used on a voluntary basis, systems logs can be used as an indicator as to the value of the system.

4   **User satisfaction.** Asking users for their assessment of the system collects this information. The areas upon which they may be asked to comment could include: quality of output; timeliness; response times; reliability (e.g. a new LAN may be often down with the result that specific applications are not available when urgently needed).

The evaluation process will require careful planning to incorporate a comparison with the previous system. The timing of the evaluation is also important; if the evaluation is undertaken too soon after implementation, the results will be distorted by the effects of introducing any new system ('teething problems'; frustration while users familiarise themselves with something new; the inevitable opposition to change, etc).

1.2   Evaluating system performance

System performance is the evaluation of all components of an existing system to determine the extent to which existing resources are being utilised and to identify resource deficiencies.

1.3   Measuring and improving systems performance

The main areas an organisation would consider when reviewing the performance of a system are as follows:

1   **Growth** in, for example, transactions processed or the size of files. With this information, trends could be identified, and future growth extrapolated (with caution). These projections could be used to identify any potential problems.

2   **Delays.** Any delays in processing should be identified and the impact of these delays assessed.

3   **Security.** The efficiency of security procedures should be assessed.

4   **Manpower.** The clerical requirements of the system should be assessed, and compared with the estimated requirements.

5   **Error rates.** If these are high, the reason/s should be identified: it may be related to the poor design of input documents, for example.

6   **System amendments.** Are any amendments to the system required?

7   **Output.** An assessment of the uses to which output is put.

8   **System documentation.** Ensuring that the documentation prepared is appropriate and of an acceptable standard.

9   **Feedback from users.** Collating users' views of the system.

10   **Operation running costs.** A close examination of individual processes: the overall costs may be satisfactory, yet costs for individual processes may be excessive.

11   **Unanticipated factors.** Ascertaining whether or not system performance has been affected by any unanticipated external factors.

1.4　Methods of improving systems performance

Outputs of the system

The value of outputs could be improved – with no increase in input resources – if the system was capable of:

- processing more transactions
- producing more management information
- increasing the accessibility of information.

Outputs of little or no value could be eradicated from the system. An example of this might be reports which are distributed too widely, too frequently and which are too lengthy. Input costs should be reduced as a result of this action.

The timeliness and quality of outputs should be reviewed. The information that is available may be out of date or lacking in other ways. The value of the information will often diminish under these circumstances. Access to information could be improved by the use of databases, file enquiry or spreadsheets. The volume of output (e.g. data processing) may be enhanced by altering the equipment used.

Inputs to the system

The systems efficiency could be improved by retaining the same volume of output, but with fewer input resources and at a lower cost. For example:

- operator efficiency can be improved with the introduction of a multi-user system. Unlike a standalone system, the multi-user system facilitates multiple accesses to the same file. Thus, operator effort can be levelled out: an operator with some free time is better placed to help out a colleague with a heavy workload
- upgrading software: a more recent version of a package may provide labour-saving features
- increasing storage capacity of computers: this can help reduce waiting time (e.g. the time taken for a particular file to become available after having been called up)
- the method of input may be changed: shared access to file means data requires inputting only once. This reduces effort and the risk of mistakes.

1.5　Use of metrics

While it may be tempting to measure 'everything that moves' in a system, it is more useful to measure certain key items when checking the success of the particular system. The most appropriate measures for most projects are:

- agreement to original specification
- time
- money
- achievement of financial objectives.

The metrics to be collected will depend on the measures being used to determine the success or otherwise of the system. Where success is measured in terms of achieving the original system specification, then a comparison between that specification and the outcome of the system will provide the appropriate information. Such metrics could include the number of transactions that can be processed per minute, the number of errors in the code, the number of 'crashes' that occur, say, per week.

However, other objectives such as time and money will require comparisons between the estimated time or budget, and the actual time and money spent. A variance analysis can be produced and reasons for significant variances determined and included in an end-project review.

Other measures concerning the financial success of the project, such as NPV or IRR also have specific information that will need to be collected. There may be some element of judgement concerning the appropriate discount rate to use, but otherwise the information should be available.

Other, less quantifiable measures such as *user-satisfaction* or *enhanced customer service* may be more difficult to quantify and measure. However, use of appropriate questionnaires or counting the number of calls to the help desk or actually contacting some users directly to assess the impact of any new system or information system can be particularly effective. It is useful to agree the data collection method and metrics to be tested in advance so that there is no dispute later, or an appearance to use the most favourable metrics at the time.

2 Computer-based monitoring

Performance monitoring can be used as an aid in systems evaluation. The main computer-based monitoring methods are hardware monitors, software monitors and systems logs.

2.1 Hardware monitors

The purpose of a hardware monitor is to measure electrical signals in specific circuits of the computer hardware. Based on these electrical signals idle time, the extent of CPU activity or peripheral activity can be measured. The sensors send data to counters, which write to magnetic tape. A program is then used to analyse the data and produce the findings as output. Inefficiencies in performance could be identified in this way.

2.2 Software monitors

The software monitor is a computer program that records data about the application in use. Software monitors might be used to identify excessive delays during the execution of the program.

2.3 Systems logs

Computer systems often produce automatic systems logs, the data from which can be useful for analysis of the system. The type of data recorded may be the times a job starts and finishes.

3 Post-implementation review and end-project reviews

3.1 Post-implementation review

A post-implementation review should be carried out after implementation of a new system or a system amendment when the system has had time to settle down (say 3 to 12 months). Its prime purpose is to establish whether the planned benefits and objectives have been achieved and whether the cost budgets and timetable of the project were met.

If there have been failings, it is important to identify why these have occurred. A knowledge of this will help to prevent similar problems in future projects and may help management to decide what corrective action might be needed now to achieve a satisfactory outcome later.

The typical structure of a post-implementation review report will be:

- executive summary of findings

- a review of system performance and user satisfaction. System performance can be assessed by recording response times, down times, errors. User satisfaction can be assessed by questionnaires

- a cost-benefit analysis comparing actual costs with actual benefits so far identified

- a comparison with the costs and benefits identified at the time of the feasibility study

- recommendations for system modification.

3.2 Efficiency of an information system project

Efficiency is a measure, or ratio, of the outputs from a process or activity in relation to the resource inputs into that process or activity.

The project can be described as efficient if all stages (development, delivery, installation and implementation):

- were concluded within the constraints identified at the outset, or within the resources specified in terms of manpower, costs and time

- exploited the resources of the members of the project team and the users' time to the full

- avoided unnecessary idle time, delays or wasted time brought about by undertaking unnecessary tasks or activities

- were effective in integrating the activities of the members of the project team, and the interactions and dependencies with other parties outside the project team (users, suppliers, consultants or managers)

- achieved timely delivery of resources including hardware, software, services and training. Note the use of the word 'timely'; resources must be delivered neither too late nor too early. Resources arriving before they are required may lead to storage problems, deterioration, unexpected fluctuations in planned cash flows and a proportion of the warranty period elapsing before equipment has been used. Much of the benefit of training will be lost if the user is unable to apply the newly acquired skills; therefore delivery of training must be carefully synchronised with the delivery of new equipment or software.

3.3 End of project review

An end-of-project (or project closure) review is a meeting held at the end of a project which concludes the project. The objectives of the meeting are to:

- bring the project to an orderly close

- confirm that all planned work has been carried out

- check that all technical exceptions and quality review actions have been closed off

- agree that all the documentation needed to maintain the delivered system is available

- confirm that acceptance letters have been signed off

- review any lessons learnt from the project for future reference.

The review itself is normally attended by the project assurance team or members of the steering committee and the project manager. A final report on the project will be prepared summarising the key points of the meeting. This report is then presented to the board of directors, or similar controlling group in the organisation, to conclude the project.

An end-of-project review will normally have the following content:

1   **Review of project initiation document**, specifically to note the objectives for the project and check whether or not those objectives have been met.

2   **Performance**. A review of achievements versus original objectives. This review provides a commentary on the way that the objectives were achieved, noting areas such as lack of clarity in objectives or whether information to run the project was made available from project staff. Project overruns will also be considered and the reasons for them.

3   **Productivity**. How efficient the project was in terms of budgets for resources and the actual resources used. Budget comparisons will normally be available for the cost of the project, number of hours spent by the different grades of project staff along with an explanation for significant variances.

4   **Quality** of the product and the process of the project itself. Comments in this section will focus on the appropriateness of the systems used within the project (such as different software packages) and issues of overall project quality caused by lack of documentation or development methods.

Project management review provides a comment on how well the project worked overall, including the effectiveness of the different meetings and other means of communication such as task lists. Any issues regarding staff such as frequent staff changes can also be commented.

Conclusion

This chapter has explained the different reviews that take place at the end of a project, and the ways that the performance of the system can be measured.

SELF-TEST
QUESTIONS

System monitoring

1   What key metrics can be used to measure system performance? (1.5)

Post-implementation review

2   List the contents of a post-implementation review report and an end project review. (3.3)

EXAM-TYPE
QUESTION

Review of implementation

A small chain of four department stores is located in and around a major metropolitan area. The company has recently implemented, in all stores, a point of sale system with linkages to a central computer. Previously, the stores all used conventional cash registers. You have been asked to assess the success of the conversion to the new system.

Produce:

(a)   An evaluation of two approaches to the system changeover.   **(8 marks)**

(b)   A checklist, in sequence, of the activities likely to be carried out during implementation.   **(4 marks)**

(c)   Suggestions as to how the new system might be evaluated after three months of operational running.   **(8 marks)**

(Total: 20 marks)

For the answer to this question, see the 'Answers' section at the end of the book.

Chapter 19

MAINTAINING SYSTEMS

While a lot of the focus on system change is actually designing and implementing a new system, the maintenance of that system and ensuring that the system continues to process correctly are also essential activities. This final section of the book reviews the need for system maintenance as well as reviewing the need to maintain quality throughout the whole project management process.

Objectives

By the time you have finished this chapter you should be able to:

- identify what procedures and personnel should be put in place to support the users of the system
- describe the different types of maintenance that a system may require.
- explain the need for a change control process for dealing with these changes.
- describe a maintenance lifecycle.
- explain the meaning and problems of regression testing.
- discuss the role of user groups and their influence on systems requirements

1 Systems maintenance

Even after they have been implemented, systems will need to be modified and adapted to make sure that they continue to satisfy user needs. The process of modifying existing systems is termed systems maintenance.

1.1 Systems maintenance

It has been estimated that 70% of software costs are incurred in maintaining existing systems. It is essential, therefore, that maintenance is strictly controlled and effectively carried out. **Maintenance** can be defined as the redoing of certain aspects of the systems development process, which implies that documentation and control procedures should be as carefully carried out as in the initial development of the system.

1.2 Systems redevelopment

Because maintenance costs are such a high proportion of overall software costs, systems analysts will try to build as much flexibility as they can into their systems. This allows changes to be made as easily and cheaply as possible, and helps to ensure that the systems can evolve to fit changing needs. Even despite this inbuilt flexibility, there will come a time where it is more cost effective to design a completely new system rather than to continue to modify an existing system. This will usually happen when new technology becomes available, or when the old system becomes too unwieldy to run effectively, or when aspects of the system environment (such as the company structure or other computer systems) change drastically.

DEFINITION

Maintenance is the redoing of certain aspects of the systems development process.

2 Types of systems maintenance

Systems maintenance is often put into four basic categories: corrective maintenance, perfective maintenance, preventative maintenance and adaptive maintenance.

2.1 Corrective maintenance

The elimination of bugs from a system is termed **corrective maintenance**. Although most of the faults in the system should be identified and eliminated during the testing process, problems may be revealed during the operation of the system. In this case the elimination of the errors is likely to be a matter of urgency, since the system will not be fully operational until it has been corrected. Indeed, expensive errors in processing could have been happening for some time.

Corrective maintenance is an expensive process, and an important facet of the design and implementation process is to try to minimise the need for corrective maintenance.

Problems are not solely caused by errors in the programs. Hardware faults can cause damage to files, and faulty procedures or incorrect operation can cause a system to fall down. Suitable back-up procedures may enable the recovery of a system without the need for programmer intervention.

2.2 Perfective maintenance

Perfective maintenance is carried out to improve efficiency or effectiveness. It may be prompted by the availability of new technology, the development of new techniques, or by a request for system enhancement from the users.

An example of perfective maintenance is the adoption of a graphical user interface (GUI) to make a system more user-friendly.

2.3 Adaptive maintenance

Adaptive maintenance enables a system to adjust to changes in its environment. User information needs may change; organisational structure may be altered; legislative changes may impose new obligations on the software.

2.4 Preventative maintenance

Preventative maintenance is maintenance carried out in advance of a problem occurring, to reduce the risk of that problem. It is the same as having a car regularly serviced in order to reduce the risk of breakdowns. In theory, more preventative maintenance means less corrective maintenance. This is good, because preventative maintenance can be carried out at a time most convenient to the organisation, whereas corrective maintenance always seems to be required during the busiest periods.

2.5 Other forms of maintenance

Sometimes system updates do not fit neatly into the categories that have been defined. The errors caused by incorrect procedures may need perfective maintenance to avoid recurrence, as well as corrective maintenance to eliminate their effect. The changes required to make a system more user friendly may also need the system to be adapted.

3 The causes of systems maintenance

When considering what causes system maintenance, we need to differentiate between the immediate spur to the maintenance activity and the underlying causes. It is important for systems designers to build in mechanisms that identify when maintenance is needed, and to start the process of updating the system.

Both the underlying causes of maintenance and the immediate spurs will vary according to the type of maintenance being undertaken, and each type of maintenance needs to be examined separately.

3.1 The causes of corrective maintenance

The basic underlying cause of corrective maintenance is a system failure of some kind. This may be an error in one of the programs, or it may be that data has become corrupted. Program bugs are likely to be caused by ineffective testing or by the failure to undertake adaptive maintenance when required.

KEY POINT

Data problems are caused by:

- human error

- poor documentation

- physical computer faults

- sabotage

- poor training

- inadequate supervision

- impact of other computer systems

- malicious damage.

Data problems are caused by:

- human error
- poor documentation
- physical computer faults
- sabotage
- poor training
- inadequate supervision
- sometimes by the unforeseen impact of other computer systems
- malicious damage to both programs and data.

Whatever the cause, it is vital that problems are identified as early as possible. Gross problems are likely to be obvious to the users who can, as long as suitable reporting procedures have been set up, inform whoever is responsible for maintenance. More subtle errors can have longer-term results because it is more difficult for the users to spot the problems.

One example of an unidentified problem of this kind affected a major international company. One of their systems relied upon a particular file being in strict alphabetical order. Because the system was not adapted to deal with changing conditions, the file had some records that were not in the correct order. The resulting errors were not sufficiently major for the system users to think it worthwhile to report them, but their cumulative effect was very costly.

The problems caused by this incorrect data file could have been nullified by a routine which could validate that it was in the correct format, and in general the best protections against subtle faults are designed into the system when it is first created. The protective measures used may be operating procedures or they may be extra validation programs.

A periodic system audit is another way in which faults can be identified. An analyst will analyse an existing program to make sure that it is still achieving the results that it should do. Although this process can be expensive, it may still be cost-justified.

3.2 The causes of perfective maintenance

KEY POINT

The causes of perfective maintenance:

- IT specialists need to monitor advances in technology

- user group meetings can help identify when improvements are needed.

Perfective maintenance may be carried out to enable a system to exploit advances in technology, or it may be to make a system more user friendly. IT specialists will need to constantly monitor advances in technology, and their input can be reinforced by including users in the monitoring process. Regular formal and informal user group meetings can be used to help identify when improvements are needed. Questionnaires can be designed to assess user satisfaction with the present system's performance. 'Wish lists' can be compiled.

Perfective maintenance may also be needed when system performance begins to degrade. The system should be constantly monitored against target indices and performance criteria, and action taken when performance declines below pre-set values.

3.3 The causes of adaptive maintenance

There are three basic reasons why adaptive maintenance may be needed:

- user requirements may have changed or have been ill-defined when the system was being designed
- the system environment may have significantly changed
- the system may have grown beyond the limits that were originally envisaged for it.

3.4 Changes in user needs

Changes in user needs may be identified through regular re-assessment of system requirements, or the users may recognise the need for change and request a system upgrade. For example, changes to legislation governing financial advisers means that clients' financial details have to be recorded. The need for change may also be predicted in advance, and the integration of IT planning in the general business planning process is an important agent for change.

3.5 Changes in the system environment

The system must relate to all aspects of its environment, and any changes must be catered for, whether they are sudden changes or evolutionary development. For example, the company may have been taken over and data now has to pass to and from head office.

It should be easy to recognise the need to respond to sudden changes such as new legislation, but recognising more gradual changes is more problematic.

3.6 Adapting to growth

The system will originally have been designed to deal with a maximum number of transactions per day, maximum file sizes, specific code lengths, etc. If these constraints have been properly documented, the system can be modified when required. The problem occurs when documentation is poor, or when no thought is given to system smaintenance. The disastrous problem described earlier (of a file not being in alphabetical order) was caused when the need for change was not recognised.

3.7 Management of change

Whatever the reason for the change, full documentation must be kept of any amendment to systems. As well as being required for ISO 9000 certification, keeping a record of changes is important for a number of reasons.

- To ensure that the systems documentation, for both user and technical systems, is updated.

- A history of changes made is available, so that the precise date of any change can be found later.

- If errors start to occur in another part of the system, these can be traced back to recent changes. Checks can then be made to find out whether the initial system change caused the error.

- Authority for each change can be recorded, and the amendment signed off by appropriate personnel.

The record of amendments must also be kept as part of the standard system documentation.

4 The systems maintenance lifecycle

It is important to see maintenance not just as a series of disconnected ad hoc reactions to problems but as a planned, formalised activity that is integrated into the system design process. The actual processes involved in maintenance can be set down as a cycle of activities.

4.1 Planning for maintenance

Good maintenance practice starts within the system design process, and a major objective in planning a new system is to make maintenance as easy as possible.

Flexibility and adaptability are major considerations when building a system. A flexible system can cope with widely varying volumes of transactions and can be adapted to cope with changes in procedures and requirements.

Another major consideration is the recognition of problems when they occur. Validation routines are built into programs to identify when data errors occur and to deal with them where possible. Not only should data be validated as it goes into the system but existing files and data should be checked periodically.

Monitoring the effectiveness and efficiency of a system is an important part of the maintenance process. Each system will have a number of performance indicators that are calculated during each run of the programs and compared with target values. When performance starts to fall below target, investigations can be carried out and remedial action taken if it is needed.

Once an existing problem has been identified, or a possible future problem predicted, action must be taken. Likely problems can be anticipated and contingency plans made during the initial design. Extra storage capacity, for example, can be made available to cope with increasing volumes of data as and when existing capacity is exceeded.

4.2 The maintenance life cycle

The procedures involved in maintaining software can be presented in the form of a diagram:

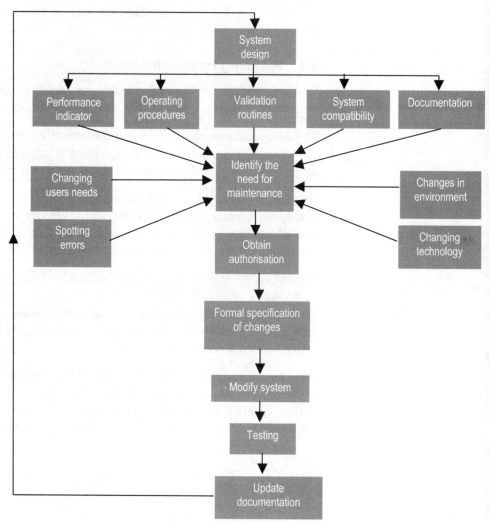

As you can see, the initial design leads into the procedures of actually producing the software along with the performance indicators that will be used to check whether or not the software is actually meeting its requirement. However, the actual need for maintenance can arise from a number of different sources:

Performance indicators show that the software is not running as efficiently as expected. This may be caused by situations such as an increase in the number of transactions being processed or higher volume of network traffic. The reason for the poor performance will need to be identified and methods of improving performance agreed.

Errors may occur, even within the final release of the software! System testing is unlikely to test all possible combinations of use of the different modules of the software, so actual use may still identify some errors.

Changes in the environment may occur, such as different taxation rules making the payroll system obsolete or possibly illegal if the new rules are not followed!

Changing technology may not actually make a system obsolete, but new technology features may be incorporated to make software, faster or provide reports in a more appropriate format.

Operating procedures can change, so making the software obsolete. For example, revised filing systems may make access and amendment of the software difficult. Alternatively, field sizes in the software may be inappropriate and require amendment.

Other issues such as validation routines and the compatability of the new system with changes to other systems may indicate that the software should be changed to avoid possible error in the future, e.g. possible incompatibility with a new operating system.

Finally, documentation may occasionally result in a change requirement, for example, new forms required by tax authorities may need additional output from the system.

Having identified the need for maintenance, then authorisation will have to be obtained for that change and a formal specification produced. The latter will be needed to help track exactly what changes are being made and so that appropriate testing can be carried out after the change has been made. An analysis will need to be made of the impact of the changes on the rest of the system.

After the change has been made and tested, documentation must be updated to ensure that users have full information about any changes made. The whole process can then start again!

5 Regression testing

When software is changed, normally as a result of a problem found during acceptance testing or maintenance, then in an ideal world, all the tests that have already been performed should be run again; as a result of the change the software is technically a different system. Changes made in one part of a system may have unexpected side effects in other parts of that system. Re-performing tests from the beginning of the testing process helps to ensure that the software has not reverted (or regressed) to a faulty state in any area or section of code. Re-performing of tests is therefore referred to as **regression testing**.

In most situations, regression testing will only be performed on part of the software. Writers of the software are normally able to identify those sections of the software that are most likely to be affected by amendments, and then focus regression testing on those areas specifically. There is obviously the risk that some errors in the software may be missed; however, this risk has to be balanced against the cost of re-running all of the tests on the entire software each time an error is found.

Computer assisted software engineering tools are available to perform some regression testing, and these do help to minimise the risk of missing an error. As noted above, the risk of error cannot be eliminated.

Regression testing is assisted where software is developed in modules. Where some modules have already completed their testing phase, regression testing can normally be limited to more recent modules where testing is not complete. As long as all modules pass a final systems test, then additional testing on completed modules is unlikely to be required.

6 User groups and help lines

When users begin to use new software and hardware they will often need help and advice – even if they have had some training. User groups and help lines can provide this.

6.1 User groups

User groups exist for most common packages. The purpose of the groups is to provide help and support to users of the software; they can also act as pressure groups to encourage the software manufacturers to correct or add certain features to their software.

The software company often starts up user groups as they can provide valuable marketing focus for additional products. Membership of these groups is made up of users from all or most companies that use the package. A committee of users will then normally run the group, rather than the software company itself. Typically, they will organise a series of meetings throughout the year where users can meet each other to discuss the software. Presentations of new software or applications of the software will often be arranged.

Some software companies run users' forums on the Internet. Users can send in queries by e-mail and receive responses from the software house and from other users.

The benefits arising from user groups are that they:

- help to solve technical problems
- aid access to other users who may use the software differently or who may be able to pass on ideas
- increase enthusiasm and motivation of the software users
- are relatively cheap
- put pressure on manufacturers for new facilities and bug fixes.

6.2 Help lines

Help lines are telephone numbers which users can ring to obtain help and advice on software and hardware. Some software and hardware companies provide help free without time limit, others provide it free for a limited period, and then the user has to take out an annual contract to provide help and backup.

Within an organisation using bespoke software, help line services are likely to be provided in-house, perhaps making use of the company's information centre.

In general, help and advice can be provided in the following ways;

- help screens, ideally context sensitive. Most software now has a help button that allows users to look up an index of topics or search for the occurrence of a term
- tool tips. When the mouse point lingers over a button on the screen, a small sign appears saying what function that button will perform
- wizards – invented by Microsoft, a wizard takes you through a procedure step by step
- help lines (see above)
- documentation
- user groups (see above)
- on-line user forums (see above)
- information centres: in-house expertise that can be called on.

Information centres have increased in importance as personal computers have become more common. Because these computers are relatively cheap, departments are often allowed to look after their own information technology requirements rather than the process being handled centrally through an IT department. This approach, known as end user computing, should give the departments more flexibility to obtain the IT system they need.

However, there are dangers in this approach. The staff in the departments are likely to be relatively unskilled in IT and may make costly mistakes. Two separate departments may duplicate development work. To avoid these dangers, an information centre can be set up by the organisation. This is like an internal IT consultancy and its roles are:

- to provide users with support and training

- to help users develop their own applications

- to advise users on suitable hardware and software

- to co-ordinate the activities of different departments to avoid duplication and to inform other departments of what has been developed

- to ensure that there is as much compatibility between systems as possible

- to advise on security and standards.

7 Time, cost and quality triangle

7.1 Project objectives

The objectives of a project must be clearly understood at the outset. Objectives often take three forms, and project management is often a delicate balancing act, as the various objectives normally conflict with one another.

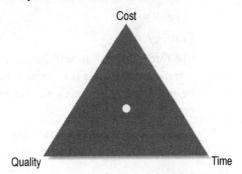

The three objectives shown in the above diagram are as follows:

Cost

There are two main aspects to cost that must be considered for any project. In almost all cases there is a budget available for project completion, and the project manager should not exceed the budget without authorisation. This may be very difficult to achieve, as often the budget is set without a clear idea of exactly what is going to be involved in the project. It is not uncommon, as a project manager, to be put in the position of having to make a project solution 'fit' the budget available.

The second aspect to cost is the need, in most projects, to prove that the benefits of the project exceed the costs. This is a major problem because often the costs are all financial or can be stated in financial terms (e.g. the time taken by staff) but the benefits are difficult or impossible to quantify.

Quality

Once again, there are two aspects to the quality dimension of a project. Firstly, there is a certain series of tasks or activities to be performed in reaching the project solution. It is important for the project manager to ensure that all the work required is completed; omitting an essential part of the project will have an overall detrimental effect of the quality of the project.

Secondly, each task will have an expected quality level associated with it. It is also important that the tasks are performed well, and that the sponsor's quality expectations are met.

Time

There are also two aspects to the time dimension of a project. Firstly, there is often an overall time constraint on a project (sometimes called a deadline) by when the project must be completed. This may be due to an internal business constraint such as a financial reporting deadline, or an external commercial constraint such as a promise made to a customer.

Secondly, there may be a 'time budget' for the project. This is often expressed in terms of resource availability and measured in person-hours or person-days. This may be due to a resource shortage within the organisation or a constraint placed on a supplier if the project is outsourced to a specialist contractor.

It is essential not only that all the objectives are achieved to the greatest possible extent, but also that a balance is maintained between them (hence the dot in the middle of the triangle).

Conflict

The three dimensions will inevitably conflict with one another. If the cost allowed to complete the project is restricted, quality will normally suffer; poorer quality staff may be employed and corners may be cut in the quality and specification of the programming.

A restriction in the available time will assist in the projects costs but will have a negative effect on the quality of the outcome.

8 Improving quality assurance

8.1 Automation and quality assurance

While there may not be a specific need for computer assistance in reviewing and monitoring systems, the time and cost savings generated will normally outweigh the initial setting up and running costs of the computer systems. Automation can assist in checking the quality of projects as well as the efficiency and effectiveness of information systems management in various ways.

- Providing tools and techniques to assist the project team in the performance of their duties, e.g. project planning software such as Microsoft Project.

- Assisting in testing new computer software using computer assisted software testing (CAST) tools. Using these tools will help to improve the quality of the completed software. Computers can perform testing faster and more accurately than humans and so, it is to be hoped, identify more bugs for the same amount of effort!

- Monitoring the use of systems and then providing appropriate metrics on those systems. For example, the amount of network traffic can be monitored and reviewed weekly or monthly in a graph or chart. Projections for the amount of traffic will assist in planning for future hardware and software upgrades to systems.

- Providing platforms for fourth generation languages to run and the processing power to convert those prototypes into deliverable systems where necessary.

8.2 The role of accountants in information systems management

The accountant's role has gradually evolved from being a recorder and controller of financial matters to one of information provider and information manager. This role has evolved in this manner largely because of the increased use of Information Systems.

In recent times the accountant has become a provider of not just financial information but also cognitive information intended to analyse an organisations strategic possibilities, identify its objectives and monitor its performance against those objectives.

Computer systems requirements have tended to grow out of the financial functions of the business. A result of this is that, in many organisations, Information Systems were under the control of accountants who had a heavy involvement in designing the information systems which sustained a business and helped it meet its strategic objectives.

The prime objective of information systems is that of provision of information to management in order that they can make timely and effective decisions.

The information provided will need to be collected from internal and external sources and must be provided at a cost which is acceptable to the business. The role of the accountant will incorporate ensuring the accuracy of the information provided by the system and also assessing the value of the information in monetary terms.

The role of the accountant in relation to Information Systems is therefore to ensure:

- Accuracy and quality of information by ensuring that transactions can be properly traced and verified for trueness and fairness.

- Ensuring that information is produced cost-effectively.

- Ensuring that information and other resources are maintained securely.

To do this the accountant must be able to:

- Assess the value of information to the organisation.

- Be aware of hardware and software developments that will improve the cost-effectiveness of information gathering and presentation.

- Be able to analyse the cost benefits of new technologies and assist with advice on the changing and upgrading of systems and in the purchasing process.

- Be aware of the security problems of systems and ensure that security and safety requirements are properly funded.

- Be able to evaluate post-introduction the use and benefits of new technologies.

Specifically the accountant will be heavily involved in the strategic planning of corporate objectives, particularly the introduction of high-cost and often high risk IT based systems. He is also likely to be one of the major providers of information during a feasibility study often producing the cost benefit analysis and offering advice on purchasing to senior management.

Strategic planning and individual feasibility studies will usually involve the production of cost, expenditure and income forecasts which will generally be produced by or under the management of an accountant.

The use of complex modelling using DSS software tools is now a pre-requisite for senior accounting personnel. The ability to collect and extrapolate information for planning, using EIS and other systems is also vital.

Conclusion

Systems have to be maintained in order for them to continue working efficiently and effectively. In this chapter, you have learnt the reasons for the different types of maintenance and how appropriate support can be provided to users to help them use the systems correctly. Finally, although they only provide a relatively small input to a project, the work of the accountant and internal auditor was also mentioned.

SELF-TEST
QUESTIONS

Types of systems maintenance

1   What are the main types of system maintenance? (2)

The causes of systems maintenance

2   State the three main reasons that adaptive maintenance may be needed. (3.3)

EXAM-TYPE
QUESTION

Maintenance

(a) A manufacturing company is about to implement a bespoke inventory control system. The implementation team is keen to collect data that measures the quality of the delivered system. A Help desk has been set up to support the users of the software.

Required

Define and show the difference between *corrective* and *adaptive* maintenance.

(10 marks)

(b) The implementation team wishes to monitor the user-friendliness and frequency of use of the system. They want to ensure that users find the software easy to use and that managers extensively use the enquiry and reporting facilities.

Required

Suggest a total of *three* appropriate measures of user-friendliness and frequency of use and describe how such data might be collected, interpreted and acted upon.   **(10 marks)**

(Total: 20 marks)

For the answer to this question, see the 'Answers' section at the end of the book.

Answers to exam-type questions

CHAPTER 1

IS strategy

There is now a growing recognition amongst organisations of the importance of information as a business resource. It follows, therefore, that the systems manipulating, storing, processing and distributing this resource must not be left to chance.

Information has in the past been collected, stored, processed and dispersed during the course of an organisation's operational activities. However, organisations have seen the introduction of information technology and such systems as management information systems, decision support systems and executive information systems as the means to gain a competitive advantage.

Previously, organisations used computers to perform the mundane tasks and computerised data processing has become a routine function. Generally organisations are now more computer literate and this, together with the low price of hardware and new technology, has made organisations more aware of the competitive advantages to be gained by the correct application of technology and its related systems.

For an organisation to invest in information technology and information systems, it will require some sort of information strategy. The IS/IT strategy would be based upon the corporate strategy, which can be defined by a study of the mission statement.

The mission statement is a statement of purpose by the organisation, and from this the aims and objectives can be ascertained. The aims and objectives state what needs to be achieved and the strategy outlines how to achieve them.

Therefore, before an IS/IT strategy can be drawn up, the corporate strategy must be studied to ensure that they are aligned.

An information strategy will comprise two parts:

1   Organisational – this is the systems management which is concerned with the collecting, processing and distribution of information.

2   Technical – this is concerned with the means by which the information will be collected, processed and distributed.

Strategic planning for IT ensures:

1   Compatibility between the various systems under development and hardware purchased within an organisation.

2   Commitment from the strategic level of management.

3   Resource allocation – the monetary commitment from the organisation.

CHAPTER 2

Centralising IT

REPORT

To:	Finance Director
From:	A Consultant
Date:	20 April 20X5
Subject:	Information Technology Management Structure

Introduction

This report was compiled for Mugen Industrial plc to recommend a management information structure within the group. It contains an appraisal of the advantages and disadvantages of centralising the management of information technology and includes other relevant, but non-IT factors.

Advantages of centralising the IT structure

The benefits to be derived from a centralised service include:

1   Improved central control with overall co-ordination in the organisation.

2   Company-wide information systems to support and exploit business opportunities, with a common approach to systems development.

3   Centralisation enhances the authority of IT staff and the overall quality of management, establishing company wide technical standards and work procedures.

4   More formalised career paths for IT specialists help attract and retain high quality staff.

5   There may be economy of capital expenditure due to the relatively high cost of computers through having only one computer for use by the group instead of several located in various units.

6   Where one powerful computer is installed, the resultant advantages are increased security, speed of operation, storage capacity and processing capability.

7   Economy in computer operating costs due to centralisation of systems analysts, programmers, operators and other data processing staff as compared with the level of costs that are incurred with each unit in the group having its own computer on a decentralised basis.

8   Centralisation would also facilitate the standardisation of applications but this would depend upon the extent of diversity in the dispersed operations regarding payroll and invoicing structures etc.

9   Centralisation will give greater bargaining power with suppliers of hardware and software. The company may also benefit from a better quality service from suppliers if its purchases are perceived as high value.

Disadvantages of centralising the IT structure

1   It may take longer to get something carried out by a centralised resource over which the user has no direct control.

2   Concentration of resources means that the organisation is more vulnerable to sudden breakdowns than it would be if resources were available in its separate units (which would have enough spare capacity to help one another out in emergencies).

3   Because the centralised staff are taking a broader view, or because they are less attuned to the circumstances of an individual unit, their contribution may be less focused than that of an insider might have been.

4   Users may feel that they lack influence and become unable or unwilling to commit time and resources to developing computer applications.

5   The reduced expertise at local level may result in delays in processing system enhancements.

Non- IT implications for Mugen Industrial plc

1   The centralised facility can reduce costs and excess capacity, can produce career opportunities for staff, and ensure consistent standards across the organisation. But the decentralised approach may give faster and more relevant service to the users and customers and is less vulnerable to problems involving an equipment failure.

2   Unfortunately, the group is not starting from scratch as far as structure is concerned, because they already have a substantial information system structure in place. This is a decentralised structure where managers are used to taking their own decisions and forming their own IS strategy. It will be expensive and disruptive to change it, especially when the benefits of doing so are uncertain.

3   The organisation needs to assess the criticality of information technology to them. McFarlan's strategic grid could be used to identify their current dependence on information systems. If the subsidiaries' use of information systems is of strategic importance to current or future operations, falling in the strategic or turnaround sectors of the grid, then they are likely to object to centralisation of these aspects of their business. However, if the usage of information technology is in the factory or support section of the grid, then the subsidiaries may not mind the IT operations being taken over by the London headquarters.

4   The existing structure with each subsidiary developing and implementing its own IT strategy to suit the local needs and culture has not been unsuccessful and might be more advantageous in its use of IT to gain local competitive advantage. The trans-border locations of the subsidiaries, with little transfer of goods across national boundaries, would make it difficult to argue for a centralised IT structure with centrally controlled databases of information. Changing the structure of the information technology management, in the hope of reducing costs, would need to be part of the overall IT strategy and its alignment to the structure, taking into consideration the diversity of styles and rate of change throughout the group.

5   A change to centralisation will result in a different management style of objective setting from that of top-down as opposed to bottom up. Mintzberg suggests that the top down objectives and strategies are intended strategy and the bottom up proposals result in emergent strategy. The management's job is to deliver the overall objective required by the organisation in a way that offers the best chance of success – which is that contributed to, supported and believed in by the employees concerned – i.e., bottom up.

CHAPTER 3	EXAM-TYPE QUESTION

National Counties Hotels plc

Memorandum

To: Head Office official

From: Advisor

Date: Today

(a)   The major components in the National organisation appear to be

- each hotel – running the local operation
- head office – co-ordinating and managing hotels; some central bookings.

Within each hotel the sub-systems are:

- the bar – sale of drinks and, perhaps, bar snacks
- the restaurant – sale of food and drink
- room letting – individuals
- room letting – group bookings from tour companies
- the housekeeping department – looks after laundry, cleaning and furnishings in rooms
- conference arrangements – liaising with conference organisers and marketing the hotel's facilities.

All of these areas are closely linked. For example:

- activities in the restaurant will affect bar takings
- lettings and conference arrangements will affect the restaurant and the bar and, for residential conferences, room lettings
- the rooms that can be let to individuals will be sometimes dependent on the rooms that have been let to groups
- housekeeping workload will depend on room lettings.

Each hotel will be linked to head office (many bookings are referred from a central booking department) and will be linked to other hotels in the chain so that onward accommodation can be arranged.

Typically, head office will carry out the functions of accounting, marketing, senior appointments, finance, strategic planning, investment decisions, pricing.

(b)   It is common for guests in hotels to be given a card showing their room number, name and period of residence. Many hotels ask to see this before items can be charged to room accounts.

The card is usually printed as the guest registers and it would be possible to include a bar code on it. This would encode the same information as was printed normally, but could be scanned by a reader each time the guest asked for an item to be charged.

The advantages of this system would be:

- accurate recording of information
- fast recording of information
- valid bar codes can be made difficult to forge
- the card would still be very cheap to produce and could be discarded by the guest after use
- guests should find the system no more awkward to use than conventional cards
- bar code scanners are cheap and can be connected to lightweight, portable recording devices.

If you have any questions regarding the above, please do not hesitate to contact me.

CHAPTER 4	EXAM-TYPE QUESTIONS

Question 1: Cost-benefit analysis

Note: The list of costs and benefits is straightforward. The need to mention factors that could distort the net present value is more complex: think about the problems of calculating NPVs for this type of project.

The costs and benefits associated with a proposed computer system can be divided into two main categories:

1 Installation

These are the costs and benefits involved in the changeover from the existing system to the new one, and will be incurred before the system begins to produce any operational benefit. Costs are likely to include:

- hardware purchase and installation
- software development or purchase
- personnel, including recruitment, training and redundancy
- file conversion
- the use of consultancy or bureau services during the changeover period.

The only benefit to arise at this stage would be the avoidance of renewal or major overhaul costs associated with existing equipment that is being replaced, and the disposal needs of any equipment being sold.

2 Operation

The costs and benefits associated with the operation of the new system will arise from year to year as the system is used. Costs will include:

- any equipment rental, maintenance and depreciation charges
- stationery and other consumables, including magnetic media
- overheads associated with office and computer room accommodation
- recurrent staff costs, such as salaries.

The benefits will consist partly of savings in these costs due to the greater efficiency of the new system, which will be taken into account in arriving at the net operation costs, and partly of the information improvement arising from a better system. This benefit is extremely difficult to quantify but without it any analysis is likely to be misleading because it is a major reason for changing processing methods.

The analysis of these costs and benefits using net present value calculations may give an inaccurate result for two main reasons:

- As can be seen from the categories of costs and benefits given above the major costs associated with the changeover are likely to be incurred at the start of the project, while the benefits will arise from the future operation of the system. This means that those benefits will only be experienced if the business has adequate resources to meet the initial costs. Any reduction caused by cash flow problems may make the new system uneconomical.

- The information benefits of the new system are usually very difficult to quantify, and any errors in their estimation may easily distort the results of the analysis, leading to an invalid decision.

Because of this, it is important that businesses should use a range of evaluation techniques and consider all the implications of proposed new systems.

Question 2: Feasibility report

(a) **Main sections of a feasibility report**

- Objective: what the report sets out to achieve.
- Terms of reference: the limits within which the report has been prepared.
- Method of study: how the study has been conducted.

- Objectives for the system: a statement of the requirements of the company that will be satisfied by the measures contemplated in the report. How the system will work in conjunction with other company systems.

- Alternatives considered: the nature and extent of other systems and methods that were taken into account before the recommended solution was put forward.

- Effect on company operations: the nature, timing and extent of the changes that would occur in procedures, practices and staffing.

- Financial effect: a summary of tangible costs and benefits that would flow from the adoption of the system.

- Achievement of company objectives: a summary of the intangible losses and benefits that would flow from the adoption of the system.

- Conclusion: a recommendation to proceed or otherwise with the system envisaged.

- Appendix 1: Present procedures: anything between a full description and a brief summary and list of working papers that sets out what was learnt about current operations in the course of the study. It is important that volumes and timing constraints are recorded.

- Appendix 2: System as envisaged: behind every feasibility study there has to be a mind's eye system. If that system cannot be implemented for any reason, the feasibility study may be invalidated and this appendix is a record against which any changes can be measured.

(b)   **Financial justification**

Note: In real-life situations, non-accountants with insufficient knowledge of 'true and fair' views often present financial justifications for new systems. In consequence, many are spurious. The title 'financial effect' is used in section (a) above as the word 'justification' assumes that all feasibility reports will make a recommendation to proceed.

There are two aspects to costs: operating costs and development costs. These are the revenue and capital sides of the proposal.

Operating costs

The marginal cost of current operations that would be displaced by the proposal:
- staff costs
- supplies – stationery, etc
- outside services
- space costs
- other.

The marginal costs of operations under the envisaged system:
- computer costs
- staff costs
- supplies – stationery, etc
- system maintenance
- other.

Development costs

Systems design and development: a cost on a full cost basis from the start of the feasibility study until the system is handed over for maintenance. This heading includes all programming and testing.

Installation costs: preparation costs of the site, delivery charges and other costs arising from any new equipment or computers required.

Capital costs: computers and equipment required for the application.

Launching costs:

- staff training
- file conversions
- systems testing
- parallel running or other change-over costs.

Policy costs: un-recovered costs of incremental capacity increases.

Cost benefits: value of equipment no longer required.

CHAPTER **5**	EXAM-TYPE QUESTIONS

Question 1: Squiggy

A project normally has a specific purpose, which can be readily defined. The statement from the FD is not specific concerning the systems to be updated or why they actually need updating. Providing this detail is essential to ensure that the project does meet the requirements and a post-implementation review can confirm that the requirements were, in fact, met.

The focus of the project on the Board may be inappropriate. Many projects are *focused on the customer* and customer expectations rather than internal requirements. As information systems are normally designed to provide some form of competitive advantage and provide appropriate customer service, the initial focus must be external. Additional sub-systems to provide Board information can be implemented later.

A project is made up of a *series of activities* that are linked together because they all contribute to the desired result. These activities range from an initial investigation into the existing systems through to implementing a new system. There is no need to stop using the existing system just because a project has started. The project manager will follow a recognised methodology that will allow for an appropriate changeover method, and it is only at this time that some processing ability may be temporarily lost.

Although the project will have clearly defined *time constraints* and a date when the results are required, these are normally suggested by the project manager and then agreed by the Board. To impose a time restriction before the project commences may severely limit the scope of the project as well as providing an information system that may not meet the organisation's needs.

Most projects are *complex* because the work involves people in different departments and even on different sites. Although there is no information about the processing systems within Squiggy, the systems change appears to be quite fundamental and so it will affect many different departments. A project team is likely to be required rather than a single systems analyst.

All projects have *cost constraints* that must be clearly defined and understood to ensure the project remains viable. The FD is therefore correct to start thinking about the cost of the project. However, agreeing a budget before the project is even started may cause some problems. There is no indication of whether the budget is for analyst costs or to cover replacement hardware/software etc. Setting a budget will normally wait until after a feasibility study; the FD may be wise to obtain a quote for this study first rather than try to constrain the whole project by an unrealistic cost estimate.

While the project will provide opportunities for new working methods, the overall control normally rests with the systems analyst. The analyst will be skilled in the running of projects, and provide a summary report for the Board on progress at agreed times. The Board input will therefore be more strategic in monitoring overall project progress rather than the operational detail.

Question 2: Skills of a project manager

Leadership. Project managers should be able to stimulate action, progress and change.

Technological understanding. Project managers need to have an accurate perception of the technical requirements of the project so that business needs are addressed and satisfied.

Evaluation and decision making. Project managers should have the ability to evaluate alternatives and to make informed decisions.

People management. Project managers should be able to motivate and enthuse their teams and have a constant personal drive towards achieving the project's goals.

Systems design and maintenance. Project managers should be able to demonstrate their individual competence and have a complete working knowledge of the internal administration of their project.

Planning and control. Project managers should be constantly monitoring progress against the plan and taking any necessary corrective action using modern planning and monitoring methods.

Financial awareness. Project managers should be proficient in risk management and have a broad financial knowledge.

Procurement. Project managers should understand the basics of procurement and be able to develop the procurement strategy for their project.

Communication. Project managers should be able to express themselves clearly and unambiguously in speaking and writing and be able to do this in a wide range of situations and with a wide range of people.

Negotiation. Project managers should be skilful in managing their clients and should be able to plan and carry out a negotiation strategy.

Contractual skills. Project managers should be able to understand the contract that defines their project and should be able to manage subcontractors to ensure that the contractual terms are met.

Legal awareness. Project managers should have an awareness of any legal issues that could affect their project.

CHAPTER 6	EXAM-TYPE QUESTIONS

Question 1: Drawing networks

(a)   There are both logical errors and departures from convention.

Logical errors

- two start events – 1 and 6
- dangling activities – H
- there is a loop joined by activities K, L, M and N.

Conventions broken

- event 7 precedes event 5
- activity J is drawn from right to left.

(b)   There are both logical errors and departures from convention.

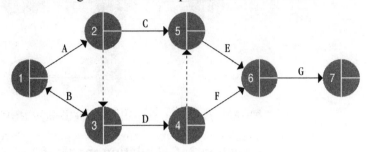

Question 2: Finding the critical path

(a)

Activity	Immediately preceding activity	Start event	End event	Duration (mins)
A	-	1	2	5
B	A	2	3	5
C	B, D	3	5	5
D	-	1	3	15
E	B, D	3	4	10
F	E	4	5	5

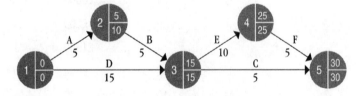

The critical path is DEF, and the duration is 30 mins.

(b)

Activity	Immediately preceding activity	Start event	End event	Duration (mins)
A	-	1	2	4
B	A	2	3	2
C	B	3	5	10
D	A	2	4	2
E	D	4	6	5
F	A	2	7	2
G	F	7	8	4
H	G	8	9	3
J	C	5	10	6
K	C, E	6	10	6
L	H	9	10	3
Dummy		5	6	

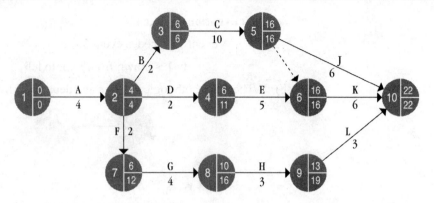

There are two critical paths – ABCJ and ABCK. The total duration is 22 days.

Question 3: Calculating the float

(a)

Activity	Duration	Manpower	IPA	From	To	Float
A	5	£1000	-	1	2	0
B	2	£200	A	2	3	2
C	2	£400	B	3	4	2
D	4	£1500	C	4	5	2
E	3	£6000	D	5	6	2
F	5	£2000	E	6	7	2
G	5	£1600	E	6	8	2
H	4	£6000	F, G	8	12	2
J	3	£250	A	2	9	3
K	4	£1550	J	9	11	3
L	12	£600	K, M	11	12	0
M	10	£100	A	2	10	0
N	11	£2000	M	12	12	1
Dummy 1	-	-	F	7	8	
Dummy 2	-	-	M	10	11	

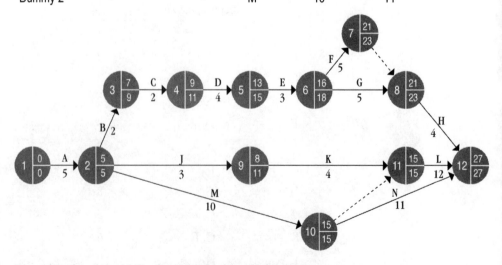

The critical path is AML, the total duration is 27 days.

The total cost is =

£1000 + £200 + £400 + £1500 + £6000 + £2000 + £1600

+ £6000 + £250 + £1550 + £600 + £100 + £2000 + 27 × £1000

= £23200 + £27000

= £50, 200

Increasing D by 2 days will use up the entire float on B, C, D, E, F, G, H but will not increase the total duration.

Decreasing L by 1 day will reduce the total duration by 1 day but will eliminate the float on activity N.

The cost is reduced by £1000.

There are now several critical paths:

A, B, C, D, E, F, H

A, B, C, D, E, G, H

A, M, L

A, M, N

CHAPTER 7	EXAM-TYPE QUESTIONS

WRF Inc

(a + b)   **Report**

To: The Board of WRF Inc

From: Chartered Certified Accountant   Date: 23 May 200X

Subject: Systems development life cycle approach to providing a successful systems changeover

1   Introduction

The systems development life cycle (SDLC) is a disciplined approach to developing information systems. It is a model that is based upon a phased approach. There are many versions of the SDLC, and different terminology may be used, but the basic intent is similar. It covers the following stages:

- requirements and specification
- design
- implementation.

SDLC is the preferred option for the following reasons:

2   The current situation

The systems analyst has prepared the initial proposal; this appears to have been done without following any formal methodology. The systems analyst is on a fixed-term contract that is due to terminate when the system installation is complete. These two factors represent a risk to the successful system changeover: the solution provided may be satisfactory, but is unlikely to be optimal; also the systems analyst's contract may terminate at a critical stage of the development.

Before embarking on the phases of the SDLC, it is worth considering that prior to a new system being designed and built, the existing system needs to be fully understood; therefore, it is important that a study of the current system is undertaken.

3   Requirements and specification

Initially it is important to ascertain the purpose of the new system, what the new system is required to do, and what level of performance is expected etc.

At this stage, business requirements are clearly defined: the inputs, files, processing and outputs of the new system. Resulting from this initial analysis, performance criteria can be set and solutions developed, resulting in appropriate specifications; the specification of a 386 processor running at 20 MHz and 2 Mb RAM running Windows® 3.1 was arrived at because the systems analyst 'thinks the users will require' this.

4   Design

This stage considers both computerised and manual procedures, and how the information flows are used. Computer outputs are normally designed first; inputs, program design, file design, database design, and security are also areas to be addressed.

It will also be necessary to consider operability at this stage i.e., who should have access and capability to do what to which data.

At this stage a detailed specification of the new system is produced. A 386 processor running at 20 MHz may well be considered to be too slow: a 486 processor running at, say, 33 MHz may be necessary to produce the required results.

5   Implementation

This stage may include the building of prototypes and the finalisation of specification requirements e.g., 2 Mb will almost certainly be considered insufficient RAM; 4 or 8 Mb may be deemed more appropriate.

The implementation stage takes the development through from design to operation. This involves acquiring or writing software, program testing, file conversion, acquiring and installation of hardware and training.

When following a formal methodology, implementation and all it embraces should be considered from the initial analysis stage so the likelihood of problems should be substantially diminished.

6   Review and maintenance

This final stage ensures that the project meets with the objectives set, that it is accepted by users, that its performance is satisfactory, and allows for future enhancements and development.

7   Recommendation

It is recommended that the Board of WRF Inc approve the utilisation of SDLC for the systems changeover. Not only does this approach encourage discipline during the development process, communication between the developers and the users, and recognition of the importance of analysis and design, but it also ensures that business needs are met and provides a useful basis for future development.

Signed: Chartered Certified Accountant

CHAPTER 8

EXAM-TYPE QUESTION

Analyst

(a)   The analyst will spend a large proportion of time during the fact-finding stage interviewing users on a one-to one basis. The purpose of the interviews depends upon the level of the person being interviewed:

- If the interviewee is at a senior level, the objectives will be to identify the boundary and constraints governing the study, and to obtain a high level working picture of the current system, and why the changes are needed. Reporting requirements and outputs will be identified.

- If the interviewee is a department or office manager, the information sought will be more to do with inputs and outputs of the department, standards and targets that the system has to meet, and a profile of the main procedures. The manager at this level will also identify the staff that the analyst will need to interview to get a detailed view of the current workings.

- If the interviewee is a 'front-line' worker, i.e. someone who handles the day-to-day transactions, and is involved with dealing directly with the customers (customers of the whole company, or customers of that department's services). This person can describe the detailed procedures to follow, highlight any problems with the way that they are specified or conducted, and give examples of all documentation used.

The interviewer needs to plan the interview programme well. As well as deciding whom to interview, in what order, where and when, s/he must also plan the course of each interview. To help in this task, it is useful to base the questions on Kipling's 'Six Honest Serving Men': What, Why, When, How, Where and Who? These specific questions allow the interviewer to direct very detailed questions, to understand in fine detail the procedures, documents, authorities and detailed sets of requirements for the new system.

As well as targeting the information using these specific questions, the analyst must also control the interview by the judicious use of open and closed questions, probing questions, linking and reflective questions.

(b)   If the study involves replacing or enhancing a current system, the analyst needs to use observation to underpin his/her understanding of the system. Formal observation involves the analyst (with the users' knowledge and permission) watching a set of tasks being undertaken, and asking questions about the procedures. Interviewing users at their own site gives an opportunity to observe the working environment informally, looking for signs of bottlenecks, issues relating to ergonomics and local cultural issues.

(c)   If the user population to be interviewed is too large, or split across multiple sites, the analyst can consider the use of questionnaires. Information from questionnaires must be easily analysable, because of the quantity of data that might be collected.

The analyst must pilot the questionnaire before sending it out, to be sure that ambiguities are found first, and loosely worded questions identified and improved. Questionnaires do not always have a high response rate, so if the information is necessary, it is a good idea to have some form of incentive. One reason for low response rates is that the questionnaires can take up too much time for the respondents; it is important, therefore to keep the questions clear and concise, preferably allowing a multiple choice style, or a 1-5 scale, for speed ease of completion.

(d)   Prototyping means producing a mock-up of the system, perhaps using a tool like Visual Basic to produce screens of the proposed input. This can be used either to design the input screens and user interface, or to confirm the requirements. When a user sees what the computer can do, by means of this mock up, they often think of new requirements. The prototype might consist of a menu screen, with their required functions shown as menu entries.

It is important to manage the users' expectations, as they may assume on seeing the prototype that it is the complete system, and expect to be able to use it straight away. While the response time will be very quick with a single terminal system, if the final system is to be multi-user and multi-terminal, the actual response time may be much slower. The prototype demonstration must take this into account, so that the users are not disappointed with the real working system.

CHAPTER **9**   EXAM-TYPE QUESTION

Process model of a mail order firm

Note: The dataflow diagram drawn below represents the procedures that take place in the existing system. The system represented is the agency system of a mail order firm.

The purpose of an initial dataflow diagram is to illustrate the analyst's understanding of the procedures carried out and to use the same as a means of communication with the user.

(a)

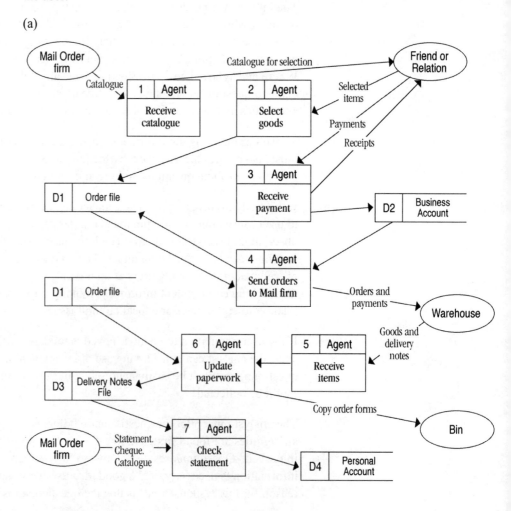

(b)   **Terms**

   (i)   An external entity is the instigator, initiator or end user of the systems data. It is a body outside of the system itself, which either provides data for the system or uses data from the system.

   (ii)   The context level is the very top level of the dataflow diagram. The context level is the starting point. At this level, it is the only process we would expect to see. The context level diagram would therefore contain the process or system being investigated plus the external entities that are the source or destination for the data used by the system.

   (iii) Decomposing or exploding is the term used for 'going deeper' into the details of the process. When drawing dataflow diagrams the major functions and processes are looked at first. These are then decomposed into their constituents. Once the context and level 1 diagrams have been drawn, each process within level 1 would be looked at in more detail and a level 2 diagram of each separate process would be produced.

   (iv)   A top down approach is the term used for starting at the highest level, and working down in a modular format. In other words, a top down approach takes a global view of the system or process and then looks at that system or process in various and increasing degrees of detail. A top down approach has the advantage of enabling rectification and amendments to take place to the dataflow diagram whilst minimising the disruption of the diagram as a whole.

CHAPTER 11   EXAM-TYPE QUESTION

Report layout

(a)   Further standard items might include:

   •   page numbering convention

   •   date to which the data in the report refers

   •   date and time the report was printed

   •   a standard identifier or code for the report

   •   distribution list for the report

   •   source of the data on the report

   •   standards for spacing between headings and sub-headings, etc.

   •   standard for denoting the end of the report.

(b)   The usability of the report might be enhanced by:

Re-ordering the columns

One of the main purposes of the report is to compare total stock value with total value at re-order level. It would help if these two columns were next to each other on the report (preferably towards the left-hand side of the layout) as this would facilitate comparison.

Re-ordering the rows

The second main purpose of the report concerns the identification of products that have gone below their re-order level. Products currently fulfilling this criterion appear to be shown by the use of eight asterisks. This is a cumbersome way of highlighting the relevant products. Re-ordering the rows so that all products below their re-order levels are shown at the top of the report would enhance its usability.

Deleting irrelevant totals

The usability of the report is reduced by the production of irrelevant totals such as total cost per unit. This has no logical meaning.

Using spacing and colour

The usability of the report might be improved by using spacing between product groups or (in a re-ordered report) between products that are below their re-order level and those that are not. Colour or emphasised typeface (bold or italic) might also be used to identify the relevant products and to show if the total percentage had exceeded 10%.

Using lines and centring column entries

The usability of the report may be improved by adding lines between the headings and body of the report and adding lines between each column so that the columns are better delimited. Most columns appear to be right justified. It might be more helpful if the column entries were centred.

(c) A check digit is a letter or number attached to the end of the code to make the code self-checking. The check digit is designed to check for transposition and substitution errors.

Check digit example

(Not necessarily required from the candidate – the question did not specifically ask for an example, but it is useful for revision purposes.)

The code may be 124127 where the last digit (7) is the check digit.

The product code (excluding the check digit) may then be weighted with appropriate weights).

Code	1	2	4	1	2
Weights	5	4	3	2	1
Value	5	8	12	2	2

Total value: $(5 + 8 + 12 + 2 + 2) = 29$

In the modulus 11 check this weighted total is divided by 11 and the remainder becomes the check digit – in this example: $29/11 = 2$ remainder 7.

Locating transposition errors

For example: 121427

Code	1	2	1	4	2
Weights	5	4	3	2	1
Value	5	8	3	8	2

Total value: 26

Check digit: $26/11 = 2$ remainder 4. This does not match with the check digit and so the error will be trapped.

Locating substitution errors

For example: 128127

Code	1	2	8	1	2
Weights	5	4	3	2	1
Value	5	8	24	2	2

Total value: 41

Check digit: $41/11 = 3$ remainder 8. this does not match with the check digit and so the error will be trapped.

CHAPTER 12	EXAM-TYPE QUESTION

Software packages

(a)   A software package is a generalised software solution usually developed by a software house for sale to an unrestricted business community. Software packages are normally developed for common business applications, such as accounts and payroll, and these are offered for sale to prospective purchasers. The software is not developed against a specific requirement (as in a bespoke solution) but is developed to provide a range of facilities usually required in the business application. It is the responsibility of the buyer to ensure that the functionality of the software fits the specific requirements of their own organisation.

A bespoke solution is where a software system has been specifically developed to fulfil a defined business requirement for a specific organisation. In this approach the business develops a functional specification defining the business requirements of the system. Software is then developed from scratch to implement the requirements defined in the functional specification. Bespoke solutions may be developed by a software house or by an in-house information systems department. It is the responsibility of the developer to ensure that the software fulfils the requirements defined in the functional specification.

(b)   **Cost savings**

The software package solution is almost certain to be cheaper than a bespoke solution, particularly at ZYNC plc where bespoke systems development is performed in-house. This is because the full cost of systems development (specification, programming and testing) has to be completely borne by the organisation commissioning the bespoke solution. In contrast the costs of package development can be spread across a number of customers (or potential customers) so reducing the cost per unit. These cost benefits will also be reflected in reduced maintenance and support costs once the package is operational. This is possible because the cost of providing support and maintenance is shared between all the users of the package. It is also likely that more financing options (such as renting or leasing) will be available from the supplier providing the software package solution.

Time savings

The software package is a product ready for implementation. In contrast the bespoke solution has a period of system construction and testing (programming, unit testing and system testing) which will mean that both the effort and elapsed time of a bespoke project is likely to be much greater than that for a software package solution. It is also likely that user requirements will change in the elapsed period of system construction and testing leading to further project problems due to changes (and subsequent implementation delays) in systems requirements. The software package approach will allow the IT department to implement systems quickly, hence exploiting any competitive edge that might exist.

Guaranteed quality

Bespoke systems should undergo unit, system and acceptance testing. However, it is unlikely that all errors will be found in the system prior to software release. It is difficult to ensure that a quality product has been released and consequently the early days of a system's use may be disrupted. This often leads to reduced user confidence in the software and it may prove difficult to restore such confidence. The software package will have also undergone relevant testing but will have been used in other installations and it is likely that most of the errors have already been located and fixed. The users at ZYNC plc have already complained about the poor quality of bespoke systems and the adoption of the software package approach should address this concern. However, it is worth pointing out that the IT director may be over-stating his case. The packages can seldom guarantee quality!

CHAPTER **13**	EXAM-TYPE QUESTION

Prototyping

(a) **Definition of a prototype**

A prototype is a working system that captures the essential features of a later implementation. It is usually used to verify parts of the system (such as requirements or dialogues) with users, or to prove (or disprove) some concept or idea. A prototype system is intentionally incomplete. It will be subsequently modified, expanded, supplemented or supplanted. Prototypes may be iteratively developed into the final system, so that each prototype represents a stage in the development of the finished product. Alternatively, prototypes may be 'thrown-away' after the objective of the prototype has been achieved.

(b) **Advantages and disadvantages of a prototype (only 2 of each are required)**

Advantages might include

1   **Pleases users**. Users have conventionally had to review paper-based screens and report layouts and sign off requirements and operations that they could not fully visualise. The prototype represents a tangible thing that they can touch and feel and the inputs and outputs of the system are represented in the medium in which they will eventually be used – on a computer screen, not on paper.

2   **Prototyping decreases communication problems.** Training takes place incrementally through the development of the software. Furthermore, excessive documentation is not needed because users gain knowledge of the software through use rather than through reading user manuals.

3   **Reduces marginal functionality.** There is evidence to suggest that prototype systems produce fewer reports and screens programmed to meet the 'I think I need' requirements that often emerge in specified systems. Prototype systems usually contain fewer validations and unnecessary controls.

4   **Prototyping provides tangible progress.** The user can see the progression of the development through a series of usable systems, rather than through abstract diagrams and models.

Possible disadvantages

1   **In most instances the prototype produces a less coherent design** than a system that has been specified. The iteration of the development means that it is difficult to produce an initial design that is likely to be applicable to the final agreed system.

2   **Prototypes can be oversold**. By definition a prototype has limited capabilities and captures only the essential features of the operational system. Sometimes unrealistic user expectations are created by overselling the prototype. This may result in unmet user expectations and disappointment. The system looks ready, but is actually very incomplete.

3   **Prototypes are difficult to manage and control.** Traditional life cycle approaches have specific phases and milestones and deliverables. These are established before project initiation and are used as a basis for project planning and control. Planning and control of prototyping projects are more difficult because the form of the evolving system, the number of revisions to the prototype, and some of the user requirements are unknown at the outset. Lack of explicit planning and control guidelines may bring about a reduction in the discipline needed for proper management (i.e., documentation and testing activities may be bypassed or superficially performed).

4   **It is difficult to prototype large information systems**. It is not clear how a large system should be divided for the purpose of prototyping or how aspects of the system to be prototyped are identified and boundaries set. In most cases, time and project resource constraints determine the boundaries and scope of the prototyping effort. Moreover, the internal technical arrangements of large information systems prototypes may be haphazard and inefficient and may not perform well in operational environments with large amounts of data or large numbers of users.

(c)   **Useful facilities in a fourth generation language include (only 2 of each are required):**

1   **Integrated screen design tool**. This allows the quick construction of example screens. Many languages allow the developer to construct the screen with the user; it is possible to discuss field positioning, display and validation as they go along. This approach provides effective user involvement and uses the medium (the VDU or PC) that will be used in the final system.

2   **Dialogue design tool**. This will be used for the construction of menus, prompts and error messages. These often change during the development of the prototype and so the language must support flexibility and ease of amendment. To many users the dialogue is the system, and so it must reflect the way users wish to go about their work.

3   **Non-procedural programming code.** Most fourth generation languages have their own development language. This language is usually concise and non-procedural allowing the quick development of programs that might later be discarded. Conventional programming languages are generally verbose and procedural. They are time-consuming to change and hence are not suitable for prototyping.

4   **Object set.** Many fourth generation languages include standard object sets that can be used in the development of the system. Thus a developer does not have to write a printer driver, merely select a printer icon from the object set. The code for printer control is already written in a program attached to this icon. This again allows fast system production.

CHAPTER **14**	EXAM-TYPE QUESTION

Disaster Recovery

DISASTER RECOVERY (DR)

From: IS Consultants Team

To: Directors of Disaster Recovery

Subject: Contingency plans for new information system.

Background

The Directors of DR have proposed a new, integrated information system to monitor and control their stocks of emergency relief supplies. The Terms of Reference stipulate that the cost should be kept as low as possible, in order not to divert DR's funds away from their primary target – disaster relief.

Non-functional requirements

Non-functional requirements are those aspects of the requirements that specify how the system should *perform*. For example, response and throughput times, security and access considerations, availability of systems, usability, ability to handle given volumes of transactions. Because the non-functional requirements involve both design and infrastructure decisions, there may be a cost involved in implementing them.

Response times

The frequency of transactions is not so great in normal times that response times could prove a problem. Most of the routine IS work is concerned with recording supplies and equipment. It is only during the handling of a disaster that the frequency and volumes of traffic increases. Even so, because the work is of a relatively short-lived intensity, there is a case for designing only for the average number and rate of transactions rather than the maximum. This means that a lower specification computer can be acceptable.

Security

The company cannot afford to lose data through mischievous hacking, or infection by viruses, so it should invest in firewall security. Because data entry can take place from remote sites, it must run on a network, either dedicated (expensive) or public (cheaper, but less secure).

The Board must make a decision as to the risk to DR's operations of contamination by a virus, or intrusion by a malicious hacker. If the data held is not personal or financial, the risk of harm is reduced, but as the essence of the organisation is rapid response, there must be a significant investment made to ensure that that response is guaranteed.

Availability

Because the nature of the system means that its use is unpredictable, (i.e. that news of a disaster can occur at any time without warning), it should be available all of the time. This means that if the system should go down for a period, whether through hardware failure or housekeeping procedures, there is a danger that a disaster could be notified during that downtime, and DR be unable to respond until the system is back. All the data regarding equipment and location of equipment would be unavailable, with the possible result of loss of lives. A way to avert this threat would be to have back-up systems working in tandem, so that should one fail, the back-up would be able to take over immediately. This is a very expensive solution, but one that would meet the problem.

The Board must calculate the likelihood of this risk, based upon the number and frequency of disasters that they need to respond to over the course of a year.

Usability

Most of the data input will be performed by dedicated staff in a stable environment, and so usability issues will be relatively minor; however, data will be entered from the field in disaster areas, and so there must be investment in robust equipment that can be taken out to e.g. earthquake zones, and simple data entered quickly and accurately.

Conclusion

Although the Directors wish to spend money only on the core functionality for this system, in order to preserve as much money as possible for the basic activities, they must be prepared to spend money on meeting extra technical requirements to be sure that the system is available when they need it, will be safe from outside attack, and can be operated both from a clean environment at home and a volatile environment in the field.

CHAPTER **15**

EXAM-TYPE QUESTIONS

Question 1: Data security

(a)   A logical access system involves a system of facilities, developed and maintained for the specific purpose of protecting a database – and in particular the confidential aspects thereof.

Initially it will be necessary to assess the security risks with regard to the computer-based applications: the data may be inaccurate; falsified; disclosed – to unauthorised individuals or to the public at large – or lost.

The next stage will be to classify the data in terms of sensitivity: e.g. public data (giving wide access to read/copy); limited access (e.g. to specific users in the personnel or finance functions); private data (access to identified individuals only).

A logical access system should, therefore, be capable of:

- establishing the user's identity be means of an ID code
- verifying the use, usually by means of a password
- confirming that the user has authorised access to the requested data.

To accomplish this the system should be capable of:

- identifying each user by means of a logical identifier
- matching the identifier with the terminal being used, to ascertain that access is from the authorised location
- controlling access to specified data and resources by users, terminals/computers
- logging accesses and usage of resources, to facilitate auditing.

(b)   (i)   **Encryption**

Encryption provides a defence to augment physical security measures.

Encryption is the technique of disguising information to preserve its confidentiality; this should occur during transmission and when stored. Encryption derives enciphered text from plain text, thus transforming the latter into an unintelligible form.

The process of encryption and decryption comprises an algorithm and a key; the algorithm is the operation itself, which transforms the data into cipher, and the key controls the algorithm; changing the value of the key can alter the effect of the algorithm so that the conversion for each key value is completely different.

Computers, because of their computational power, facilitate sophisticated encryption techniques that would otherwise be unrealistic. The cryptanalyst must devise a system with a cost of decoding which is sufficiently high to deter a potential unauthorised decoder but which has, at the same time, a level of sophistication no higher than necessary as this slows down the processing time – which costs money.

(ii) **Hacking**

Hacking is the deliberate accessing of on-line systems by unauthorised persons. Often this activity is considered by the offender as fun and may often not be done with malicious intent. As modems and micros have become more widespread, the threat of hacking has increased. Many systems now have dial-up facilities due to changing working practices; this facilitates entry into the system by the hacker after the telephone number has been obtained, or by means of an auto dialler. Once a number has been obtained, hackers make them available over the Internet.

A knowledgeable hacker can hide any evidence of their deeds by disabling the journal or console logs of the main CPU.

Once the hacker has gained access to the system there are several damaging options available to him. For example, he/she may:

- gain access to the file that holds all the ID codes, passwords and authorisations
- discover the method used for generating/authorising passwords
- develop a program to appropriate user's IDs/passwords
- discover maintenance codes, which would render the system easily accessible
- interfere with the access control system, to provide the hacker with open access to the system
- generate information which is of potential use to a competitor organisation
- provide the basis for fraudulent activity
- cause data corruption by the introduction of unauthorised computer programs and processing onto the system (computer viruses)
- alter or delete files.

(iii) **Computer viruses**

A computer virus is a small program that, having been introduced into the system, proliferates; its purpose is to spread extensively impairing both data and software.

The potential for the damage a virus can cause is restricted only by the creativity of the originator; once a virus has been introduced into a system, the only course of action may be to regenerate it from back up. However, some viruses are written so that they lie dormant for a period, which means that the back-ups become infected before the existence of the virus has been detected; in these instances, restoration of the system becomes impossible.

It is extremely difficult to guard against the introduction of computer viruses. Steps may be taken to control the introduction and spread of viruses, but these will usually only be effective in controlling the spread of viruses by well-meaning individuals. The actions of hackers or malicious employees are less easy to control. Preventative steps may include:

- control on the use of external software (e.g. checked for viruses before use)

- use of only tested, marked disks within the organisation

- restricted access to floppy disks on all PCs and workstations.

Software is written to protect against viruses, but all these may only detect and cure known viruses; they will not restore data or software that has been corrupted by the virus. As new viruses are being detected almost daily, it is virtually impossible for the virus detection software to be effective against all known viruses.

Question 2: Security factors and the Computer Misuse Act

(a) (i) The potential physical threats that an organisation should be aware of are:

Weather. This is a constant threat to buildings; high winds, rain and storms can have a destructive effect on the building which might result in it becoming structurally unsound or being penetrated by water which could cause damage to equipment.

In addition, storms could affect the power supply, by reducing power or by power surges. The company should fit lightning conductors, and anti-surge equipment. Where necessary a back-up generator should also be installed.

Fire. Fire, smoke and excessive heat can all cause damage to sensitive equipment. Data records can also be destroyed causing, at the very least great inconvenience to the company. Precautions should include the use of low-flammable materials and smoke detectors. Water sprinklers may be used in areas where there is no electronic equipment. In addition, back-up copies should be taken regularly and kept at a separate physical location.

Water. This might also be a common threat if the building is situated on low-lying land. Computer rooms should be situated above ground level and flood defences installed.

Environment. High temperatures, dust and static electricity can all affect electronic equipment. Controls should be introduced to minimise the risk from these environmental factors.

Unauthorised access. Entrances and exits to the building should be kept to a minimum. Emergency exits should be alarmed to prevent their use as an illegal back entrance. Guards, receptionists etc, should control public access to the building. Visitors should be issued with special recognition; signature recognition can be used where appropriate as a control measure.

(ii) Contingency planning is the planning process set up to deal with an unplanned or disastrous event. So far as computing is concerned this usually means the breakdown of the system.

In most businesses very few areas are not computerised or would not be affected by a breakdown in the computing facilities. Organisations now have to cope with unauthorised access to systems and the possible theft of valuable data.

The losses that would be incurred in the breakdown of a computer system would increase with the amount of time it was unavailable; it is therefore important to make plans to keep the computer downtime to an absolute minimum.

Management must fully realise the impact of the loss of computing facilities because any contingency plans will involve considerable expense.

Standby plans to be considered should include:

- the company can set up a distributed support system whereby the work is transferred to another site in the event of computer breakdown

- an arrangement can be made with another company to use their equipment, but this would depend upon their having the capacity available to cope with increased processing

- a spare computer room can be set up in the event of a disaster occurring. This is a very expensive option, but if the computer is vital to the operation of the organisation then this might be the best option

- a portable computer room can be installed on the user's site, but there would be a time delay in setting this up.

The key feature to disaster recovery is the regular back up of data and software. Contingency plans must specify the procedures to be taken in the event of computer breakdown, and until normal processing is restored.

The better the contingency plans, the more likely a company will survive a disastrous event.

(b)   **The Computer Misuse Act 1990**

The Act produced three new criminal offences.

(i)   The *Computer Misuse Act* now makes it unlawful for anyone to obtain or attempt to obtain unauthorised access to computer systems. A person is guilty of an offence if he/she 'knowingly' gains unauthorised access into a computer system.

(ii)   A person is guilty of an offence if they gain unauthorised access to a computer system with the intention of committing a further offence, for example, accessing the personnel records with a view to blackmailing an employer or employee.

(iii)   In addition, a person is also guilty of an offence if he/she deliberately causes unauthorised modification to computer programs. A person is guilty under this offence if the intention is to prevent or hinder access to any program or data or to compromise the reliability of the data by causing modification of any sort to the computer system.

CHAPTER 16

EXAM-TYPE QUESTIONS

Software testing

(a) **Systems testing**

Individual programs are usually tested by the programmers who wrote them and by their team leader who has certain testing responsibilities. Once a program has passed, program or unit testing it is passed on for systems testing. Systems' testing is usually undertaken by a systems analyst or project leader.

Systems' testing considers whether the individual units or programs fit together properly. In doing such tests the analysts will wish to verify that the programs interact successfully (passing data from one to the other) and correctly.

Systems testing will also usually consider the error trapping and reporting facilities of the system. Consequently, the tester will enter values that will cause the system to fail or undertake procedures that will lead to sudden or unpredictable failure – such as switching off the machine in mid-process. The systems tester will also need to ensure that the error reporting messages are correct and that appropriate messages are displayed.

The systems tester may also take responsibility for ensuring that the interface is consistent (for example, the same function key is always used to quit the system) and, where appropriate, it conforms to agreed industry conventions and standards.

Finally, systems' testing ensures that the system fulfils its functional requirements (as defined in the systems specification). It is the last chance to do this prior to the release of the system out of the department to its user.

User acceptance testing

After the completion of systems testing the system is passed on for user-acceptance testing. In this stage, users, or their representatives, are asked to formally consider whether the system fulfils their requirements. In theory users should evaluate the system against the formal specification (defined in entity-relationship models, dataflow diagrams etc.) they approved earlier in the project. In practice, it is the time when deviations between the system's operations and the user's actual requirements become known.

User acceptance testing will consider the functional characteristics of the system but it is unlikely to replicate the detailed range and format checks undertaken in systems testing. By this stage users should expect error-trapping to work successfully. In contrast, user acceptance testing will focus on the usability of the system, checking that the natural flow of the business process is reflected in the way that the software works.

User acceptance testing may also be concerned with:

- testing and agreeing cyclical activities (such as end of month and end of year routines)

- testing and accepting generalised housekeeping functions (such as back-up and restore)

- testing and accepting documentation.

(b) **Systems testing**

Systems and user acceptance testing is usually undertaken for physical working deliverables – programs or systems whose behaviour can be executed and documented. For example, a program to calculate the average price of timber can be tested to see if it performs (by not failing during operation) and that it performs the calculation accurately. This procedure is not always possible for deliverables early in the systems development life cycle – such as dataflow diagrams and logical data structures. Consequently these are usually reviewed in structured walkthroughs. A structured walkthrough is a formal meeting where a product is presented and checked for its:

1   **Functional accuracy.** This is usually undertaken by the user representative at the walkthrough. Their role is to confirm that a business process has been properly understood.

2   **Technical accuracy and adherence to standards.** A standards or audit representative is present to ensure that the product meets the quality standards defined in the methodology.

The walkthrough may also be attended by the presenter or author of the product, a chairperson and a scribe. The product will be formally accepted at the meeting or referred back for further work.

Walkthroughs are also appropriate for testing working deliverables such as programs and systems and so they are appropriate in all stages of the systems development life cycle. However, many analysis deliverables can only be checked by walkthrough – execution testing is just not possible.

CHAPTER 18	EXAM-TYPE QUESTION

Review of implementation

(a)   **Essentially, there are four approaches from which to choose:**

Direct changeover

The existing system is abandoned for the new at a given point in time. *Prima facie* this seems an economical approach, but this is balanced by the risk that the new system will not work perfectly. Furthermore, there will be no safety net, in terms of existing procedures and staff, with which to recover the situation. It is not suitable for large systems crucial to the well-being of the organisation. If the new system bears little or no similarity to the old, this may be the only route. In the context of the department store, it should be obvious that this is not a viable option; if the new system collapses, then the store potentially loses all sales until it is remounted.

Parallel running

This involves the running at the same time of both old and new systems, with results being compared. Until the new system is proven, the old system will be relied upon. This is a relatively safe approach, which also allows staff to consolidate training in the new system before live running commences. It is expensive, however, because of the extra resources required to run two systems side by side. Parallel running is necessary where it is vital the new system is proven before operation. In the case of the POS system, this would be the most suitable method of changeover.

(b) **Checklist of implementation activities should include:**

- development of a changeover timetable
- involvement of all affected personnel in planning
- advance notification to employees, followed by periodic progress bulletins
- development of training programme
- possible need for external resources
- delivery of POS equipment
- testing of equipment
- installation and testing of software
- completion of documentation
- training for systems operators
- system trials
- changeover period
- acceptance of new system
- operational running.

(c) **Systems evaluation**

The objective of systems evaluation is the systematic assessment of system performance to determine whether the established goals are being achieved.

Several criteria are commonly used to measure the performance of the systems:

Time, i.e. the time required for a particular action to be performed. Response time is the time that elapses before a system responds to a demand placed upon it; for the POS system, this must be measured in seconds. Turnaround time is the length of time required before results are returned; for a POS system, little processing is done, and this may not be significant.

Costs, sometimes the only measure applied, are used to determine whether the various parts of the system are performing to financial expectations, and include labour costs, overheads, variable costs, maintenance costs, training costs, data entry costs, data storage costs, etc. For the POS system, all of these should be considered.

Hardware performance should be measured in terms of speed, reliability, maintenance, operating costs and power requirements. The performance of the POS devices in the various store departments, the central computer servicing the POS system and any networking components must be evaluated.

Software performance should be measured in terms of processing speed, quality and quantity of output, accuracy, reliability, maintenance and update requirements. Again, this is necessary for all software involved in the POS system.

Accuracy is a measure of how closely an output agrees with a given set of input instructions and can be measured in several ways. It is important that the type of errors as well as volume is analysed to ensure that serious errors are quickly identified. In the POS system, it is essential, for example, that the prices charged to customers are accurate.

Security means that all records are secure, that equipment is protected and that unauthorised or illegal access is minimised. It is important that the central database containing product prices is not corrupted, for example.

Morale is reflected in the satisfaction and acceptance that employees feel towards their jobs. Absentee rate and employee turnover are two factors that can be used to assess morale of the POS operators in the stores.

Customer reactions are an important factor in the context of the POS system; large numbers of complaints from customers would indicate that the system is not performing satisfactorily.

All the data gathered from the various components of evaluation should be studied to assess the success or otherwise of the system and, if the latter, to help pinpoint the reasons why performance is not reaching expectations.

CHAPTER 19	EXAM-TYPE QUESTION

Maintenance

(a) *Corrective maintenance* is the term often applied to the fixing of programming errors in the software. It can also be applied to hardware faults and to operational errors that cause the system to become unusable. Corrective maintenance is often required to return the system to a fully operational state. The system is 'down' until corrective maintenance has been completed.

Many companies log 'downtime' system failures. It must be determined whether these are due to operational problems (for example, the user switching the system off leaving files partially updated) or due to programming errors or mistakes in file use and updating. Each of these errors must be logged and investigated. The investigation must focus on the development and testing process so that it is understood how the error was introduced into the system in the first place. The results of the investigation may lead to changes in procedures and standards.

Adaptive maintenance is concerned with changing the software to reflect alterations in the business environment. These changes may be due to new user requirements or (more usually) refined user requirements in the light of experience in using the software. New user requirements are often triggered by changes in the business environment or perhaps by new users. In most instances the system can still be used whilst adaptive maintenance is performed.

Measuring the number of functional user changes after implementation is useful as long as the changes are correctly diagnosed and categorised. For example, some changes will actually be 'what we wanted in the first place'. In such instances there has been an error of specification and so specification methods must be reviewed to reduce these problems. In other instances the user's understanding of the requirements has only become clear after experimenting with and using the software. These changes can be expected although there may be a case for seeing whether these might have been uncovered earlier in the systems development lifecycle, perhaps through prototyping. Finally, there may be amendments due to unforeseen changes in the business environment. Hopefully a flexible design will reduce the effect of such changes but in general these amendments are difficult to predict.

(b) Appropriate measures might include the following:
- *Calls to the help desk* must be categorised and the statistics produced analysed. It may emerge that problems keep recurring and the reasons for this must be understood. There may be confusion or ambiguities in the dialogue, training may have been unsuccessful or inappropriate, or the system may not be able to cope with the variety of circumstances met in practical use. The reasons must be investigated and remedies suggested – changes in dialogue wording and structures, refresher training courses, new documentation etc.

- *Software monitoring of errors* records information about what errors have been made. It will include errors that never get reported to the help desk because the user has solved the problem themselves – after some confusion and wasted time and effort. Consequently the help desk statistics and the software monitoring of errors are important complementary sources of information. The overall usability of the software can also be assessed through the following.

- Recording the time required for users to become proficient in the software. This may emerge from training courses, where users may still not be confident in the use of the software after the allocated course time. The trainers may also observe common problems and feed these back to the development team.

- Suitable questions in a user-satisfaction questionnaire.

- Software monitoring of the use of the system by discretionary users.

The last of these examples illustrates how software monitoring can be used to assess the use of the system. For example, the number of times a particular report is requested can be logged together with the user and the time taken to produce the report or fulfil the enquiry. This can be used to provide statistics of actual use. This is very important with discretionary users such as managers who do not have to provide operational input into the system. Managers may elect not to use the system because of the following.

- It does not provide useful information. Hence requirements must be reviewed.

- It is too difficult to use. This may lead to changes in dialogue wording and structure.

- It is too slow to use. This may lead to changes in programs or data structures.

Index

FTC Foulks Lynch
A **Kaplan Professional** Company

STUDY TEXT REVIEW FORM
ACCA Paper 2.1

Thank you for choosing this text for your ACCA professional qualification. As we are constantly striving to improve our products, we would be grateful if you could provide us with feedback about how useful you found this publication.

Name: ....

Address: ....

....

Email: ....

Why did you decide to purchase this Study Text?		**How do you study?**	
Have used them in the past	☐	At a college	☐
Recommended by lecturer	☐	On a distance learning course	☐
Recommended by friend	☐	Home study	☐
Saw advertising	☐	Other (please specify)...........................	
Other (please specify)...................................			

Within our ACCA range we also offer Exam Kits and Pocket Notes. Is there any other type of service/publication that you would like to see as part of the range?

CD Rom with additional questions and answers ☐
A booklet that would help you master exam skills and techniques ☐
Space on our website that would answer your technical questions and queries ☐
Other (please specify)...

During the past six month do you recall seeing/receiving any of the following?

Our advertisement in *Student Accountant* magazine? ☐
Our advertisement in any other magazine? (please specify) ☐

....

Our leaflet/brochure or a letter through the post? ☐
Other (please specify)...

Overall opinion of this Study Text

	Excellent	*Adequate*	*Poor*
Introductory pages	☐	☐	☐
Syllabus coverage	☐	☐	☐
Clarity of explanations	☐	☐	☐
Clarity of definitions and key terms	☐	☐	☐
Diagrams	☐	☐	☐
Activities	☐	☐	☐
Self-test questions	☐	☐	☐
Practice questions	☐	☐	☐
Answers to practice questions	☐	☐	☐
Layout	☐	☐	☐
Index	☐	☐	☐

If you have further comments/suggestions or have spotted any errors, please write them on the next page.

Please return this form to: The Publisher, FTC Foulks Lynch, FREEPOST NAT 17540, Wokingham RG40 1BR

Other comments/suggestions and errors

....
....
....
....
....
....
....
....
....
....
....
....
....
....
....
....
....
....
....
....
....
....
....
....
....
....
....
....
....
....
....

Other comments/suggestions and errors

....
....
....

FTC Foulks Lynch
A **Kaplan Professional** Company

ACCA Order Form

Swift House, Market Place, Wokingham, Berkshire RG40 1AP, UK
Tel: +44 (0) 118 989 0629   Fax: +44 (0) 118 979 7455

Order online: www.financial-training.com
Email: publishing@financial-training.com

Examination Date: Dec 05 ☐   Jun 06 ☐
(please tick the exam you intend to take)

	Study Text £26.00	Exam Kit Dec 05 £13.00	Exam Kit Jun 06 £14.00	Pocket Notes £10.00	Drill & Practice £10.00
Part 1					
1.1 Preparing Financial Statements (UK)	☐	☐	☐	☐	☐
1.1 Preparing Financial Statements (International)	☐	☐	☐	☐	☐
1.2 Financial Information for Management	☐	☐	☐	☐	☐
1.3 Managing People	☐	☐	☐	☐	N/A
Part 2					
2.1 Information Systems	☐	☐	☐	☐	N/A
2.2 Corporate & Business Law (English)	☐	☐	☐	☐	N/A
2.2 Corporate & Business Law (Scottish)	☐	N/A	N/A	N/A	N/A
2.3 Business Taxation – FA 2004	☐	☐	N/A	☐	N/A
2.3 Business Taxation – FA 2005	☐	N/A	☐	☐	N/A
2.4 Financial Management & Control	☐	☐	☐	☐	N/A
2.5 Financial Reporting (UK)	☐	☐	☐	☐	N/A
2.5 Financial Reporting (International)	☐	☐	☐	☐	N/A
2.6 Audit & Internal Review (UK)	☐	☐	☐	☐	N/A
2.6 Audit & Internal Review (International)	☐	☐	☐	☐	N/A
Part 3					
3.1 Audit & Assurance Services (UK)	☐	☐	☐	☐	N/A
3.1 Audit & Assurance Services (International)	☐	☐	☐	☐	N/A
3.2 Advanced Taxation – FA 2004	☐	☐	N/A	☐	N/A
3.2 Advanced Taxation – FA 2005	☐	N/A	☐	☐	N/A
3.3 Performance Management	☐	☐	☐	☐	N/A
3.4 Business Information Management	☐	☐	☐	☐	N/A
3.5 Strategic Business Planning & Development	☐	☐	☐	☐	N/A
3.6 Advanced Corporate Reporting (UK)	☐	☐	☐	☐	N/A
3.6 Advanced Corporate Reporting (International)	☐	☐	☐	☐	N/A
3.7 Strategic Financial Management	☐	☐	☐	☐	N/A
Research and Analysis Project Guide (supporting Oxford Brookes University BSc (Hons) in Applied Accounting)	☐				

Postage, Packaging and Delivery (per item):   **Note**: Maximum postage charged for UK orders is £15

TOTAL

Study Texts and Exam Kits	First	Each Extra	**Pocket Notes and Drill & Practice**	First	Each Extra
UK	£5.00	£2.00	UK	£2.00	£1.00
Europe (incl Republic of Ireland and Channel Isles)	£7.00	£4.00	Europe (incl Republic of Ireland and Channel Isles)	£3.00	£2.00
Rest of World	£22.00	£8.00	Rest of World	£8.00	£5.00

Product Sub Total £.................   **Postage & Packaging £**.................   **Order Total £**.................   **(Payments in UK £ Sterling)**

Customer Details

☐ Mr   ☐ Mrs   ☐ Ms   ☐ Miss   Other ....

Initials:................... Surname: ....

Address: ....

....

Postcode: ....

Delivery Address – if different from above

Address: ....

....

Postcode: ....

Telephone: ....

Email: ....

Fax: ....

Payment

1 I enclose Cheque/Postal Order/Bankers Draft for £...................

   Please make cheques payable to '**The Financial Training Company Ltd**'.

2 Charge MasterCard/Visa/Switch/Delta no:

Valid from: ☐☐☐   Expiry date: ☐☐

Issue no:

(Switch only) ☐   Verification No. ☐☐☐

Signature: .... Date: ....

Declaration

I agree to pay as indicated on this form and understand that The Financial Training Company's Terms and Conditions apply (available on request).

Signature: .... Date: ....

Notes: All orders over 1kg will be fully tracked & insured. Signature required on receipt of order. Delivery times subject to stock availability. A telephone number or email address is required for orders that are to be delivered to a PO Box number.

Delivery please allow: United Kingdom – 5 working days
Europe – 8 working days
Rest of World – 10 working days

ACCA Approved Publisher

FTC Foulks Lynch
A **Kaplan Professional** Company

SPECIAL OFFER - Our Distance Learning Students consistently achieve pass rates above the ACCA global average. Increase your chances of success and upgrade your Official ACCA Study Text to a Distance Learning Course for only £88 per paper and gain

- Personal Tutor Support by telephone and email (local rate 0845 number for UK callers)
- The whole range of Official ACCA Publications including Exam Kits and Pocket Notes
- Work Programme
- Unique 5-Star-Guide written by a Specialist Tutor
- Two Progress Tests which you can send to us for marking and feedback
- Hints and Tips Audio CD on study skills and exam technique
- Student Handbook packed with practical information about your course
- 10% discount on any FTC revision course.

This offer is only available if you already own the Official FTC Foulks Lynch ACCA Study Text for the December 2005 or June 2006 Examinations.

ACCA Distance Learning Enrolment Form

Surname _____ First Name _____ Mr / Miss / Mrs / Ms

Home Address _____

_____

Post Code _____ Country _____

Home Tel _____ Office Tel _____

Mobile _____ E-mail _____

Date of Birth _____ ACCA Registration Number _____

Exam sitting: ☐ CBE ☐ December 2005 ☐ June 2006

EMPLOYER DETAILS (Sponsor must be UK based company)

Company Name _____

Manager's Name _____

Address _____

Post Code _____ Country _____

Telephone _____ Email _____

SPONSORED STUDENTS: EMPLOYER'S AUTHORISATION

If the above employer is responsible for the payment of fees, please complete the following:

As employer of the student for whom this form is completed, we are responsible for payment of fees due on receipt of the invoice in respect of the student named above and undertake to inform you in writing of any change to this arrangement. We understand that we are fully responsible for the payment of fees due in all circumstances including termination of employment or cancellation of course.

Purchase Order Number _____

Manager's Name _____

Manager's Signature _____ Date _____

DATA PROTECTION ACT:

Your sponsor can be informed of your test results unless we are otherwise notified.

HOW TO ENROL:

By phone: If you are paying by credit card, please telephone +44 (0)113 200 6363

By post: Complete this enrolment form and return to:
FTC Foulks Lynch Distance Learning, 49 St Paul's Street, LEEDS LS1 2TE

By fax: Fax both sides of your completed enrolment form to +44 (0)113 243 0133

Distance Learning Courses include VAT and all materials. Add postage & packing – applicable to both Distance Learning options (for rates see below).	Distance Learning		Distance Learning (excluding Official ACCA Study Text applicable for the December 2005 and June 2006 examinations sittings only)	
	£	✓	£	✓
Part 1				
1.1 Preparing Financial Statements (UK)	114		88	
1.1 Preparing Financial Statements (International)	114		88	
1.2 Financial Information for Management	114		88	
1.3 Managing People	114		88	
Part 2				
2.1 Information Systems	114		88	
2.2 Corporate & Business Law	114		88	
2.3 Business Taxation	114		88	
2.4 Financial Management and Control	114		88	
2.5 Financial Reporting (UK)	114		88	
2.5 Financial Reporting (International)	114		88	
2.6 Audit & Internal Review (UK)	114		88	
2.6 Audit & Internal Review (International)	114		88	
Part 3 Options				
3.1 Audit & Assurance Services (UK)	114		88	
3.1 Audit & Assurance Services (International)	114		88	
3.2 Advanced Taxation	114		88	
3.3 Performance Management	114		88	
3.4 Business Information Management	114		88	
Part 3 Core				
3.5 Strategic Business Planning & Development	114		88	
3.6 Advanced Corporate Reporting (UK)	114		88	
3.6 Advanced Corporate Reporting (International)	114		88	
3.7 Strategic Financial Management	114		88	

FEES	£
Postage & Packing	£
Total	£

POSTAGE & PACKING
Distance Learning (per paper):
UK & NI £6, Europe & Channel Islands £15, Rest of World £40

DISTANCE LEARNING TERMS AND CONDITIONS OF ENROLMENT:
1. A completed enrolment form must be accompanied by the full fee or employer's authorisation.
2. Where an employer's authorisation is received, the full fees are payable within 30 days of the invoice date. The employer is responsible for the payment of fees due in all circumstances including termination of employment or cancellation of course. FTC reserves the right to charge interest on overdue accounts.
3. A deferral can be processed to the following exam sitting subject to a deferral fee of £25 if notified in writing. If new study materials are required due to syllabus changes or changes in Finance Acts, they will have to be paid for in addition to the deferral fee.
4. Refunds are only available on study materials returned within 14 days in a saleable condition.
5. Courses are not transferable between students.
6. Distance Learning fees include VAT and all materials but exclude any taxes or duties imposed by countries outside the UK.

METHODS OF PAYMENT:
☐ Please invoice my employer (details completed overleaf).
☐ I enclose a cheque made payable to The Financial Training Company Ltd. for £ _____
Payments will only be accepted in UK Sterling.
☐ Please charge my Credit/Debit Card Number for the fees indicated above.

Valid from ☐☐☐☐   Expiry ☐☐☐☐   Solo/Switch Issue No ☐☐   Security Code ☐☐☐

I agree to the terms and conditions of enrolment which I have read.

Student Signature _____   Date _____